Researching New Literacies

new literacies

AND DIGITAL EPISTEMOLOGIES

Colin Lankshear and Michele Knobel
General Editors

Vol. 76

The New Literacies and Digital Epistemologies series
is part of the Peter Lang Education list.
Every volume is peer reviewed and meets
the highest quality standards for content and production.

PETER LANG
New York • Bern • Frankfurt • Berlin
Brussels • Vienna • Oxford • Warsaw

Researching New Literacies

Design, Theory, and Data in Sociocultural Investigation

Edited by Michele Knobel and Colin Lankshear

PETER LANG
New York • Bern • Frankfurt • Berlin
Brussels • Vienna • Oxford • Warsaw

Library of Congress Cataloging-in-Publication Data

Names: Knobel, Michele, editor. | Lankshear, Colin, editor.
Title: Researching new literacies: design, theory, and data in sociocultural investigation / edited by Michele Knobel, Colin Lankshear.
Description: New York: Peter Lang, 2017.
Series: New literacies and digital epistemologies; vol. 76 | ISSN 1523-9543
Includes bibliographical references and index.
Identifiers: LCCN 2016032921 | ISBN 978-1-4331-3146-2 (hardcover: alk. paper)
ISBN 978-1-4331-3145-5 (paperback: alk. paper) | ISBN 978-1-4539-1649-0 (ebook pdf)
ISBN 978-1-4331-3833-1 (epub) | ISBN 978-1-4331-3832-4 (mobi)
Subjects: LCSH: Internet literacy. | Media literacy. | Computer literacy.
Technological literacy. | Digital media—Research. | Qualitative research—Methodology.
Classification: LCC TK5105.875.I57 R419 2016 | DDC 025.042072—dc23
LC record available at https://lccn.loc.gov/2016032921
DOI 10.3726/978-1-4539-1649-0

Bibliographic information published by **Die Deutsche Nationalbibliothek.**
Die Deutsche Nationalbibliothek lists this publication in the "Deutsche Nationalbibliografie"; detailed bibliographic data are available on the Internet at http://dnb.d-nb.de/.

The paper in this book meets the guidelines for permanence and durability of the Committee on Production Guidelines for Book Longevity of the Council of Library Resources.

29 Broadway, 18th floor, New York, NY 10006
www.peterlang.com

Printed in the United States of America

This volume is dedicated to Brian Street,
who was there for us right from the start.

Table of Contents

Acknowledgments

We want to acknowledge the generous efforts of the chapter authors who have made this volume possible. They are exemplary colleagues, and we have greatly enjoyed working with them.

Our appreciation is also owed to the many anonymous people who participated in the various research projects reported in the chapters that follow. Such participation requires much goodwill, effort and trust, without which researchers simply could not explore our social world.

As always, we are indebted to Bernadette Shade for her care and oversight during the production of this book, as well as for her work on numerous other volumes in the New Literacies series.

Thanks are also extended to the many permissions holders who have allowed the authors to reproduce material necessary for the integrity of their chapters.

We acknowledge the institutions with which we and the chapter authors are affiliated, for supporting the research activity reported in this volume.

Finally, as reflected in our dedication, we are truly grateful for the contribution Brian Street has made over the past 35 years to the study of literacies as social practices. And we are especially appreciative of the support he gave us, individually and together, as newbies to the field, and thereafter: initially through written comments on typewritten hard copy received and sent by post; subsequently in face to face communication; and, since the early 1990s, via email and whenever we get the chance to meet up. Brian's career has exemplified the very best of academic collegiality, and we count ourselves among the many fortunate beneficiaries of his generosity and his passion for literacy research and scholarship.

CHAPTER ONE

Researching New Literacies

Addressing the Challenges of Initial Research Training

COLIN LANKSHEAR AND MICHELE KNOBEL

THE AIM

This book aims to provide guidance and support for students and academic and professional researchers involved in initial (or novice) research training in the area of empirically based qualitative studies of new literacies. Our observations during the past 20 years of involvement, in varying roles and capacities, with graduate research training and mentoring, have convinced us of three things.

1. Students who enroll in graduate programs offering opportunities to learn how to conduct empirical qualitative research in the area of literacy generally, and literacy practices more specifically, typically arrive with strictly limited prior knowledge and understanding of academic research as a distinctive kind of engagement. A high proportion have come through teacher education programs that provide little direct exposure to the academic disciplines and their constitutive theories and research literatures (Bridges, 2006; Krishnan, 2009). Typically, so far as becoming academic researchers from a broadly social science standpoint is concerned, these students are very much "starting from scratch."
2. Academics responsible for overseeing the initial research training of students undertaking empirical qualitative studies of literacy practices often struggle with the demands of their roles. Graduate research student numbers have grown exponentially since the 1980s, without corresponding growth in staffing. Academics find themselves with increased numbers

of students to advise or supervise. Furthermore, they are often obliged to supervise or advise outside their areas of strength or expertise. In many universities, increased research student numbers have necessitated pressing into research training roles academics whose own research experience is limited or otherwise fragile.

3. The quality of the final outcomes of initial research training, in the form of dissertations and theses, is often disappointing, even allowing for the fact that this has been initial research training (Boote & Beile, 2005).

In light of these observations, we conceived a book comprising chapters written by new literacies researchers whose work we regard as exemplary in terms of our view of what counts as elegant, robust, and cogent qualitative research that is empirically based (see Lankshear & Knobel, 2004). Furthermore, we deliberately selected a high proportion of early career researchers, and asked them to base their chapters directly on their graduate research studies and/or research that grew out of their graduate work and followed immediately upon it. This was done to ensure that the discussion in their chapters pertains as closely as possible to the kinds of situations, issues, challenges, and decisions to be made that commonly arise within initial research training and experiences.

THE UNDERLYING RESEARCH IDEAL

Empirically based qualitative studies of social phenomena involve looking in depth at a typically small number of research subjects in order to obtain rich and detailed data about such things as what they are doing, how and why they are doing it (in those ways), what happens in the course of doing it, and how we (as researchers) make sense of certain aspects of what has gone on. To do this well a researcher has to aim for the most powerful and economical *coherence* they can get between (i) a set of research goals or purposes (aims, objectives, research questions); (ii) relevant theory; (iii) data collection approach and methods; (iv) data analysis approach and methods; and (v) interpretive techniques to be applied to the results of data analysis. In other words, they must ensure that there is an optimal degree of "fit" between what they aim to describe, understand, and explain, and the way they *design* their study.

So, for example, they have to be able to show that their data collection approach and the methods and techniques they develop and use are consistent with and grow out of their research purposes and their informing theory and key theoretical concepts. Researchers have to be able to describe and demonstrate how they have "translated" their research purposes and theory and concepts into a data collection strategy and a set of data collection components (instruments) that will help them address their research question. Readers have to be able to see and understand (and accept) that there is a rational connection between, say, an interview question or a questionnaire item or types of artifacts to be collected, and the research purposes and theoretical and conceptual framing of the study. Researchers can't hope to do *everything*; it is better to do *something* (that is worth doing) *well* than to try to do too much and end up achieving little. Therefore, at each point in the overall research process, such as developing a data collection approach and generating data collection instruments or guides and procedures, researchers have to learn to make hard decisions about what to leave in and what to set aside. The guiding principle here is to get as much as one can that is relevant and valid from as little complication as possible, and to make the case for how it is done.

In the case of graduate students in the process of learning to become researchers, the point here is as much about learning how to take those decisions, and how to pursue and demonstrate coherence and elegance, as it is about what they actually end up doing and producing. It's as much about learning to play the game as it is about the result of the game. The temptation is often to try and "do too much"—certainly, to do more than is necessary to get a convincing finite result—and, in the process, fail to learn the need to achieve and demonstrate coherence and elegance, and to see how and why less is often more.

The same applies to data analysis. The types of data analysis tools and techniques developed and employed in a study must fit coherently, and as economically or elegantly as possible, with the research purposes, theoretical and conceptual framings, and the data to be collected. Here again, less is often more, and the main point during research training is to learn how to make good decisions, how to achieve depth, and how and when to let go in the interest of learning one's craft well. Trying to juggle multiple data analysis approaches and methods can, and often does, get in the way of becoming a good data analyst of one kind or another. There is no need to try to master multiple data analysis approaches at the outset. Similarly, learning to apply one data analysis approach—and knowing what data to use it with—expertly is time well spent in learning to become a researcher. There is ample time later to diversify if one wants to try on a different researcher identity. The researcher one becomes during initial training may or may not be the same researcher one ends up as. One thing, however, is sure. It is much more likely that one will become a good and competent Type Y researcher later if one has already become a good Type X researcher in one's initial research formation.

To elaborate further on the point at issue, a key goal of graduate research (training) is to acquire a strong and clear sense of research as a *structure* of knowing. It is about seeing how research purposes, theory and concepts, data collection approaches and techniques, data analysis approaches and techniques, and interpretive procedures *hang together* as a *system*. To get control of this system and to be able to operate it, and make adaptations within and between the different components in order to get a more efficient and tighter "operation" is, precisely, to develop a certain kind of *mind*. It is to "get" research logic and to be able to apply it as an extended *argument*. Doing research is a sophisticated form of argumentation. Once one has that kind of mind in the first place it is easy to make variations upon it, just as one can make variations within any kind of argument structure by, say, modifying one or more premises. Within research training, what committees and advisers/supervisors and examiners should be looking for in the first instance is the *demonstration* of the presence of that kind of mind through the dissertation and defense.

. Each key step in the process, from conceptualizing the research design and methodology to interpreting the analytic results, needs to be demonstrated and justified as being at the very least a defensible option and, at best, an optimal one. This involves a lot of argumentation. Getting to the decision about why data analysis method A is appropriate and is better than B (which may also be appropriate), and reporting the process of getting to that decision, may involve as much or more "work" and demonstration than is involved in actually applying the method to data and reporting the application. To have grounds for believing that a novice researcher has acquired a "researcherly" *mind* we need to see that a sound case has been made for decisions about design and methodology, as well as being able to see that the study components have been implemented competently. This is why less is often more. There is less to have to provide detailed justification for, and justice can be done to providing the underlying rationale for what is actually conducted in the study.

In the course of providing the rationale aspect of a study, it may (and often will) become apparent that something needs to be pruned or modified somewhere else within the overall study design. Seeing this and doing it is as much a learning achievement as is wielding a data collection or data analysis method. When researchers talk about a study being robust and cogent they mean, among other things, that the logic of the inquiry has been laid bare—made transparent—and that it has been implemented competently (LeCompte & Schensul, 2010; Maxwell, 2012; Miles, Huberman, & Saldaña, 2014).

A NEW LITERACIES RESEARCH FOCUS

In a seminal statement, and one that underlies this book, Silvia Scribner and Michael Cole (1981, p. 236) claimed that literacy comprises "a set of socially organized practices which make use of a symbol system and a technology for producing and disseminating it." Brian Street (1984, p. 1) subsequently rendered a key part of this idea in his claim that literacy "is best understood as a shorthand for the social practices and conceptions of reading and writing." From this standpoint, then, we can talk about literacy in the singular, but really there are very many different literacies. Each is a "socially organized practice" and collectively they make up the set that constitutes literacy as a singular term. From this standpoint, then, if we think of English language literacy during the age of print, we might say that it comprises all the various socially organized practices that are mediated by a Latin alphabet and a technology that ranges from pencils to printing presses.

Going further, Scribner and Cole clarify their idea of socially organized practices. They talk about practices as "socially developed and patterned ways of using technology and knowledge to accomplish tasks" (1981, p. 236). So, for example, if someone is a lawyer and needs to complete some conveyancing, s/he can use a typewriter (involving knowledge of how to use it) to prepare the appropriate documents (again using knowledge of what the appropriate documents are for the purpose). The appropriate documents are recognized publicly as such, which is another way of saying that they reflect socially recognized and patterned ways of doing something. Therefore, in this case, the lawyer may need to prepare a certain kind of contract, a certain kind of deed, a certain kind of covering letter, and so on. In other words, there are multiple specific *literacies* involved here: a socially organized practice of "deed writing," a socially organized practice of legal letter writing, a socially organized practice of drawing up a contract. There is, then, much more to it than just using knowledge of a given symbol system and how to use a particular technology. As Scribner and Cole put it, it's also a matter of "applying this knowledge for specific purposes in specific contexts of use" (1981, p. 236). So, there are lots of "knowledges" here. The knowledge needed for legal letter writing differs from that for deed writing, and our lawyer needs both, as well as knowledge of when each is appropriate. In Street's terms, deed writing and letter writing are different *conceptions* of reading and writing inherent in different *practices* of reading and writing.

There is something else that is important here; something that is often muddled or confused in thinking about literacy and social practice. It concerns the idea of "contexts of use." Contexts of use are themselves often social practices in which literacies as social practices are embedded. We *can* think of conveyancing as a *literacy*, a literacy that involves multiple more specific literacies (letter writing, deed writing, contract writing). Ultimately, however, conveyancing is much more than (just) a social practice of literacy. It is, of course, a legal practice of *transferring* things from one party to another. This is not just literacy. It transfers property and obligations and so on.

And in the middle of all of this—indeed, all *through* all of this—is the matter of meaning. Everything that goes on in social life is meaningful. That's how socially organized and socially recognized routines come into existence and function within human lives. All of the documents created in the multiple literacies involved in conveyancing create and communicate meanings. The overall practice of conveyancing is meaningful. And these meanings bring about and mediate material effects. In our own words, literacies are socially recognized ways in which people generate, communicate, and negotiate meanings, as participants (with roles and identities) in larger social practices, through the medium of encoded texts. If we can convert the conveyancing example into others such as a parent writing a list that a child can recognize as a set of grocery items they are requested to get before the parent arrives home from work, or a child writing a note to Santa, or whatever, then we will have the idea of literacies as social practices sorted out.

When it comes to the idea of *new* literacies we need to think in terms of some differences to the kinds of examples provided above. And we need to bear in mind that there are all kinds of continuities between conventional literacies of the print age and "new" literacies of the digital age. Indeed, literacies get modified and invented all the time, in the analogue print world as much as in the digital "multimedia" world. But in the present context we will be dealing with "new" literacies in terms of literacies that are mediated by digital technologies.

With the advent of digital electronic technology/media, radical changes occurred in the means of encoding texts, the nature of encoding texts, and the "reach" of encoding texts. This had vast implications for the creation, communication, and negotiation of meanings, and the scale and distribution of involvement in social practices and meaning-making and exchange within those practices. As social practices mediated by digital technologies, new literacies differ fundamentally from conventional print literacies on the basis that their inscriptions are rendered in pixels on screens rather than by impressions on paper, by means of digital code rather than material analogue means (whether printed and illustrated/imaged/diagrammed by hand, typewriter, or press). That is, new literacies involve a shift from material inscription to digital coding, from analogue to digital representations. Consequently, "new" kinds of texts are seamlessly multimodal rather than involving distinct processes for different modes (text, image, sound). You basically click for everything, since beneath the clicks lies the digital code that renders multiple modes. With the right kind of knowledge someone who cannot draw a straight line or play a note on a conventional instrument can create an impressive image and compose a significant piece of music (although conventional artistic and musical knowledge remain powerful assets). In addition, the development of electronic networks vastly extends the reach and "real-time" immediacy of new literacies beyond anything remotely possible under print. Meaningful expression and cultural artifacts can be shared with the click of a mouse and as extensively as one chooses via digital networks.

All of a sudden anyone with access to a modern computer could do things that previously could only be done by big enterprises with expensive equipment. Ordinary people could make movies, music videos, music remixes, and create sophisticated fan art. They could play games with people anywhere in the world in real time, organizing themselves into units and sides to play against oppositions of considerable scale, and strategize by communicating instantaneously with one another. They could organize and administer online spaces in which like-minded people sharing interests could "meet" and share expertise and resources, growing the scale of shared "affinities" and pursuing mutual growth in competence. They could even be "in" each other's text. They could cooperate and participate and collaborate in forms of meaningful practices with a degree of interactivity and immediacy previously unthinkable. This can be thought of as a new "ethos."

"New" literacies emerged, flourished, and, sometimes, declined—to be replaced by "newer" ones. Ways of "writing" often became highly interactive. Participants in collaborative endeavors worked out how to use the affordances of their hardware and software to undertake tasks and achieve purposes—such as finding ways to communicate with other players on one's own side in an online game to strategize effectively and defeat their opponents; or using wiki software to create and maintain the world's largest encyclopedia, which could be continually updated and improved and edited by anyone. These changes can be thought of in terms of "new" literacies involving a new "ethos."

As social practices characterized by a new "ethos," new literacies are more participatory, collaborative, and distributed, and less "published," less "author-centric," and less "individual" than conventional (print-based) literacies. Typically, although—regretfully—not universally (Gee & Hayes, 2013), engaging in social media sites, (passionate) affinity spaces (Gee, 2013), and within environments and practices of participatory cultures (Jenkins et al., 2006) involves deep interactivity, openness to feedback, sharing of resources and expertise, and a will to collaborate and provide support that is writ large into myriad contemporary everyday practices. Participants in new literacy practices actively seek out memberships and peers in areas of affinity and shared interest, and pursue different kinds of relationships between "authors" and "audiences" from those characterizing many conventional literacy practices. They generally value attending to the interests and knowledge of others, recognize that quality is judged by groups rather than appointed experts, welcome diversity of opinion in decision-making, and so on.

This broad "ethos" of new literacies sets them apart from simply being conventional literacies in digital form. As such, paradigm cases of new literacies include such practices as creating fan fiction, blogging and microblogging, remixing cultural artifacts, photo curating and sharing, video gaming, video game modding, online social networking, editing wikis, creating machinima, editing anime music videos, sharing and contributing to memes, building apps, creating animations, and participating in interest-driven online forums, to name just a smattering.

Empirical qualitative studies of new literacies, then, focus on the ways people use knowledge, skills, and tools to create, communicate, and negotiate meanings within contexts of undertaking tasks and pursuing purposes in the kind of everyday settings we associate with the conditions of new media. The point of this book is to contribute toward maximizing the quality of such studies, by learning to research well.

FINDING THE AUTHORS

Consequently, when it came to identifying authors to contribute to this collection our key question was: "Who do we think of as counting among empirical qualitative researchers of new literacies who exemplify our view of the research ideal (as described above)?" Who, in other words, makes crystal clear the way their research purposes cohere with theory and key concepts; the way their purposes, theory, and concepts get "translated into" or rendered as appropriate data collection tools and techniques; the way their economical and elegant choice of data analysis tools and techniques fit with and grow out of their theory, concepts, and data collection strategy; and who has conceptualized these multiple and economical "fits" and "coherences" into an elegant and powerful design for their study as a whole?" "Who lives out the principle that less is often more when it comes to generating significant and convincing research outcomes?"

Of course, there are two broad types of empirical qualitative research. One is what we call "theory-guided" or theory-based research, and the other is grounded theory. This book is concerned *only* with research that proceeds from some conventional theoretical option or other (e.g., symbolic anthropology, ethnomethodology, social semiotics, activity theory, sociolinguistics, symbolic interactionism, sociocultural theory) or from components of some such theory. This is a purely personal preference, although we believe that since so many graduate research students in the area of literacy studies have such limited prior knowledge and understanding of the nature and role of theory in social inquiry they might as well learn something about this during their initial research training by trying some theory on and seeing how it runs.

This means that in addition to exemplifying the research values underpinning this book, participating authors also had to have engaged in theory-guided research. In addition, as previously noted, we wanted a good proportion of authors who were either in their own research training at the time of the study their chapter is based on, or at a very early point after that. A number of authors approached were unable to participate, and others we did not know sufficiently well to feel comfortable inviting "from out of the blue." Hence, the authors who contributed to this volume certainly meet our selection criteria, but they're by no means an exhaustive set of those who are conducting good quality new literacies research.

We also tried to ensure that the book as a whole would cover a reasonable range of new literacies. Potential participants were identified in part on the basis that they collectively addressed a number of new literacies.

THIS BOOK'S APPROACH

Drawing on our experiences with initial research training, we selected what we see as four key "pressure points" in the research training enterprise to orient this book: study design, the nature and role of theory within a study, the approach to and conduct of data collection, and the approach to and conduct of data analysis. The aim is that the book as a whole will speak substantially to each of these pressure points, but that authors of individual chapters would emphasize one or other of them. We identified for each invited author the particular emphasis we hoped they would take.

We asked all authors to address the same set of items organized as a template, but to pay greater attention to some items than others in accordance with the emphasis we had assigned to them. Authors would reflect upon and spell out how the particular study (or studies) on which their chapter was based speaks to these items. The template was as follows:

- The research problem/question(s)/issue you addressed
- How it was informed theoretically and conceptually, and why
- The kinds of data you collected, how were they collected, the amount of data collected (and used), etc.
- How data were analyzed (including actual, concrete, worked-through examples)
- How data analysis outcomes were interpreted and discussed in light of theory, etc., and the extent to which you revised initial positions, assumptions, etc.
- Reporting the conclusions—how you arrived at the "so what" dimension of your study
- Ideally, the chapter should also include reference to glitches and revisions, etc., encountered along the way in order to provide a "warts and all" account of how new literacies can be studied.

ORGANIZATION AND CONTENT

The book has aimed for a mix of depth and scope on multiple dimensions. It was important to try and cover a range of new literacies, but at the same time to achieve some concentrations that might indicate options and diversity within a particular field or area. Accordingly, two new literacies that are especially well-represented in the overall literature are prevalent here: namely, fan fiction writing and gaming. In addition, chapters give at least a nod to mobile phone use, social media, audio and visual media remix, and classroom-based digital literacies. Similarly, in terms of theory and methodology, multiple chapters reflect the considerable interest currently evident in researching new literacies in terms of participation in affinity spaces, as well as the use of discourse analytic approaches of one kind or another. These concentrations are augmented by chapters based on interests in social semiotics and multimodal analysis, ethnomethodology and conversation analysis (CA), actor-network theory and a sociomaterial perspective, and sociocultural theory, social practices, and the New Literacy Studies.

Because each chapter addresses a common template, albeit with a particular emphasis, the content is too varied to be organized accurately in distinct parts or sections. Instead, it has been organized as a single sequence of chapters arranged to reflect as well as possible the emphasis as well as the range and continuity within and between individual contributions. The opening chapters are intended to reflect an emphasis on designing a study and how theory informs research design and implementation. These chapters transition into an emphasis on data collection around Chapter 5 and then into data analysis and findings around Chapter 8. Some small liberties have been taken here and there with emphasis to try to maximize balance and continuity while moving through the content.

Following this introduction, the book opens with Jayne Lammers' discussion of key design decisions and decision points she faced during the initial design and data collection phases in an ethnographic study of a fan fiction affinity space. She identifies a series of critical junctures, or "points of convergence" among "theoretical, contextual and methodological factors," where the decisions researchers make "propel a study down a particular path." For Lammers, the earliest critical junctures occurred when initially getting into an affinity space and getting experience of participating from the inside and, subsequently, crafting some research questions. Further junctures followed during the university research review for gaining necessary permissions, generating an initial sense of the affinity space, and working out how to access insider perspectives (whose, and how). These were followed at the points of recruiting participants for the research and determining how to collect participant data (kinds of data to be collected and methods to be used). Her discussion concludes by identifying four lessons based in her retrospective analysis of this research experience that could potentially inform others' work in the area of new literacies research.

In Chapter 3, Aaron Hung introduces researching new literacies from the standpoint of CA—"the study of social organization through the close analysis of naturally occurring talk" (this volume, p. 37)—with a focus on videogaming. He identifies the underlying premise of CA as the idea that everyday talk is "the most fundamental unit of social life," and that researchers can reveal and describe the ways people make sense of their activities and interactions—moment by moment—by transcribing naturally occurring talk in a specialized and detailed way and analyzing it closely. Although CA has rarely been used in new literacies research to date, it seemed an obvious choice to Hung for his doctoral research because he was more interested in players than in game design. Moreover, he wanted to understand the game from the player perspective as a *process*. Hung outlines some basics of CA research and illustrates them with detailed examples and informed references to the primary literature. He then draws on his own doctoral research (subsequently published as a book) to describe and demonstrate the hows and whys of data collection. The heart of the chapter consists in demonstrating some of the CA "basics" previously identified by working with some of his own data. He shows how the careful and specialized development of transcripts of naturally occurring talk among his research participants reflects the underlying theory of CA and constitutes the core of the analytic work involved in generating research findings. The net result is an informative and accessible guide for graduate students open to considering CA as an option for researching new literacies.

Alecia Magnifico's account of a design-based analysis of an online affinity space shows a researcher opening up a new research angle on a recently developed and evolving theoretical construct. The idea of affinity spaces was originally introduced into research on participatory cultures as an alternative to the established concept of communities of practice (Gee, 2004). To date, affinity space research has mainly focused on how aficionados mobilize, use, and extend the resources provided by such spaces to grow the affinity and enrich the experiences and expertise of participants. This research has involved ethnographic and other qualitative investigation of what people do and how they do it within affinity spaces. By contrast, Magnifico moves inquiry from the level of investigating activity mediated by the resources of affinity spaces toward looking at structural features of the resources themselves, and how their very design may significantly shape what goes on in the space. She does this by studying the design of a commercially sponsored, multisited online fiction writing affinity space, Figment.com, which is owned by Random House Children's Books. Originally intending to conduct an interview-based study of some aspects of participation on the site, Magnifico's experiences of immersing herself in the site for 6 months prompted a radical shift in her research direction. What caught her attention were "the very different and sometimes contradictory messages and interaction" that traveled across Figment.com and social media (Tumblr, Instagram, Facebook, Pinterest, Twitter). Magnifico shifted her research focus to studying the *design* of Figment, with a view to theorizing "the *context* of affinity spaces that have multiple portals, goals, and audiences for communication" (this volume, p. 64). The chapter outlines the two concise and focused research questions underlying her study and presents the elegant suite of standard data collection procedures she employed. This is followed by a detailed account of her analytic methods and results. Magnifico concludes by articulating a fresh focus for affinity space research in new literacies suggested by her work.

In Chapter 5, Jen Scott Curwood and Carly Biddolph report a field-based study of how a small population of Australian English teachers active in Twitter's #ozengchat group used this space for nonformal professional learning. The main emphases of the chapter are on conceptualizing what constitutes a "site" when conducting a field-based study largely online; determining which posts to collect, and how and why to collect them; and conducting qualitative thematic analysis. Curwood and Biddolph describe how participants were recruited and selected for study, and describe and explain in detail their overall suite of data collection tools. Survey and semi-structured interviews were used to tap teachers' self-reported uses of Twitter for professional learning purposes. The researchers supplemented these accounts by collecting—in consultation with the creator of #ozengchat—all the tweets posted to four #ozengchats synchronous chat sessions that run weekly at an appointed time. Curwood and Biddolph argue for the importance of making data collection tools available to readers to enhance the trustworthiness of any study and, accordingly, provide their survey and semi-structured interview questions in the chapter. They used an approach to thematic analysis informed by Saldaña (2012) and provide a clear demonstration of how they developed codes and subsequently generated themes in the original study. The authors make a valuable contribution to new literacies research by advancing a concept of "networked field studies" that grew out of their data collection experience. This concept provides a theorized way of designing, speaking about, and collecting data within multisited qualitative studies that are neither ethnographies nor case studies.

In Chapter 6, Mark Chen describes a complex series of iterations during the 7-year span of his doctoral dissertation, from the origins of data collection during a preparatory course on grounded theory to the eventual publication of his study as a book. Chen conducted an ethnography of a guild's communication and raiding practices within the online multiplayer game *World of Warcraft*. Citing John Law (2004), Chen describes the whole practice as being "messy as hell." Within the context of this book, Chen's study is an outlier. It is unorthodox. Data collected for a grounded theory course prior to beginning the dissertation are subjected to intense reverse engineering in order to assign research purposes and to identify potential theoretical and conceptual frameworks for an academically viable doctoral-level investigation. The chapter chronicles a protracted search for coherence in the midst of numerous unforeseeable circumstances. Of particular significance here are the ways Chen organized and managed (in his word, "massaged") the data for analytic purposes, and the extent to which this responded to contingencies. One such contingency, associated with the guild's use of a third-party add-on during raiding (the KLH threat meter), led directly to Chen appropriating Actor Network Theory as a resource for guiding data analysis and interpreting results.

Ibrar Bhatt focuses on some practicalities of data collection in Chapter 7. The study context is classroom-situated digital literacies involved in student assignment tasks for assessment within a Further Education College in the U.K. Bhatt approaches assignments as "entities made in the world," and to describe and understand such entities involves investigating the practices and sociomaterial relations that constitute them and give them their features and characteristics. In Bhatt's research, this entailed understanding how ways (of doing and being) and tools and tool use grounded in "worlds" beyond the classroom were mobilized in the process of creating new kinds of entities and their constitutive digital literacies. Accordingly, Bhatt frames his study theoretically at the intersection of the New Literacy Studies and sociomaterial theory, with particular emphasis on the context of practice and a sociomaterial conception of performativity: approaching what all of those who were involved came to see and recognize as an "assignment" as something that is "assembled by a choreography of practices and performances of those practices" (this volume, p. 133). The core of the chapter focuses on what this kind of approach requires in the form of data for analysis. Bhatt makes clear the links between his research purposes, the theory he employs, and his data collection approach and methods. From the overall set of ethnographic data collection procedures he adopted, Bhatt focuses particularly on the approach he developed to generating a videographic record of student activity, describing this in detail and providing its rationale. He describes how the data were subsequently assembled into "accessible videologs" for analysis, and illustrates key steps (digital transcriptions and narrative vignettes) in his process of preparing the data for analysis.

Rebecca Black's chapter, based on her virtual ethnography of fan fiction writing by English language learners (ELL) celebrating *Card Captor Sakura* anime, provides a transition from an emphasis on aspects of data collection to one on data analysis and the production of research findings. Black identifies issues and challenges involved in recruiting study participants following her three-year "advance preparation" for her research as a participant observer in the affinity space (in this case, Fanfiction.net). The main components of the three-year data collection phase are then presented, followed by the rationale for the data collection approach and an overview of the final data set. The main focus in the chapter, however, is on the discourse analysis approach Black used to address a particular subquestion that emerged in the course of the study. This asked what kinds of "work" ELL writers and reviewers are performing with their texts on the site. Black draws on complementary elements of discourse analysis approaches developed by James Paul Gee, J. Amos Hatch, and Norman Fairclough and shows how these go to the heart of the question at issue. She provides illustrative segments of coding based on the analytic approach taken, as a prelude to an extended worked example that simultaneously encapsulates and demonstrates the coherence of the study as a whole.

In Chapter 9, Andrew Burn draws on social semiotics to present frameworks for multimodal analysis of film, videogames, and machinima, respectively. He approaches each of these as a "relatively settled cultural form" characterized by "particular clusters of modes and media" (this volume, p. 169). Each combines a range of modes (e.g., language, visuals, music) to create meaningful productions and performances. Multimodal analysis seeks to understand, describe, and explain how such modes can be mobilized and combined to create meaningful "wholes," and how the ways they are combined end up in the production of something we can recognize as a video game, or a film, or a machinima creation. Burn identifies and outlines multiple analytic approaches appropriate for each of the forms under discussion, and the kinds of steps that can be taken in these approaches. These constitute frameworks for multimodal analysis, and Burn works them through in concrete examples of how creators combine modes to produce texts that are "systems of potential meaning" (this volume, p. 192). He concludes with an important cautionary note, observing that while multimodal analysis—as a form of textual analysis—can be used to render the meaning potential in (multimodal) texts, further methodological approaches are needed for identifying and explaining the particular meanings that get made in particular instances in the negotiation between *film* (as text and a system of potential meaning) and *viewer*; between *game* and *player*.

In Chapter 10, Sean Duncan focuses on affinity space research, with an emphasis on data analysis, drawing on research he has been involved in during the past decade. He notes that methodological concerns associated with researching learning in affinity spaces have been discussed in the literature, but that to date there have been no step-by-step accounts of scholarly ways to characterize, understand, and track practices within affinity spaces. The chapter seeks to redress this gap, with reference to three connected studies of different sets of gaming affinity spaces. Duncan builds an argument for how affinity spaces can be studied, in the course of which he outlines "a specific mixed-methodology approach that can leverage the benefits of quantitative analyses as well as qualitative approaches" (this volume, p. 196). He begins by describing and discussing early approaches to content coding used with Constance Steinkuehler to analyze data in a study of informal scientific reasoning within affinity spaces. This is followed by an account of subsequent work that sought a productive combination of content coding methods and discourse analysis. These sections, which constitute most of the chapter, include detailed worked examples that clearly explicate the approaches taken. The chapter concludes with a brief report of methodological innovations Duncan has explored in order to address structural and interactional changes within online discussion spaces over the study period, and the challenges such changes present to affinity space research.

The book concludes with Anita Charles' chapter on cell phone use within schools whose rules officially forbid their use by students, but where students use them nonetheless. Charles' study was framed within the scope of her larger interest in how young people learn to be literate across a range of sociocultural contexts and practices. Its emphasis on analyzing interview and observational data and generating research findings is central to our purposes here. The study was framed theoretically and methodologically by Gee's "building tasks" component of his version of Discourse theory, and Michael Agar's (2006) ethnographic approach to making sense of behavior in social settings by exploring interconnections between meaning and content. From Gee's list of the things people use language to build, Charles focuses on significance, relationships, identities, activities, and sign systems that "work" within particular contexts. From Agar she takes a conception of ethnographic research as involving attempts to identify differences and conflicts between points of view and then seeking to build coherence by constructing a context, or a "logic-in-use" that makes sense. Charles shows how these informing ideas underpin her coding of observational and interview data, and her subsequent development of substantial findings. These findings explain, among other things, how students negotiate cell phone use—practices based on understandings and kinds of knowledge—outside the school's rules in ways that they can reconcile as being appropriate and acceptable within the school setting and in keeping with the educational purposes of school. These are ways that at least some teachers are able to accept as a form of shared negotiation with students' infringements of official rules: infringements that enable a kind of literacy across discourses within the school context.

REFERENCES

Agar, M. (2006). Culture: Can you take it anywhere? *International Journal of Qualitative Methods*, 5(2), 1–16.

Boote, D., & Beile, P. (2005). Scholars before researchers: On the centrality of the dissertation literature review in research preparation. *Educational Researcher*, 34(6), 3–15.

Bridges, D. (2006). The disciplines and the discipline of educational research. *Journal of Philosophy of Education*, 40(2), 259–272.

Gee, J. (2004). *Situated language and learning: A critique of traditional schooling*. New York: Routledge.

Gee, J. (2013). *Good video games + good learning* (2nd ed.). New York, NY: Peter Lang.

Gee, J., & Hayes, E. (2013). Nurturing affinity spaces and gamebased learning. In J. Gee, *Good video games + good learning* (2nd ed.) (pp. 103–124). New York, NY: Peter Lang.

Jenkins, H. (2006). *Convergence culture: Where old and new media collide.* New York, NY: New York University Press.

Krishnan, A. (2009). What are academic disciplines?: Some observations on the Disciplinarity vs Interdisciplinarity debate. Southampton, UK: Economic and Social Research Council National Centre for Research Methods. Working Paper.

Lankshear, C., & Knobel, M. (2004). *A handbook for teacher research.* Maidenhead, UK: Open University Press.

Law, J. (2004). *After method: Mess in social science research.* New York: Routledge.

LeCompte, M., & Schensul, J. (2010). *Designing and conducting ethnographic research: An introduction* (2nd ed.). Lanham, MA: Altamira Press.

Maxwell, J. (2012). *Qualitative research design: An interactive approach* (3rd ed.). Thousand Oaks, CA: Sage.

Miles, M., Huberman, A., & Saldaña, J. (2014). *Qualitative data analysis: A methods sourcebook.* Thousand Oaks, CA: Sage.

Scribner, S., & Cole, M. (1981). *The psychology of literacy*. Cambridge, MA: Harvard University Press.

Street, B. (1984). *Literacy in theory and practice*. Cambridge, UK: Cambridge University Press.

CHAPTER TWO

Critical Junctures IN THE Design AND Conduct OF Affinity Space Research

JAYNE C. LAMMERS

During the winter break of 2008–2009, I was just starting my investigation of *The Sims Writers' Hangout* (*SWH*), an online discussion forum created and maintained by young fans of writing stories using *The Sims* videogames for character and storyline ideas. I spent much of my time over that holiday reading *Sims* fanfiction stories and posts on the *SWH* forums, trying to make some initial sense of what exactly was happening on this site. As it happened, some of *SWH*'s own members seemed to be trying to make sense of their hangout as well. On the afternoon of December 30, 2008, a new thread in the Chit Chat forum appeared: "Is The Hangout … The Hangout?" As an end-of-year reflection and conversation starter, a relatively new member of *SWH* posted this message:

> The title pretty much explains it all; doesn't anyone (and I'm *sure* that I'm not the only one) else think that the hangout has changed this year? Even though I've only been a member since July, I've seen some people on here who don't really care about what other people came on here for; ex. their creations for *Sims*, stories, ideas, and everything else that includes it. I'm not saying that the Hangout doesn't need to have fun every once in a while, but don't you guys just think that the Hangout has changed a little **too** much? If this is offensive in any way, I'm sorry … and if it's in the wrong place … but I was just wondering … Anyone willing to share opinions? (emphasis and ellipses in original; *SWH* post, December 30, 2008)

I read with great investigational interest as 46 responses to this message appeared over the next seven days, giving me glimpses into the varied opinions of some *SWH* members as they claimed that "the Hangout has changed because the people have changed" (*SWH* post, December 30, 2008) and encouraged the group to "revitaliz[e] this forum with the upcoming year" (Pamela, *SWH* post, December 31, 2008). The thread remained active for six months, eventually collecting 87 responses to the original post, in which members argued for a return to the "Golden Age"—a time when great writers and stories got attention—of *SWH*, debated what practices they truly valued, and in part, led the site's leadership to "revamp" the site in June 2009. My research gave me a front row seat to the entire discussion, and this thread and the resulting changes to the Hangout became the subject of the first published analysis in my study of *SWH* (Lammers, 2012).

That my inquiry coincided with *SWH* members' own examination of their practices and purposes was happenstance. While researchers can certainly benefit from recognizing the lucky opportunities that present themselves in a project, much of our work derives from intentional design decisions made throughout the research process. Like many of my contemporaries who were also interested in understanding the nature of literacies, learning, and participation in digital affinity spaces (see Hayes & Duncan, 2012), I entered *SWH* with questions that sought to make sense not only of the site's culture and practices, but also of James Paul Gee's theories of affinity spaces (Gee, 2004; Gee & Hayes, 2010). To that end, I brought virtual ethnographic research methods (Hine, 2000) together with methodologies that emphasize the discourse of online interactions (Androutsopoulos 2008) and the connective nature of adolescents' digital literacies (Leander & McKim, 2003) to design an interpretive exploration of *SWH*—conducting what I later came to call an *affinity space ethnography* (Lammers, Curwood, & Magnifico, 2012).

This chapter aims to lay bare the realities of study design and data collection in affinity space ethnographic research, opening them up for examination, because, as Sean Duncan (2012) noted, "one of the challenges in moving affinity space research forward to date has been primarily methodological" (p. 52). Though Duncan's concerns centered on the need for methods to uncover more generalized practices within and across affinity spaces, I want to take up his charge to move affinity space and new literacies research forward by unpacking the numerous decisions researchers face when designing and conducting these studies. Inspired by Alan Peshkin's (2000) revelatory article describing his "journey of interpretation" in a research project, in this chapter I, too, provide a "retrospective account" (p. 5) of my two-year affinity space ethnography to reveal *critical junctures* in the design process. In keeping with this book's focus, I highlight those critical junctures—crucial points when decisions made based on a convergence of theoretical, contextual, and methodological factors propel a study down a particular path—that occur in the earlier design and data collection phases of affinity space research. To continue, I first offer additional background information about my study of *SWH* and then move to illuminating a series of critical junctures, reviewing what other researchers have decided at each, and indicating how my choices shaped my data collection approach. This chapter concludes by discussing the lessons I've learned about designing and conducting affinity space research by examining these crucial decision points.

STUDYING *THE SIMS WRITERS' HANGOUT*

From 2008 to 2010, I was involved in projects aimed at understanding women's trajectories in information technology learning (Hayes, King, & Lammers, 2008) and developing afterschool programs that might build young girls' interest in technology. We used the videogame *The Sims*, the most popular PC game in the world at the time (EA Play Label, 2010), as a vehicle for introducing girls to programming, 3D modeling, and digital storytelling. In my efforts to show our participants some of the creative possibilities connected to this game, I found numerous fan sites where *Sims* players from all over the world were creating and sharing their work online. Thus, I discovered *SWH*, a site with more than 12,000 members who had contributed over 665,000 posts organized into 31,000 topics across 22 forums and 72 subforums (as of May 12, 2010).

As a former English teacher whose interests in literacy learning were struggling to find a place in our technology-focused projects, I explored *SWH* with great interest, immediately seeing connections to the workshop models I had implemented in literacy classrooms in the past (cf. Atwell, 2014). On *SWH*, I found young people soliciting assistance from proofreaders and technical collaborators to create stories that paired images from their *Sims* games with narratives they wrote—creating what I call *Sims* fanfiction (Lammers, 2012)—and then sharing those creative works back within the forums for reader feedback. Initially, the fact that young people seemed motivated to do all of this work on their own, with little tangible reward, intrigued me most about *SWH* as it stood in stark contrast to all of the efforts that I as a teacher had put into trying to incentivize my former students to read and write in our classroom-based literacy workshops. Thus began my research focused on better understanding the nature of literacy and learning in this out-of-school, youth-inhabited, online affinity space. In this section, I aim only to provide a brief overview of my study as an orientation to the project's scope, recognizing that many more details will be revealed through the discussion of critical junctures presented later.

After discovering *SWH*, the first phase of data collection involved 12 months of systematic observation (cf. Androutsopoulos, 2008). During this observation period, I not only followed current *SWH* discussion threads, including the one referenced at the beginning of this chapter, but also read past threads. I worked to get a situated sense of what participation looked like in *SWH*, focusing on where different comments got posted, what reactions *Sims* stories received, and what resources were available to authors in this site, paying particular attention to how practices evolved over time. Through my observations, I learned that *SWH* was not a repository to store *Sims* fanfiction itself. Rather, authors hosted their creations on other websites, such as *Sims* corporate sites like "The Exchange" or their own websites and blogs, and then provided hyperlinks in their *SWH* posts that directed readers to various story repositories across the Internet. This prolonged period of time spent reading and tracing participation allowed me to develop an initial sense of *SWH* as "a place where people do things" (Hine, 2000, p. 21) as I mapped out the content of each forum (see Table 2.1).

Table 2.1. Sims Writers' Hangout Forums.

Forum Name	Topics	Posts	Description
		General Section	
Welcome to the *Sims 2* Writers' Hangout	2997	38171	"Please introduce yourself to the group here."
Help, FAQ and Tutorials	895	4315	"Forum, *Sims 2*, picture, and general computer questions"
The Hangout Reporter	23	1013	"*Hangout* extras: feature interviews and special announcements"
Idea Box	66	1151	"Do you have a great new idea? Come inside to discuss making the *Hangout* a better place."
Hangout Activities	4	223	"Daily, weekly, and monthly games to keep our members connected!"
Chit Chat	11578	381525	"This board is for the regular chit chat. Just chit and chat."
		The Sims 2 Section	
Sims 2 Talk	1016	26896	"Chat about our favorite game! Remember: questions go in *Help & FAQ*."
The Sims 2 Bookshop	1900	36046	[A space for authors to share links to their *Sims 2* stories and for readers to post responses]
Sims 2 Inspired	1192	16743	"*Sims 2* Creativity at its best! Pictures, Movies & Requests"
Sims 2 Couturier	1792	23163	"Share your *Sims 2* creations, from clothing to genetics to make-up, Sims, objects and lots."
Sims 2 Custom Content Links	3863	26361	"Looking for the great hair style or piece of clothing you saw in one of our stories?"

Forum Name	Topics	Posts	Description
			The Sims 3 Section*
Sims 3 Talk	14	762	"Chat about the latest addition to our favorite game! Remember: questions go in *Help & FAQ*."
The Sims 3 Bookshop	15	168	"Read all the latest *Sims 3* stories."
Sims 3 Inspired	9	220	"*Sims 3* creativity at its best! Movies, Pictures & Requests"
Sims 3 Couturier	2	10	"Share you *Sims 3* creations, from clothing to genetics to make-up, Sims, objects and lots."
Sims 3 Custom Content Links	9	32	"Whatever you want we've got it or we'll be able to find it for you."
			Sims Stories Section
Sims Stories: Advice, Ideas, and Tips	4407	35316	[A space to share general ideas and advice for creating *Sims* stories.]
The Vault	36	745	"The secrets of great *Sims* stories—Tutorials, tips, articles, exercises, name banks, etc. can be found in the *Vault*."
Writers Lounge	47	751	"Original poetry, prose, or non-*Sims* stories? Post them here!"
			Contests Section
HNTM Season 4	48	1141	"The Hangouts Next Top Model—Season 4—The teachers and tantrums of Male & Female teen models."
Member Contests	156	3138	[A space for on-going contests and for members to create their own contests.]
Special Contests Archive	1249	67416	"Winners and archives of finished contests."

Note: As of May 12, 2010. When available, descriptions are quoted directly from the *SWH* website.
* Indicates forums created as a part of the 2009 *SWH* revamp.

As I studied the layout of *SWH*, I also generated a nascent understanding of who participated here and what roles were available to them. In addition to the obvious roles of writers, readers, and moderators that I was able to easily detect, spending extended time in *SWH* allowed me to cultivate a richer catalog of the varied pursuits available in this space. I followed the work of many different writers, from those who wrote longer, multichapter *Sims* fanfiction to those who posted single-chapter stories, called "one-shots." I also took note of writers who posted initial story ideas, but never shared a finished product. With an interest in how members served as resources for each other in this space, I reviewed posts in the Classified subforums, where members asked for and received assistance from proofreaders and *Sims* custom content creators, and studied the member-created tutorials shared in *SWH*. To get a sense of how newbies were welcomed into the space, I observed the Welcome forum and followed where new members went on *SWH* to begin participating. In addition to focusing on practices specifically linked to the creation of *Sims* fanfiction, I also spent a great deal of time studying how members participated in the Chit Chat forum, in contests, and in the Writers Lounge forum (a space to post non-*Sims* writing such as original poetry or prose) to round out my understanding of *SWH*. All of this intense focus on the participants and roles in *SWH* led me to the next phase of data collection: contact with key informants.

The remaining 12 months of my affinity space ethnography centered on interactions with eight young women who agreed to participate in my study. Table 2.2 provides a brief introduction to these participants and their *SWH* activities. To gather these insiders' perspectives on *SWH*, I conducted semi-structured virtual interviews with each either through e-mail or through the private message (PM) system in *SWH*, personalizing my interview questions based on what I had observed them post in the forums. For some participants, I also exchanged numerous follow-up messages to help clarify my understanding of what I was seeing in the forums or in my later analysis. Lastly, I gathered and organized artifacts documenting their individual *SWH* participation, *Sims* fanfiction creations, and related activities, including tracing their *Sims*-related practices to other online spaces such as Flickr, YouTube, The Exchange, and more. The full data corpus for this affinity space ethnography includes hundreds of pages of downloaded *SWH* posts, 15 virtual interview responses, and copies of PMs or follow-up e-mails from participants, 12 *Sims* fanfiction stories authored by my participants, numerous screen shots to capture visual images, a log of hyperlinks to other websites, and multimodal, ethnographic field notes documenting my systematic observations.

As I moved on to the data analysis phase of the study, I worked to make sense of different aspects of literacies and learning in *SWH* through various analyses. My first analysis drew on Gee's (2004) affinity space theory to explore the tensions revealed, in part, through the "Is the Hangout … the Hangout?" discussion thread and the subsequent revamp of *SWH* in 2009 (Lammers, 2012). I also pursued answers to questions about the nature of pedagogy in *SWH*, using Basil Bernstein's (2000, 2004) pedagogic discourse theory as a lens to understand how social behaviors were normed and how discourses relocated from other media spaces served as pedagogy in *SWH* (Lammers, 2013). A later analysis focused on one newer member, Angela, and used the New London Group's (1996) Designs of Meaning

Table 2.2. Information about Study Participants.

Participant*	Date Joined SWH	Total SWH Posts	SWH Status**	SWH Activities
Angela 15 United States	Aug. 10, 2009	280	Full Member Active	Chit Chat posts, reading and writing *Sims* fanfiction, sharing story ideas, posting requests, using proofreaders, writing non-*Sims* stories
Eastwood 19 England	Apr. 4, 2006	633	Seniority Active	Chit Chat posts, reading and writing *Sims* fanfiction, using proofreaders, entering contests
Eleanor 18 England	Aug. 24, 2005	5675	Demi Goddess Inactive	Chit Chat posts, reading and writing *Sims* fanfiction, role play, writing My Chemical Romance (a band)-inspired fanfiction, writing non-*Sims* short stories
Eve 23 Hawaii, United States	Oct. 17, 2005	3843	Royal Member Inactive	Chit Chat posts, reading and writing *Sims* fanfiction, creating *Sims* movies, entering contests, creating photo editing tutorials
Missy 23 England	Feb. 17, 2006	1591	Senior Staff Active	Chit Chat posts, reading and writing *Sims* fanfiction, moderating and entering contests, moderating forums
Naomi 18 United States	May 22, 2008	714	Seniority Inactive	Chit Chat posts, reading and writing *Sims* fanfiction, proofreading, using proofreaders, writing non-*Sims* short stories
Pamela 18 Canada	May 11, 2007	3409	Senior Staff Active	Chit Chat posts, reading *Sims* fanfiction, moderating and entering contests, moderating forums, welcoming new members, managing the site
Zahrah 22 United States	Dec. 9, 2007	2228	High Priestess Active	Chit Chat posts, reading *Sims* fanfiction, answering requests, moderating contests, creating custom content

Notes: All participants identified themselves as females. Data are as of June 1, 2010.

* Pseudonym, age, and place of residence.

** Status markers were displayed on all *SWH* profiles, and changed as members posted more or took on moderator roles. This column indicates whether or not the participant was actively posting in *SWH* during data collection.

framework to make visible the multiple factors influencing this writer's choices as she leveraged her participation in *SWH* to create and share her *Sims* fanfiction (Lammers, 2016). In addition, I have brought data from this study into conversation with others' research of adolescents' videogame and fan-based literacies to make claims about methods for conducting affinity space ethnography (Lammers, et al., 2012), writers' motivation to share their creative works with affinity space audiences (Curwood, Magnifico & Lammers, 2013), and the features of belongingness in videogame affinity spaces (Abrams & Lammers, forthcoming 2017). With this background about the study articulated, I now move to discussing critical junctures in the initial design and data collection phases of this research project.

CRITICAL JUNCTURES

As noted earlier, I conceptualize critical junctures as crucial points in the research process when decisions made based on a convergence of theoretical, contextual, and methodological factors propel a study down a particular path. For each of the critical junctures below, I present the factors I considered when making a decision and a discussion of how my choices shaped the design and conduct of data collection in my study of *SWH*.

(a) Starting an Affinity Space Study

The very beginning of any study presents a critical juncture in which factors, such as time, capacity, and a researcher's beliefs, converge with the spark of an idea to influence how a project gets started. Ideas come from myriad sources, including one's own professional and personal life or the launch of a new technology or media product. Inspiration for a study may also derive from calls for additional research encountered while reading literature in the field or reviewing funding agencies' requests for proposals. However, recognizing an intriguing phenomenon, discovering a new online space, wanting to know more about interesting people or practices, or responding to a call for more research serves as only part of what impacts a study's design at this initial critical juncture. Researchers also need to consider how material factors like time and resources shape the feasibility or "do-ability" (Marshall & Rossman, 2006, p. 11) of their affinity space research. Assessing an individual's or research team's capacity to collect and analyze data within the allotted time and with the available resources can play an important role in shaping the design of a study. Finally, a researcher's philosophical worldview (Creswell, 2014), or what may also be referred to as a paradigm or epistemology, will impact what approach is taken in designing an affinity space study.

Published accounts of new literacies research do not often include discussions about how a project or line of inquiry got started. Some notable exceptions include Gee's (2003) account of being intrigued as he watched his four-year-old son play challenging videogames and other scholars' acknowledgments that their own participation in an affinity space or new literacies practice sparked their research (e.g., Black, 2008; Chen, 2012; Davies, 2006). As mentioned earlier, my affinity space research began with a desire to understand an online space—the *Sims Writers' Hangout*—that I had stumbled upon when looking for models of *Sims* stories to share with the girls in our afterschool program. In addition, my choice to pursue this line of research was informed by the scholarly conversations I was aware of through my doctoral course work and the academic conferences I had attended, particularly with respect to Gee's (2004) theory of affinity spaces and New Literacy Studies notions of literacies as situated, social practices (e.g., Barton, 2007; Lankshear & Knobel, 2011; New London Group, 1996). My own past as an urban middle school English teacher and high school Reading teacher also factored into how I saw *SWH* as a writing workshop of sorts, and informed the educational worldview I brought with me into my study of this affinity space. Finally, my alignment with Christine Hine's (2000) notion of viewing the internet as a culture shaped how I conceptualized *SWH* and the situated practices of its inhabitants.

In starting my study of *SWH*, I made a variety of decisions at this critical juncture that shaped the direction my research would take. First, I chose to enter into the space with an exploratory purpose. Affinity space research was relatively new at the time, and while other new literacies studies already offered relevant insights into the phenomenon of fanfiction writing (e.g., Black, 2008; Chandler-Olcott & Mahar, 2003; Thomas, 2007), I believed there was still more to explore with respect to the multimodal nature of *Sims* fanfiction and the structure and practices of *SWH* as a "portal"—that is, "anything that gives access to the content and to ways of interacting with that content" (Gee, 2004, p. 81)—to the *Sims* affinity space. Then, because I had no prior experience participating in this affinity space, I also decided it was crucial to build extended time for observing in *SWH* into my study design, which aligns with recommendations that online researchers commit to the space as a means of showing respect (Knobel, 2003). Additionally, I began playing *The Sims 2* more and created my own *Sims* fanfiction, in an effort to deepen my understanding of the cultural practices key to this space. Coupling these decisions with a commitment to the extended time in a field site required by ethnographic research dictated that my project timeline grow to at least two years, a period long enough for me to conduct this research but short enough to accommodate external factors related to my status as a graduate student conducting a dissertation study.

(b) Crafting Research Questions

Many of the factors outlined above, which shape the start of an affinity space study, also direct the work of crafting research questions that will guide the inquiry. One's worldview and approach to research again inform the decisions made at this critical juncture, pointing the project in specific methodological directions. Initial knowledge of the field site and awareness of current conversations in relevant research also factor into how questions will be asked to better understand the phenomenon under study and fill identified gaps in the field's literature. Qualitative, ethnographic research questions, of the type that guided my study of *SWH*, often consist of a limited number of overarching or "central" questions (Creswell, 2014) and then more specific subquestions. Collectively, these questions articulate the specifics of a project in terms of research site and focus of the study and reveal the theoretical orientation being brought to bear on data collection and analysis. They set the study on a path of inquiry that has consequences for what and how data will be collected, from whom and where, and to what ends. However, qualitative research questions evolve in response to the researcher's developing understanding throughout the data collection process, and thus must remain flexible (Marshall & Rossman, 2006). At this early juncture in the design process, then, an affinity space ethnography's research questions should be specific enough to direct the researcher's attention but open enough to allow for discovery and responsiveness as the project unfolds.

Examining others' affinity space research reveals some factors influencing the research questions they crafted to guide their studies. For example, Rebecca Black (2008) noted that her adoption of a sociocultural framework allowed her the "theoretical and methodological flexibility" necessary to "best answer key questions that emerge … in response to the growing salience of media, popular culture, and technology in youths' lives" (p. 25). Many of these "key questions" guided her ethnographic study of English language learners writing anime fanfiction and sharing it on Fanfiction.net. Relatedly, Constance Steinkuehler (2007) made the argument that the massively multiplayer online game *Lineage* was a "robust social and virtual-material world" warranting "full investigation in its own right" (p. 299). Conceptualizing the videogame and surrounding affinity space as a cultural world directed her study down an ethnographic path, and, coupled with her theoretical perspectives of literacy and cognition, guided her to craft research questions about what people "learn through participation in such spaces" and whether the "knowledge and skills leveraged in virtual worlds 'pay off' in the purportedly 'real' one" (Steinkuehler, 2007, p. 299). These examples reflect how most accounts of affinity space research focus on theoretical factors impacting this critical juncture.

Sharing the evolution of my own study's research questions reveals the numerous factors that shaped them. My earliest documented articulation of possible research questions exists in an Excel workbook created on November 9, 2008. This multitabbed collection of more than 25 questions indicates that I was initially interested in three broad categories of exploration: mapping the *Sims* fanfiction affinity space, studying how learning happened in *SWH*, and understanding how adolescents constructed identities as writers in this space. Clearly, having two-dozen research questions would not have been reasonable given my time and capacity constraints, nor would it have helped me design a focused study. Therefore, I engaged in an iterative process of revising my project's research questions, informed by my continuing observations in *SWH*, my reading of empirical and theoretical literature, and my conversations with advisors and critical friends. In a later funding proposal, I articulated the following research questions:

1. How is an online Pro-Am affinity space organized to create a collaborative learning environment?
   a. How does the space create and promote high standards for literacy learning?
   b. What is the role of multigenerational mentorship in this space?
2. What is the nature of the multimodal literacies recruited by the space?
3. How might an intervention within this space affect the literacy learning of participants?

These questions reflect numerous influences, including my reading about Charles Leadbeater and Paul Miller's (2004) Pro-Ams—professional amateurs—concept, my desire to investigate Gee's (2004) claim that affinity spaces allow people of all ages to learn together, and an early idea Gee and I had about introducing an intervention into *SWH.*

However, subsequent factors, particularly that this proposal was not funded and that my situated understanding of *SWH* continued to evolve, moved me away from some of these questions. Ultimately, I crafted the following research questions to guide my affinity space ethnography:

1. How is *SWH*, an online affinity space, organized to create a collaborative learning environment?
   a. How does this space create and promote high standards for literacy learning?
   b. How does participation in this space shape the creation of participants' *Sims* fanfiction?
2. What is the nature of the multimodal literacies recruited by this space? (Lammers, 2011, p. 14)

Thus, my study remained exploratory and ethnographic, rather than becoming an intervention study, and I focused my attention on understanding *SWH* as an affinity space that promoted literacy learning through creating and sharing multimodal *Sims* fanfiction. These questions guided my data collection process and directed how I gathered particular types of data and how I interacted with *SWH* insiders.

(c) Navigating Review Board Approval

While securing the necessary approval to conduct an affinity space study may not immediately follow the crafting of research questions, I turn now to focusing on this critical juncture to unpack how ethical and institutional factors may also shape a study's data collection and overall design. With the increase in research about, including, or taking place—at least in part—within online spaces, there has been an evolution in thinking about online research ethics and the consent process. Some researchers argue that the same ethical principles that apply to physical space research also apply online, whereas others contend that there needs to be special consideration for the consequences of gathering data online (Knobel, 2003). Factors particularly important to ethical considerations in online research include determining whether data are public or private, how to obtain informed consent, and whether or how to ensure anonymity. Addressing these issues needs to be informed by the practices and technical specifications of the online space being studied. Adding to the complexity of this critical juncture, institutions and their research review boards vary in terms of how they handle online research (Buchanan & Ess, 2009), and the guidelines of the particular institution will impact study design decisions that get made in the process of securing approval for affinity space research.

Discussions about how a researcher navigated human subjects review rarely make it into published reports of new literacies research. However, some insights about ethical decisions made during a research project are available. For example, regarding the protection of anonymity, Black (2008) includes a discussion of how she changed participants' names and story titles, particularly when they were "highly Googleable" (p. 23). Ensuring that data shared in publications does not lead back to a participant expecting anonymity becomes more challenging when a simple internet search of that data can reveal a person's identity. Obtaining informed consent from research participants, another factor important to securing review board approval, can also present affinity space researchers with challenges, especially when they only know their participants through online spaces and communication. To help researchers with these and other questions about ethical decision-making at this critical juncture, guidance is available (see Boellstorff, Nardi, Pearce, & Taylor, 2012; Markham & Buchanan, 2012).

Before submitting my materials to Arizona State University's institutional review board, I first had a conversation with Rebecca Black, who was generous enough to share copies of what she submitted to the board that approved her study of Fanfiction.net and to offer insights about how she navigated this process at a time when online ethnographic research was very new. Based on this conversation, I created a Google site for participant recruitment—a site that displayed the content of the approved study information letter and a form for participants to indicate their desire to participate in my research by providing their e-mail address and birth date. Once participants provided the requested information, I used the birthdate to determine if follow up was required to obtain parental consent via the multistep process the review board required for any participant under the age of 18 years. This process included e-mailing the participant to get a parent's e-mail address, sending the parental consent and youth assent forms electronically and receiving signed copies back, and then following up with a phone call with the parent to verify consent. The Arizona State University review board was very concerned that I not alert minors that they would undergo a different consent process than adults, so the Google site collected birthdates from every interested participant and made no mention that the process was different depending upon one's age. As it turned out, this consent process for youth did deter one *SWH* member from being in my study, as she did not want her mother to know about her online practices. In the end, all but one of my study's informants was an adult. I did, however, feel assured that my participant recruitment and data collection methods met the field's and the institution's standards for ethical practice in online research.

(d) Generating Initial Understandings

Once data collection begins in earnest, researchers face decisions about how to generate initial understandings about the affinity space. This can be challenging regardless of whether the researcher is an insider, who may be overly familiar with and not recognize the uniqueness of a phenomenon, or an outsider, who could misinterpret the practices observed. Factors to consider at the critical juncture of entering the field as a researcher include: the time available for the project, the vastness of the space, and the extent to which offline contexts and practices need to be considered to fully understand the affinity space. An important part of the research process comes from "getting a 'feel'" (Knobel, 2003, p. 196) for the field site, becoming familiar with the organization, people, and practices that make up the affinity space. At this juncture, researchers must make decisions about the nature and duration of the observations they will conduct.

Stances on conducting observations in online affinity spaces vary. Some researchers prefer to conduct participant observations, continuing to engage as contributors to the space while also collecting data as a researcher. This seems to be the preferred method for literacy researchers who decide to study a space to which they already belong (e.g., Black, 2008; Magnifico, 2012). Others enter into an unfamiliar space and conduct observations to gain the familiarity needed to make sense of what insiders will share in later steps of data collection. One benefit of conducting research in online affinity spaces is that platforms such as discussion forums, message boards, blogs, etc., provide researchers with historical records to include as data (Lammers, et al., 2012). However, such data may disappear at the whim of the site's creators, so researchers need to consider how they will capture and preserve as much of this record as possible during data collection.

To generate my initial understandings of *SWH*, I followed Jannis Androutsopoulos' (2008) advice for conducting systematic observations in online ethnography. He recommends the following six guidelines:

1) Examine relationships and processes rather than isolated artifacts
2) Move from core to periphery of a field
3) Repeat observation
4) Maintain openness
5) Use all available technology
6) Use observation insights as guidance for further sampling. (Androutsopoulos, 2008, p. 6)

Using these guidelines gave my observational work direction and focus, and helped me to feel as if I was doing more than just aimlessly reading posts on *SWH*. I started by going into each of the forums to capture the rules—what I later came to call "moderator-created norming texts" (Lammers, 2012)—and read initial posts and their responses, to get a sense of what was posted in each area. I followed hyperlinks to observe the *Sims* fanfiction stories, *Sims* custom content, and other outside material connected to the practices within *SWH*, developing a sense of the interconnected portals that made up the larger *Sims* fanfiction affinity space. To stay organized at this critical juncture, I created a system of file folders on my hard drive to catalogue the screenshots, downloads, and field notes I generated. I arranged the data by discussion thread type (e.g., story threads, norming texts, requests), by date (separating "before the revamp" data from "during and after revamp" data), and later by study participant. I downloaded a list of the top 100 *SWH* members, based on number of posts, and followed links in some of these members' posts to read their *Sims* fanfiction. All these data helped me to generate initial understandings about *SWH* that informed my focus and direction in data collection, my selection of study participants, and my later interpretation of data.

(e) Gaining Insiders' Perspectives

Though the field's understanding of affinity spaces has benefitted from knowledge gained through studies that relied primarily on online data (e.g., Duncan, 2012; Magnifico, Curwood, & Lammers, 2015), gaining insiders' perspectives is an important component of affinity space ethnography. The numerous factors that converge to shape a researcher's decisions at this critical juncture include the types of roles available in the space and people's willingness to contribute to research, and decisions made here will inform both who a researcher invites to participate in the study and how data are collected to gain these insiders' perspectives. Androutsopoulos (2008) recommends that contact with potential "informants" be "limited, non-random, and include various participation formats" (p. 6), allowing the researcher to develop a targeted understanding of a fuller range of how people interact in the space. It is also important to realize that decisions made at earlier junctures shape and direct what happens as the project continues into this phase of contacting insiders. For example, the focus and research questions will guide who to solicit for participation in the study, and the time spent to develop initial understanding of the space will help a researcher establish the crucial rapport needed to gain insiders' trust and encourage them to participate in the study. Finally, researchers need to consider how best to document an insider's participation in the affinity space, drawing on a range of methods for data collection.

Examining existing affinity space research reveals how these factors shape the selection of participants and data collection process at this critical juncture. Shree Durga's (2012) desire to recruit participants with varied technological expertise and interest in the game modding practice she was studying guided her selection of the three focal participants in her study. However, Black (2008) recruited participants whose similar interests, shared status as English language learners, and friendship allowed her to gain insights into how they supported each other's fanfiction writing. No guidelines exist for determining how many participants should be recruited, as rich studies of affinity spaces stem from data gathered from as little as three people, as with these two studies, to 16 key informants (Steinkuehler, 2007) or more. Whereas some see the ability to access participants outside of one's geographic area as a benefit to online affinity space research (Lammers et al., 2012), in her study of eBay, Knobel (2003) insisted on only interviewing people she had met face to face or from whom she had purchased something, so practices vary in terms of the researcher's connection to possible study participants. Generally, much of the affinity space research relies on a variety of data collection methods, including interviews conducted via e-mail, private messaging within a system or service, internet chat, telephone, or Skype, and artifact collection, for gaining insiders' perspectives. Based on the scope of their project, some studies focus on the practices within a particular website (e.g., Duncan, 2012; Magnifico, 2012), while others trace people's practices across portals (e.g., Curwood, 2013).

(i) Recruiting participants

In connecting back to my own study of *SWH*, let me begin with outlining the decisions I made that relate to recruiting participants. As Androutsopoulos (2008) recommends, my selection of participants was non-random and based upon the 12 months of systematic observations I had conducted thus far. I sought these insiders' perspectives because they exemplified a range of participation practices within *SWH*, including moderating, organizing and participating in contests, and asking for and providing help. Following the procedures dictated by the institutional review board, when making initial contact with participants, I included links to my recruitment Google site, my Arizona State University e-mail address, and an Arizona State University webpage with additional project information, all in an effort to clearly identify myself as a researcher affiliated with this university and to offer necessary information to help participants decide whether or not to join in the study.

It should be noted that connecting with potential research participants is not always a smooth process. For example, I first reached out to the head moderator (Pamela) of *SWH*, as a way of showing respect for her role in the site by informing her about my study, and to ask her to participate. After she agreed, I then used the e-mail address Pamela provided on the Google site to send her a set of initial interview questions. This approach to maintaining contact with her failed, as my e-mail (and the follow-up messages I sent) went unanswered for a couple of painful weeks. It turned out that my preference for e-mail as a communication tool was not shared by this teenager who said she did not even remember which of her e-mail addresses she had provided on the form. So, communicating with Pamela through the private messaging system within *SWH* was the best way to maintain our connection. Learning from this initial contact experience, I explicitly asked subsequent participants whether they preferred to communicate with me via private messaging or e-mail going forward. After Pamela, I later recruited popular writers with numerous comments on their story threads, long-time participants who had been around before the site's revamp, and a new contributor to the space, all in an effort to document the "many different forms and routes to participation" (Gee, 2004, p. 87) available in this affinity space. My recruiting efforts resulted in the eight *SWH* participants listed earlier in this chapter.

(ii) Collecting participant data

To collect data that captured each of these young women's participation in *SWH* and their connection to the practices of creating and sharing *Sims* fanfiction, I decided to incorporate a variety of data collection methods into my study design. The primary data source came from semi-structured virtual interviews. I started with an existing interview protocol from our earlier study of women's trajectories in technology learning (Hayes, King, & Lammers, 2008), giving me a base to work with, and then adapted it in two ways: first to reflect the practices within *SWH* and then to reflect what I had observed about each participant. I also decided to break up the long original protocol into a series of two or three sets of questions. Doing so allowed me to keep the amount of questions manageable for participants, respecting their time, and allowed me to further adapt subsequent questions based on earlier responses. However, breaking up the protocol into multiple interviews also presented the risk that participants may not stay engaged through the entire interview process, though I attempted to mitigate this risk by letting no more than one day pass between receiving responses and sending out the next set of questions.

Another crucial data source involved collecting participants' posts in *SWH*, from the past (which was possible given that all of the posts from 2005 on were still available on the site) and as they happened during the data collection period. Here again, my earlier conversation with Rebecca Black helped inform my data collection process, because she relayed the experience of missing data when her participants deleted something before she could capture it. As a result, I developed a practice of scheduling regular time each day to visit *SWH* and capture new forum data. Finally, because I decided to follow my participants' practices of *Sims* fanfiction wherever they occurred online, rather than bounding my study to only include artifact data from *SWH*, I also collected data from other sites, including participants' *Sims*-related websites and blogs, Flickr accounts, YouTube channels, Twitter posts, and the corporate-sponsored sites that hosted *Sims* fanfiction. To capture these multimodal data for later use in analysis, I copied and pasted web content into Word documents, which sometimes had the effect of not preserving the format of these data, so I also took screenshots to preserve the "look" of the data.

LESSONS LEARNED ABOUT AFFINITY SPACE RESEARCH

My examination of how researchers make decisions at each of these critical junctures early in an affinity space project highlights the impact of numerous theoretical, contextual, and methodological factors on the design and implementation of data collection. This chapter's retrospective analysis of how I made decisions at these critical junctures in my study of *SWH* and *Sims* fanfiction points to the following lessons learned that could inform new literacies researchers as they conduct their own studies.

Lesson 1: Read the Research

Though it is widely recognized that reading relevant studies is necessary for writing literature reviews and background sections in proposals and manuscripts, this reading also can serve an important role in sparking inspiration for a study as the researcher develops a sense of what conversations are happening in the field. Not only might an idea arise from direct calls for additional research on a particular topic, reading through what others have done can also provide insights into strategies that work, pitfalls to avoid, or factors to consider when making certain methodological decisions.

Lesson 2: Talk to Others

Reading published scholarship only allows a researcher to see part of the data collection picture, however, because often there is not enough space for writers to reveal all of the factors that went into their study design decisions. Conversations among researchers allow for more honest and revelatory sharing of this kind of information. Talking to others can shape a study's design by introducing new theories or methods, and allowing researchers to articulate their own assumptions and decision-making process.

Lesson 3: Document Everything

Even though much of the work researchers do to document their process may never make it into a published account of the study, capturing as much as possible during the study design and data collection phases of research remains important. By this I mean not only thoroughly documenting and categorizing the data collected, which can be particularly important for researchers studying impermanent and unstable online spaces, but also logging the decisions made along the way. Doing so has the benefit of providing a historical record of the process to which researchers can refer when entering later phases of a project.

Lesson 4: Refer to Theory

Establishing a cohesive and appropriate theoretical framework provides researchers with a touchstone to refer back to throughout their data collection process. Theory will help direct the researcher's attention in the initial framing of a study, making some choices more fitting than others. Theory should also guide the process of selecting participants for a study.

While the critical junctures identified in this chapter were connected back to my own affinity space research, my hope is that the critical junctures concept and the lessons articulated here can inform the work of new literacies researchers more broadly. Taking the time to articulate and systematically analyze the various factors that shaped my data collection decisions in retrospect has already had the benefit of making me more intentional as I design a new research study. Recognizing that the decisions made during early stages of the process have implications for later phases of a study, forces researchers to be more deliberate in their design decisions.

REFERENCES

Abrams, S., & Lammers, J. (forthcoming 2017). Belonging in a videogame space: Bridging communities of practice and affinity spaces. *Teachers College Record.*

Androutsopoulos, J. (2008). Potentials and limitations of discourse-centered online ethnography. *Language@Internet,* 5, 1–20. Available from: http://www.languageatinternet.org/articles/2008/1610

Atwell, N. (2014). *In the middle: A lifetime of learning about writing, reading, and adolescents* (3rd ed.). Portsmouth, NH: Heinemann.

Barton, D. (2007). *Literacy: An introduction to the ecology of written language* (2nd ed.). Malden, MA: Blackwell.

Black, R. (2008). *Adolescents and online fan fiction.* New York: Peter Lang.

Bernstein, B. (2000). *Pedagogy, symbolic control, and identity: Theory, research, critique* (revised ed.). New York, NY: Rowman & Littlefield Publishers.

Bernstein, B. (2004). Social class and pedagogic practice. In S. Ball (Ed.), *The RoutledgeFalmer reader in sociology of education* (pp. 196–217). New York: RoutledgeFalmer.

Boellstorff, T., Nardi, B., Pearce. C., & Taylor, T. (2012). *Ethnography and virtual worlds: A handbook of method.* Princeton, NJ: Princeton University Press.

Buchanan, E., & Ess, C. (2009). Internet research ethics and the institutional review board: Current practices and issues. *ACM SIGCAS Computers and Society,* 39(3), 43–49.

Chandler-Olcott, K., & Mahar, D. (2003). "Tech-savviness" meets multiliteracies: Exploring adolescent girls' technology-mediated literacy practice. *Reading Research Quarterly,* 38, 356–385.

Chen, M. (2012). *Leet noobs: The life and death of an expert player group in* World of Warcraft. New York, NY: Peter Lang.

Creswell, J. (2014). *Research design: Qualitative, quantitative, and mixed methods approaches* (4th ed.). Los Angeles, CA: Sage.

Curwood, J. (2013). *The Hunger Games*: Literature, literacy, and online affinity spaces. *Language Arts.* 90, 417–427.

Curwood, J., Magnifico, A., & Lammers, J. (2013). Writing in the wild: Writers' motivation in fan-based affinity spaces. *Journal of Adolescent & Adult Literacy,* 56, 677–685. DOI: 10.1002/JAAL.192

Davies, J. (2006). Affinities and beyond! Developing ways of seeing in online spaces. *E-Learning,* 3, 217–234. DOI: 10.2304/elea.2006.3.2.217

Duncan, S. (2012). Kongregating online: Developing design literacies in a play-based affinity space. In E. Hayes & S. Duncan (Eds.), *Learning in video game affinity spaces* (pp. 51–83). New York: Peter Lang.

Durga, S. (2012). Learning to mod in an affinity-based modding community. In E. Hayes & S. Duncan (Eds.), *Learning in video game affinity spaces* (pp. 84–102). New York: Peter Lang.

EA Play Label. (2010, February 4). EA's groundbreaking franchise *The Sims* turns ten. Retrieved February 21, 2010 from: http://news.ea.com/news/ea/20100204005467/en/EA%E2%80%99s-Groundbreaking-Franchise-Sims-Turns-Ten

Gee, J. (2003). *What video games have to teach us about learning and literacy.* New York: Palgrave Macmillan.

Gee, J. (2004). *Situated language and learning: A critique of traditional schooling.* New York: Routledge.

Gee, J., & Hayes, E. (2010). *Women and gaming:* The Sims *and 21st century learning.* New York: Palgrave Macmillan.

Hayes, E., & Duncan, S. (Eds.) (2012). *Learning in video game affinity spaces.* New York: Peter Lang.

Hayes, E., King, E., & Lammers, J. (2008). *The Sims2* and women's IT learning. In *AERC 2008 Conference Proceedings* (pp. 1–6). St. Louis, MO: AERC. Available from: http://www.adulterc.org/Proceedings/2008/Proceedings/Hayes_King_Lammers.pdf

Hine, C. (2000). *Virtual ethnography.* Thousand Oaks, CA: Sage.

Knobel, M. (2003). Rants, ratings and representation: Ethical issues in researching online social practices. *Education, Communication & Information,* 3(2), 187–210. DOI: 10.1080/14636310 32000092028

Lammers, J. (2011). "The Hangout was serious business:" Exploring literacies and learning in an online *Sims* fan fiction community. (Unpublished doctoral dissertation). Arizona State University, Tempe, AZ.

Lammers, J. (2012). "Is the Hangout ... The Hangout?" Exploring tensions in an online gaming-related fan site. In E. Hayes & S. Duncan (Eds.), *Learning in video game affinity spaces* (pp. 23–50). New York: Peter Lang.

Lammers, J. (2013). Fangirls as teachers: Examining pedagogic discourse in an online fan site. *Learning, Media and Technology,* 38, 368–386. DOI: 10.1080/17439884.2013.764895.

Lammers, J. (2016). "*The Hangout* was serious business": Leveraging participation in an online space to Design *Sims* fanfiction. *Research in the Teaching of English,* 50, 309–332.

Lammers, J., Curwood, J., & Magnifico, A. (2012). Toward an affinity space methodology: Considerations for literacy research. *English Teaching: Practice and Critique,* 11(2), 44–58.

Lankshear, C., & Knobel, M. (2011). *New literacies: Everyday practices and social learning* (3rd ed.). New York: Open University Press.

Leadbeater, C., & Miller, P. (2004). *The pro-am revolution: How enthusiasts are changing our economy and society.* London: Demos.

Leander, K., & McKim, K. (2003). Tracing the everyday "sitings" of adolescents on the Internet: A strategic adaptation of ethnography across online and offline spaces. *Education, Communication, and Information,* 3(2), 211–240.

Magnifico, A. (2012). The game of Neopian writing. In E. Hayes & S. Duncan (Eds), *Learning in video game affinity spaces* (pp. 212–234). New York: Peter Lang.

Magnifico, A, Curwood, J., & Lammers, J. (2015). Words on the screen: Broadening analyses of interactions between fanfiction writers and reviewers. *Literacy,* 49, 158–166. DOI: 10.1111/lit.12061.

Markham, A., & Buchanan, E. (2012). *Ethical decision-making and internet research: Recommendations from the AoIR ethics working committee (version 2.0).* Association of Internet Researchers. Available from http://aoir.org/reports/ethics2.pdf

Marshall, C., & Rossman, G. (2006). *Designing qualitative research (4th ed.).* Thousand Oaks, CA: Sage.

New London Group. (1996). A pedagogy of multiliteracies: Designing social futures. *Harvard Educational Review,* 66(1), 60–92.

Peshkin, A. (2000). The nature of interpretation in qualitative research. *Educational Researcher,* 29(9), 5–9.

Steinkuehler, C. (2007). Massively multiplayer online gaming as a constellation of literacy practices. *E-Learning,* 4, 297–318. DOI: 10.2304/elea.2007.4.3.297

Thomas, A. (2007). Blurring and breaking through the boundaries of narrative, literacy, and identity in adolescent fan fiction. In M. Knobel & C. Lankshear (Eds.), *New literacies sampler* (pp. 137–166). New York: Peter Lang.

CHAPTER THREE

Conversation Analysis, Transcription, and Local Productions of Order

AARON CHIA YUAN HUNG

INTRODUCTION

The New Literacy Studies expands our understanding of literacy as a purely cognitive phenomenon to account for social, cultural, political, material, and historical contingencies (Gee, 1996; Street, 2003). New literacies studies extends "literacies" to look at "socially recognized ways in which people generate, communicate, and negotiate meanings, as members of Discourses, through the medium of encoded texts" (Lankshear & Knobel, 2011, p. 50). This position focuses on how people engage with digital texts and media through collaboration, sharing, remixing, meme-ing, and play (Jenkins, Ito, & boyd, 2015; Lankshear & Knobel, 2011).

Of the various research methods used in new literacies studies, conversation analysis (CA) is seldom among them. CA, the study of social organization through the close analysis of naturally occurring talk, is also interested in the nature of negotiated meanings. The underlying premise is that everyday talk is the most fundamental unit of social life and that, through detailed transcription and close analysis, we can uncover and describe how people make sense of their interactions and activities on a moment-by-moment basis. CA grew out of ethnomethodology, a sociological tradition that studies how people practically make sense of their world and the actions within it. Like the New Literacy Studies, CA does not consider talk as simply an expression of what a speaker has in her mind; instead, CA considers talk as a tool that people use to achieve practical actions, which can be as simple as a greeting or invitation, or as complex as establishing and maintaining social organization (Goodwin, 2006) or making sense of a piece of technology (Suchman, 2002). This chapter gives readers a quick overview of CA, using data I collected with video game players, and provides sample analyses to show how CA can contribute to new literacies studies research.

RATIONALE

Interest in games for learning can be traced back to the 1960s, when games and simulations were considered promising ways of teaching complex concepts such as systems thinking and language learning (Abt, 1970; Crookall, 2000; Duke, 1974, 2000). In the 2000s, renewed interest in games, led largely by literacy researchers (e.g., Gee, 2003, 2005; Shaffer, Squire, Halverson, & Gee, 2005; Squire, 2006, 2011) and game designers (e.g., Bogost, 2005; Fullerton, 2014; Prensky, 2006; Salen & Zimmerman, 2003), reignited optimism over games. Educators began wondering what it is about video games that compel players to keep playing, despite the time and effort it takes to master them (Gee, 2003). A logical extension was to consider whether games could help educators rethink the way people learn in formal and informal contexts.

As a novice researcher entering into this field, I was excited by this interest in games but was more curious about players than game design. I wanted to examine what actual players who are not academics, not game designers, not imagined "ideal" gamers, and not myself have to say about games. I wanted to understand the game from a player's perspective, not as a statistic in a survey but as a process, and process is best studied *as* a process that unfolds in time (Hung, 2011). This drew me to CA and ethnomethodology.

BASICS OF CA

CA uses naturally occurring talk as data, in which the focus is not only on the content of the talk but how the talk is sequenced and organized by speakers. "Naturally occurring" generally refers to talk that is not structured or prompted by a researcher, as would be the case in questionnaires and interviews. These data are usually audio- or video-recorded because the method of transcription requires the researcher to be able to play the recording repeatedly in order to capture the details of the talk in the transcription, including gaps in conversation, overlapping talk, false starts, and so on. Some of the earliest findings in CA come from technology-mediated talk, namely the telephone. Harvey Sacks, who pioneered CA as a methodology, did his early work studying recorded talk of a suicide prevention hotline (Sacks, 1995). Telephone conversations, being an example of naturally occurring talk that is easily recordable without being too obtrusive, became a significant source of data for many CA researchers.

While everyday talk is a basic component of social life and is easily taken for granted, CA researchers show that even the most basic features of talk are quite complex and have to be locally managed between the speakers (Hutchby & Wooffitt, 2009; Sacks, 1984; Sacks, Schegloff & Jefferson, 1974; Sidnell, 2010; ten Have, 1990; Wooffitt, 2005). CA researchers often refer to this local management as a "joint accomplishment" or "achievement"; in other words, for speakers to establish a shared orientation, or intersubjective understanding, of what they are trying to accomplish in their talk, they must collaborate with each other by attending to the details of how things are said and how people respond (Sidnell, 2010). A comprehensive overview of CA findings is beyond the scope of this chapter. Instead, I introduce three core concepts in CA—turn-taking, adjacency pairs, and repair—to help readers better understand the sample analyses that follow.

Transcription notations

The CA transcription system used today is attributed to Gail Jefferson, who came up with a set of conventions to capture not only what was spoken, but how it was spoken (Jefferson, 2004). Being familiar with these notations is important in knowing how to transcribe and read recorded data in CA research. Some of these are:

[	Overlapping talk, with bracket marking the point of overlap
:	Lengthened syllable, indicated by number of colons
-	Cut off utterance
?	Rising intonation
=	No interval between end of prior sentence and beginning of next
.hh	Audible breathing intake
hh	Audible breathing out
( )	Uncertainty over verbatim transcription
(( ))	Action or other non-linguistic feature
(0.0s)	Number of seconds of silence

Below are two sample transcripts: the first one is a cleaned-up version that removes repetition, false starts, and other details usually captured in CA; the second one shows it as a CA transcript. These examples come from a conversation between two adolescent boys, Grant and Mitch, who were talking about the 2012 Presidential elections on Xbox Live:

G: Obama is projected to be re-elected.
M: Wow.

G: We won't know officially till tomorrow but it's really gay because Romney won more states than Obama, but Obama won the bigger states. There were more delegates for those states.
M: All right.
G: Like Ohio and Florida.
M: Whatever, I'll find out tomorrow. California I'm guessing.

While this version might be more readable, it lacks the details that allow those who do not have access to the audio to have a better idea of how the conversation unfolded. Here it is as a CA transcript:

G: Obama is projected to be re-elected but- hh
M: =wo:::w=
G: =we won't know we won't know officially till tomorrow bu:t it's really gay because Obama- I mean Romney won more states than Obama .hh.. but- Obama won the bigger states. ( ) there were more delegates for those states.
M: [all ri::ght
G: [(like) Ohi- like [Ohi:::o::: and Florida
M: [whatever I'll find out tomorrow, I'll find out tomorrow. (California) I'm guessing.

Mitch's drawn out "=wo:::w=" comes as Grant briefly pauses to breathe, and serves as an assessment of what Grant was saying. These types of assessments, placed before a turn is complete, function as a display of the listener's orientation (e.g., surprise, outrage, etc.) toward the speaker's talk (Goodwin, 1986). The overlapping talk toward the end, in which Mitch begins before Grant is complete, indicates Mitch's intention to close the conversation. Even so, he adds "California" to show that he had heard Grant's talk and understands that he was referring to U.S. states that have a large number of electoral delegates.

Note that all forms of transcriptions are imperfect and selective. CA notations are used to highlight what features are analytically important. In this way, CA researchers have been able to accumulate and share large sets of data and use them to describe basic rules of talk that have been surprisingly generalizable.

Turn-taking

Harvey Sacks, Emanuel A. Schegloff and Gail Jefferson's (1974) paper, "A simplest systematics for the organization of turn-taking for conversation," is a seminal piece in CA research, in which they lay out the basic framework that guides how turns are locally allocated by speakers in everyday conversation. The basic rules are:

1. When the current speaker is approaching the end of her turn (a "turn-transition"), then:

a. *Current speaker selects next*: The current speaker selects the next speaker, for example, by directing a question at a specific person and/or by indicating the next speaker using eye contact; if (a) doesn't occur, then:
b. *Self-selection*: If no speaker is identified, then anyone can take the next turn;
c. If neither (a) nor (b) occurs, the current speaker may continue the turn.

2. When a turn completes, the rule set restarts.

As unremarkable as this seems, this basic set of rules governs much of everyday talk in English, including new forms of communication such as texting and chatting. A big part of managing everyday conversation is to ensure that participants know when turns are still in progress and when they are about to end. This is usually more apparent in talk than in texting or chatting. However, features in texting, such as ellipses to indicate that someone is typing or automated receipts to indicate when someone has read a message, can be seen as ways of managing turn-taking in a digital context.

Adjacency pairs

Adjacency pairs are paired sequences that consist of a first pair part (FPP) and second pair part (SPP). Some examples include greeting-greeting, question-answer, summons-answer, invitation-response, request-response, compliment-response, and so on (Sacks et al., 1974; Sacks, 1995; Schegloff & Sacks, 1973). Adjacency pairs are oriented in such a way that, when a FPP is uttered, the SPP is expected; in its absence, the speaker of the FPP will look for reasons why the SPP did not occur, for example, by checking to see if the recipient did not hear the FPP or had misunderstood its meaning. Schegloff (1968) refers to this as "conditional relevance," in which the first part being uttered leads to the second part being anticipated. Adjacency pairs govern many aspects of talk, including how conversations open and close. In his study of telephone conversation, Sacks (1995) notes that the answerer always speaks first. Schegloff (1979) argues that the telephone ring itself can be described as a FPP of a summons-answer adjacency pair, in which the answerer's greeting is a SPP. The SPP is also an opportunity for the caller to identify who picked up the phone and whether the caller is the intended recipient.

Repair

When a speaker suspects that something is misunderstood or misheard, for example, when a SPP is missing, then a repair is initiated to remedy. Schegloff, Jefferson, and Sacks (1977) note that there is a general preference toward self-correction. A simple example can be seen from the excerpt above:

G: =we won't know we won't know officially till tomorrow bu:t it's really gay because **Obama- I mean Romney** won more states than Obama

Grant starts with "Obama" but then self-corrects and follows with "I mean Romney".

Repairs initiated by someone other than the speaker can take on different forms, ranging from a simple "Hello?" to a check of understanding (e.g., "You mean X?"). With repair, then, speakers and listeners hold one another accountable for what is spoken, how it is understood, and whether repairs are needed.

Lucy Suchman (2002) extends CA to studies of human–computer interactions, arguing that the interaction between humans and machines, such as, for example, when someone is trying to follow instructions on a photocopier, constitutes a turn-taking system similar to a conversation. She argues that the expert help system consists of a plan of action designed by the designers of the photocopier that is intended to guide any potential user through a set of rules. As such, the designer has to anticipate a user's needs and map them onto the expert help system. The user has to discover the plan through the process of using the machine and following the rules, which involves following them exactly as the designer had planned. However, miscommunication can arise when the designer's plan and user's plan do not coincide. For example, when a speaker repeats a statement in a face-to-face conversation, the repetition is usually taken as a form of repair, such as when we repeat something to make sure it was heard properly. In machine instruction, repetition may be intended as a request for the previous step to be repeated. Using CA to analyze the recorded talk between the novice users and their reactions to predesigned instructions, Suchman was able to identify how communication can break down between users and the photocopier instructions when one misinterprets the other's actions. Unlike conversations between humans, human–machine communications cannot be remedied by repair sequences and can become potential sources of trouble and misunderstanding.

DATA COLLECTION

CA studies talk primarily, so clear audio- or video-recordings are crucial. Since my research looked at players interacting around games, it was also helpful to collect data on what they were interacting with on the screen. Back in the mid-2000s, the best way to collect the game data was through a VCR. For the audio data, I used a digital voice recorder placed near the players. The video data, recorded on a VHS tape, had to be later converted into a digital format and then combined with the digital recording in Final Cut Pro, a video editing software program. The VHS tapes caused an unanticipated problem. VHS tapes tend to stretch; while it is usually not noticeable when viewed in isolation, it became apparent when compared to the digital audio, causing them to go out of sync over time. Fortunately, the audio recording captured the sounds from the video game as well so I was able to correct this in Final Cut Pro through careful editing. Today, it is possible to collect this kind of data more easily. Game capture devices that players use to capture and stream their gameplay in high definition are relatively affordable. I was able to use one such device, made by Elgato, to collect gameplay data in a digital form. Video editing software can also help you clean up static or other noises to help boost the quality of the data. In CA, the analyst typically presents ideal but representative examples from a larger set of data to best illustrate the features of talk they want to describe. For my dissertation, I had collected data from 16 sessions, each roughly three to four hours in length, totaling around 50 hours. My next study looked at how adolescents socialize on Xbox Live, for which I was able to use the game capture device, and collect roughly 60 hours of recorded data. Since I was present during all these sessions, I also took notes as a passive participant observer during the sessions to generate a written record of what incidents occurred. These written notes made it easier to go back and sort through the data.

Much of the analysis occurs during transcription. As such, it is best to do your own transcribing because the process of capturing the details for the transcription often reveals patterns and features that might not be as noticeable if you are passively listening. When patterns do manifest, it is important to see whether these patterns are isolated incidents or phenomena that are also present in other occasions, and whether they can be meaningfully explained against other CA studies as well as in the context of their occurrence. It is also important to have good equipment, both for data collection and for data analysis. A good set of headphones can make previously inaudible things audible, for example.

FINDINGS

Below are a few examples of data that are analyzed using CA and ethnomethodological approaches. The first set of examples comes from data collected from party chats on Xbox Live, in which the participants were not copresent (i.e., sharing the same physical space); the second set comes from data collected for my doctoral dissertation, in which the players were in the same room.

Opening sequences in party chats

The data for this example came from a group of adolescent boys who had given me permission to record their Xbox Live party chats. I became interested in this age group because increasingly more adolescents, particularly boys, are using party chats as a way to maintain friendships and socialize (Bennett, 2008; Lenhart, 2015). Since studies of naturally occurring talk of adolescents are comparatively rare, I wanted to investigate how they talk and what they talk about. My participants spend a lot of time after school on Xbox Live, usually in a party chat. Sometimes they play games together, but more often than not, they are engaged in separate activities but still talking to each other. When I log on, I usually wait for one of them to send me an invitation to their party. After I join, I am usually on the Dashboard menu, which shows me what activity each user is doing and who is speaking. Sometimes I am invited to join a game. The game capture device records what I see on my screen, the party chat, and any audio from the system (e.g., sound effects, music from games or movies). While this limits my data to what I can see on my end, this is not unlike earlier CA studies of phone conversations, where the researcher only has access to the talk.

Conversations do not simply begin. The way we begin conversations with friends is different from the way we do with strangers (Hutchby & Wooffitt, 2009; Sacks, 1995; Sidnell, 2010). In face-to-face conversations with friends, conversations typically begin with a greeting adjacency pair (e.g., "Hi," "How are you?"). Phone conversations also begin with an adjacency pair, but unlike face-to-face conversations, where turns are not predetermined, phone conversations begin with the answerer saying "Hello" first. As noted earlier, Schegloff (1968) suggests that the phone ringing can be considered the first part of a summons-answer adjacency pair, in which the answering "Hello" constitutes the second part of the pair.

Are party chats like phone conversations? The general setup is similar. Each member of the party is in his own physical space and connected to the others via a communication technology. In the case of Xbox Live, it is a headset and the console itself. In the following examples, I focus on the opening sequences of players, including myself, who enter the party chat. In Xbox Live, a notification pops up for a few seconds whenever someone on your friends list logs onto the system. It also notifies you when someone sends you an invitation and when someone joins your party. Excerpts 1 through 5 show examples of when I accept an invitation to join a party chat. In each case, the transcription begins as soon as I can hear what is being said in the chat. In bold are the opening sequences and the responses:

Excerpt 1 (Perry (P), Mitch (M), Kevin (K), and Grant (G) are in the party; G sends invitation)

A: **Hello::?**
P: **[=Hey what's up Mister Hu:::ng?**
K: [( )

Excerpt 2 (M and G are in the party; G sends invitation)

A: **Hello?**
(1.8)
M: **He::y**

Excerpt 3 (M, G, K, P, and Joseph (Jo) are in the party; G and M both sent invitations)

M:	((laughs)) (You know it) You kno:w he's Mexican when he says
	something like that.
	(2.9)
P:	Are you using [( ) (map)?
M:	[((coughs))
	(4.0)
M:	((coughs))
	(1.5)
A:	**Hi=**
M:	=I lo::ve this ma::p. (1.5) **Sup Mister Hu::ng?**
A:	How are yo::u?
	(2.0)
M:	Goo::d. Ti::red.

When I join a party, my instinct is usually to greet first, in part because I want to alert them that I am there and am recording. In Excerpts 1 and 2, which are parties consisting of more than one member, the person who sends the invitation is not necessarily the same person who responds to the greeting. From these examples, which are fairly representative, we can make three preliminary observations: (1) the greeting does not have a specific recipient; it is addressed to the party as a group and anyone can respond; (2) someone usually does respond; (3) only one person needs to respond. A fourth observation, which is not overtly supported in the data, but is one I can hypothesize for now, is that the party chat does not have a leader who "owns" the party. While the party technically does have a host, this is not usually relevant in the usual business of the party. In other kinds of multigroup interactions that do have a leader, for example, a classroom led by a teacher or a meeting with a chairperson, we typically expect the leader to do the greetings and introductions, and manage overall communication. From the way people are greeted, we can get a sense of what kind of social context the participants create for one another.

Sacks, Schegloff and Jefferson (1974) note that people try to avoid gaps in conversations, such as when a turn ends and no one picks up the next turn, or when an adjacency pair lacks its SPP. CA studies show that people can be seen to begin their turn when they anticipate that the speaker's turn is about to end, thereby creating a brief moment of overlapping speech, in part to avoid any potential gap in conversation. When gaps do occur, it often means that people are waiting for someone else to start a turn or to respond. In Excerpt 2, a gap of 1.8 seconds is noticeable (line 2). When no one responds to my greeting (line 1), Mitch responds (line 3). We see the same phenomenon in Excerpt 3 (line 10), in which there is a 1.5 second gap before Mitch attends to the greeting.

There are times when I do not always greet first, often because I had not finished setting up my recording equipment or because I had to do a software update. For example:

Excerpt 4 (Jensen (Je) is in the party; Je sends invitation)

A: **Hello?**
(8.0)
Je: **Hello?**
(1.0)
A: **Hey** (2.0) Hey (2.0) oh (1.0) sorry my mic was off

Excerpt 5 (Je is in the party; Je sends invitation)

(8.0) ((software update in progress))
Je: **Hello?=**
A: **=He:::y** (1.0) He:::y
Je: Hey how you doin'?

"Hello" is a versatile term that can take on different meanings depending on where it is placed in conversation. We cannot have a stable definition of it without knowing its context of use. The fact that we can usually tell the difference between "Hello" as a greeting or sarcastic retort or repair (in the CA sense) demonstrates how we usually are able to establish a shared orientation to the term's proper meaning when it is used. What does Jensen's "Hello?" in Excerpt 4 (line 3) mean? I had greeted Jensen but my microphone was off, so he was not able to hear me. A significant time had elapsed before he says "Hello?" not as a greeting but as a repair to remedy any possible communication breakdown. The SPP of a "Hello" greeting is typically not a "Hello?" in the form of question and is heard as a trouble, which made me realize that my microphone was off (line 5). Likewise, in Excerpt 5, Jensen greets me again after I hadn't said anything after joining the party. The "Hello?" is again a repair, because the person already in the chat does not typically greet with a "Hello?" in the form of a question. In this sense, the "Hello?" does not function the same way it does when someone answers a phone; in other words, it is *not* the SPP to a summons-answer sequence initiated by the party chat invitation. In both cases, the "Hello?" can be heard as a "Can you hear me?" or "Are you there?", which is not uncommon in party chats because technical issues do crop up, either due to connectivity issues or malfunctioning headsets or because the microphone is off. In fact, many of the participants would join the party chat and then later walk away, mute the party, or even go to sleep without logging off.

Similar opening sequences can be seen when someone else joins a party, for example:

Excerpt 6 (G, M and myself (A) are in the party chat)
P joins the party

M: -sent me a (text) what the fu::ck?
(1.0)
P: **Why hello::: there**
(1.8)
M: **Hi Perry**

Excerpt 7 (Je and A are in the party)
G joins the party

1	Je:	Yeah i- i- like I said you don't need to take anything that- is said
2		[into consideration 'cause it doesn't matter
3	G:	**[whasu::::p?**
4	A:	((chuckles))
5		(2.0)
6	(Je):	((chuckles))
7	Je:	**Sup?**

The transcription here begins when I see the notification that a new member has joined the party. We don't know at what point the new member is able to hear the party chat, but the talk is included to show that people usually wait for the turn in progress to end before they greet the party. This is most noticeable in Excerpt 6, when Perry waits for Mitch to finish his turn before his greeting. This is not the case in Excerpt 7, although Jensen does wait for the topic to end before responding to Grant's greeting (line 7).

While greetings in conversations are common, they are not inviolable laws. There are circumstances in everyday conversation when greetings are not used, especially when the speakers know each other well or when there is something urgent to convey. This is the case with these participants, who either see each other in school or talk on Xbox Live every day. Greetings may also be skipped when an activity is in progress among the others in the party, such as when they are playing a game together. For example:

Excerpt 8 (M, G, K, and A are in the party chat, playing *Call of Duty: Black Ops 2*)
P joins the party

1	M:	O:::H! (one hit one hit)	
2	Ca:	Da:mmit! right when I get it (to::)	
3	G:	O::h Dra::gunov	
4		(2.0)	
5	C:	( )	
6	M:	Oh can I ple:ase hit it? I have a spe:ctre sti:ll please please	
7		[please please please	
8	G:	[ye::a::h	[( ) go ahead ( )
9	P:		**[( ) I'm so ( ) pissed**
10		(1.0)	
11	G:	**Wh::y?**	
12	P:	That was a terrible way to end it	
13	G:	Oh! With Hershel getting bit in the leg? Yeah I kno::w ri::ght?	

Perry's opening (line 9) is vague, but serves as a potential preface to a storytelling sequence (Sidnell, 2010) and specifically one that is part of a complaint (Traverso, 2009). It is not addressed to anyone in particular, which means it potentially can be picked up by anyone or be ignored by everyone. Grant does respond with a "Wh::y?" (line 11), which again could be intended for anyone in the party but is heard relevantly by Perry, who continues his complaint. Perry's response is an example of what Sacks, Schegloff and Jefferson (1974) call "recipient design," which refers to how conversation is designed with the hearer in mind. This includes not overexplaining or telling the recipient what he already knows. Had I been the one to ask "Why?" Perry would probably have given me more detail. Perry's response is designed for Grant (line 12) because it was Grant's question he was responding to and he knew that Grant was a big fan of *The Walking Dead* and would understand that he was referring to the episode he had just watched. Even though "That was a terrible way to end it" is a nonspecific statement, it was properly understood by its recipient, as can be seen by Grant's response (line 13). This exchange also illustrates how conversation in multiparty talk has to be a collaborative effort between the whole group, and not just those who are currently speaking. This is especially important in talk where participants are not copresent and cannot rely on resources like achieving eye contact as a way of directing attention (Goodwin 1980, 1981). In this case, the coherence is achieved not only by Grant and Perry knowing what to say to each other, but also by the rest of the party *not* responding to Grant's question and understanding that it is meant for Perry.

Fairness

The issue of fairness is a common preoccupation in any competitive game. In sports, there are referees, umpires, timekeepers, judges, and spectators to keep an eye on fairness; in video games, the game's design—its set of rules that determines who wins and loses—can be a resource for judging fairness but is often not enough. In my observations, I noticed that "fairness" was a persistent topic in players' conversations, during which they spent time discussing whether a particular action committed by a player, or whether some aspect of the game, could be considered "fair."

Another way to look at this is to think of fairness as an emergent and contingent property of interaction, which includes not just their talk but also their onscreen actions and the extent to which their actions onscreen confirm or contradict their talk. Here, it is important to point out how the participants were physically positioned. Since they were playing a multiplayer fighting game, they were all looking at the same screen and not at each other. The single screen format of multiplayer fighting games is also important. Unlike split screen games, in which players see the screen split into the different players' points of view, a single screen means they are visually oriented to the same field, even if their eyes might be tracking different parts of the screen. This also means that they can be assessing the same action from the same point of view. CA studies in workplace settings describe how the act of seeing is a locally, contingent activity, in which people pay attention to the visual environment at the same time they attend to the talk (Goodwin, 1994; Goodwin, 1995; Goodwin & Goodwin, 1996). Charles Goodwin (1994, p. 606) calls this "professional vision," which comprises "socially organized ways of seeing and understanding events that are answerable to the distinctive interests of a particular social group." For example, we can all look at an X-ray or crime scene photo or geological map, but doctors and crime scene examiners and geologists are able to see them through unique lenses and use them to make professional interpretations according to their expertise. Studying these "practices of seeing" help us uncover how "visual phenomena become meaningful through the way in which they help elaborate, and are elaborated by, a range of other semiotic fields—sequential organization, structure in the stream of speech, encompassing activities, etc.—that are being used by participants to both construct and make visible to each other relevant actions" (Goodwin, 2001, p. 179). Related to this is the concept of "accountability" in ethnomethodology, which refers to how we make our actions intelligible, observable, and reportable by others (Dourish & Button, 1998; Garfinkel, 1967; Garfinkel & Sacks, 1970). In conversation, features such as adjacency pairs help orient recipients toward particular actions such as greetings, apologies, or conversation closings. It is not simply that we use words like "Hello" and "Sorry" and "Good-bye"; they have to be observable and understood by the recipients as those particular kinds of action. In video games, players who claim to be playing fairly also have to display their actions in an accountable way in order for them to be observed and reported as fair play. These actions are themselves contingent on how the players define "fairness" and what activity they are in. As such, "fairness" is not a notion that can easily be defined ahead of time or outside the context of play.

My dissertation data collection procedures were largely inspired by Suchman's (2002) work on users and photocopiers and Goodwin's (2006) research on how young girls manage their social organization through talk during playground games, gossip, and other activities. I wanted to study the gaming practices of Asian adolescent immigrants in New York City because I had observed their attachment to games and the ways games helped bridge their transition from Asia—in this case, China—to the United States. I asked a group of adolescents to pick a video game they might play together within the same physical space and recorded their sessions, looking to see what kind of talk would emerge. Jason, Kevin, and Andrew were three of the participants in this study. Since they spoke only Cantonese, a gloss and a translation are provided. For example:

gaau keoi waan	*romanization*
teach her play	*gloss (by morpheme)*
Teach her how to play	*translation*

They had picked *Super Smash Brothers Melee* on the Nintendo GameCube, a fighting game in which players choose characters from different Nintendo games, each with unique abilities. I initially was concerned that the participants picked fighting games because it was not a genre that I enjoyed playing myself. To me, it was just a flurry of noise and movement. I was therefore surprised at how much the players were able to get from the game, and how much of their talk was spent on analyzing features of the game and discussing how they wanted to approach it.

In the examples below, they had established what it meant to be in "dueling" mode, which was when two players compete against one another, while the third observes. After that, the losing player switches with the observer. The observer often ends up playing the role of a commentator, making assessments of the ongoing gameplay.

Excerpt 9 (Kevin (K) and Andrew (An) playing; Jason (J) observing)

1	J	Kevin *waan bobo godi haijau*
		Kevin play Jigglypuff those there.is
		When Kevin uses Jigglypuff, he does it
2		*geiseot ( ) keoi janwai keoi zeon*
		style he because he accurate
		with style, because he's a good shot.
3		*keoi jau geiseot*
		he has style
		He plays with style.
		((Kevin laughs))
4		*nei lidi mhai wo nei*
		you these isn't final particle you
		You're not like that. You only know how
5		*zinghai sik zapje haijan dou sik*
		only know pick.up anyone also know
		to use items. Anyone can do that.
6		*laa::::::::::::*
		final particle

Andrew problematizes Jason's use of items, which are random objects that appear for the characters to use. As a "house rule," they had decided that during dueling sessions, no one should use items because it would give one an unfair advantage over the other (Hung, 2011). This was one of many rules that emerged in the midst of play, a phenomenon that can be seen in other forms of play (Goodwin, 2006). Goodwin also notes that players often tend to push the rules to their boundaries, testing them to see how much they can get away with.

These assessments do not go uncontested. In the excerpt below, Andrew protests Jason's assessment (lines 4–5), arguing that he is just a sore loser when he lost to him earlier. Kevin sides with Jason's assessment (line 7).

Excerpt 10 (Jason and Kevin playing; Andrew observing)

1	J	Kevin *godi hai daadak hou leng* Kevin those is can.fight very beautiful **Kevin here fights really beautifully**
2		*lo::::: houci ngo daa ngo* final particles like I fight I **Like when I fight I use**
3		*jung peikaaciu* use Pikachu **use Pikachu**
4	An	*=aai daklaa daklaa daklaa* =exclamation okay okay okay **Oh, okay, okay, okay,**
5		*daklaa [aai::::::: zenghai syumhei* okay [just cannot.afford.to.lose **okay, you're just a sore loser.** [( )
		(0.9)
7	K	*diu zanhai gowo* fuck really final particles **Fuck, it's true.**
8	J	*hailo* Kevin *godi zanhai daadak* that's right Kevin those really can fight **That's right. Kevin can really fight**
9		*leng houci* Andrew *godi gam me?* beautiful like Andrew those such question marker **beautifully, (un)like Andrew.**

In this exchange, we see how the properties of "being a skilled player" emerge from the talk. Andrew may have violated the house rules, but he never violated the game rules. In other words, he did not cheat by entering special codes that might have given him an unfair advantage. He was playing by the rules of the game but not necessarily following the player-generated rules. Note also that Andrew was outnumbered. If either Jason or Kevin had sided with him, agreeing that it was fine to use anything the game provides, then the definition of "being a skilled player" would have shifted between them.

As an example of how players make one another accountable, see what happens when Jason picks up an item:

Excerpt 11 (Jason and Andrew playing; Andrew observing)

	((Jason's character picks up an item))	
1	J	*wai mhai jiu nibaa* (1.2) *wai dim* hey not want this.one hey how **Hey, I don't want this [item]. Hey how**
2		*dam aa::[:::?*

drop question marker
do I drop it?
((K also picks up an item))
3 K [*wai mhou (gamjoeng)*
[hey don't be (like this)
[Hey, don't (like this)
4 *mhou mhou dam je*
don't don't drop thing
don't drop the item [yet].
((Kevin shoots at Jason, causing him to drop the umbrella. Jason picks up an orb item. Kevin laughs.))
5 J *nei waa mhou dam aa?*
you say don't drop question marker
You said not to drop the item?
6 *dam!*
drop
Drop it!
7 K *dam lo:::::::::*
drop final particle
Then drop it.
((Both players stop using their items and go back to hand-to-hand combat))

We cannot tell whether Jason picked up the item on purpose or by accident, but we see here that he makes a declaration to signal that it was not intentional (line 1). At this point, dueling mode turns into training mode, during which one is allowed to attack the other in order to test out the impact of a weapon or attack move. By picking up the item, they had done precisely the kind of action they had criticized Andrew for carrying out earlier. They both make a declaration that they did not mean to pick it up (lines 1, 2, and 3), although Kevin changes his mind and asks Jason not to drop it yet (line 4). Jason repeats, "You said not to drop the item?" (line 5) to signal to Kevin that he is still holding onto the item because he is complying with Kevin's request. Finally, they declare that they will both drop their items at the same time (lines 6 and 7) and follow through. In doing so, they were able to establish their fairness to one another, and to Andrew, who was observing.

DISCUSSION

A common critique of CA is that it focuses too much on mundane features of talk. However, there is a lot we can understand from a detailed analysis of how the context of talk is locally produced and maintained by the participants. The participants in the Xbox Live party chat designed their party in a particular way through the way they interact, including the way they open their talk when they join a party. Other parties, for example, ones that are more focused on gaming and less on socializing, may design their talk in different ways. Opening sequences orient the speakers to their relationship with one another and the context they are in. As I noted in the analysis, not everyone in the party greets a person when they enter the chat. There are occasions in face-to-face encounters when it is appropriate, even expected, for us to greet everyone in turn, for example, when we are meeting friends or family we have not encountered in a long time. There are other occasions when it is not appropriate. The context and the relationships between the people determine what is appropriate.

CA can also help us better understand how adolescents socialize. The participants on Xbox Live were not just using Xbox Live as a place to play video games. They were using it as a place to "hang out," in the way adolescents might be expected to in the past, except that the places where they spend their leisure time has increasingly shifted from public to private spaces (Bennett, 2008; boyd, 2014; Ito, et al., 2010; Watkins, 2009). Xbox Live was where they went to talk about their school life, their social and political views, their complaints about parents, siblings, and friends, their aspirations, and so on. While there are many studies of naturally occurring talk between young children, studies of adolescent talk are comparatively rare. As adolescents begin to spend more time with their peer group instead of their parents, studies that use CA as well as other qualitative methods, such as ethnographies or participant observation, can help us better understand the social lives of adolescents.

Another common critique of CA is that it is overly descriptive, and that it does not adequately account for how social categories such as gender, ethnicity, class, and so on affect what people say and do. The CA response is that those factors are taken into account only to the extent that they are invoked or made relevant in the conversation (Sidnell 2010). We all belong to multiple categories at any given time. We cannot assume that some or all aspects of our identities are always activated when we are in conversation. I often found myself wondering whether these external factors affected talk in ways that are less visible from the talk alone. For example, when I was collecting data for my dissertation, I sometimes met my participants at Internet cafés or walked them to the subway. On a few occasions, when the digital recorder was off, I heard Jason and Kevin make oblique references to Andrew's privilege, calling him a "rich kid." To what extent did that impact their relationship? Was it possible that Jason and Kevin teamed up against Andrew as a result? To what extent did something uttered in the past or in another context still matter when analyzing any particular piece of conversational data? Marjorie Goodwin's (2006) study of young girls playing indicates that social status and power relations do surface in their talk in the form of labels and directives they give to a marginalized member of their social group. Children construct their own values and moral codes during play (Goodwin & Kyratzis, 2007). Amy Kyratzis

(2004) notes that children use games as a means to maintain social order by deciding who can play, what order they play in, who is performing well, who is playing fairly, and how conflicts are resolved. To that end, a CA response to my concerns would be that it is sometimes too tempting to speculate on external factors that may or may not be the reason why people say or do certain things. The reason why Jason and Kevin sided with one another against Andrew *could be* attributed to his perceived privilege, or it could be any number of reasons. What we can see empirically is what we can work with concretely and analyze with some confidence. Empirically, Kevin and Jason can be observed to have "teamed up" against Andrew, but that is all I can say from the data. This is not an easy position to assume, but ultimately one that gives me welcome restraint and focuses my attention on what is observable and reportable.

CONCLUSION

When the Millennium Bridge opened in London in June 2000, tens of thousands of pedestrians celebrated the occasion by crossing it on foot. To the surprise of the engineers, the bridge began to wobble laterally in an unexpected way. This was finally attributed to the way people achieve balance when they walk, which amplified the bridge's sway. To me, that has always been a fascinating illustration of the limits of design. That is not to say that the engineers did not do their jobs properly, but that there are often unpredictable outcomes when a designed object or experience encounters real people. This is true for bridges and lesson plans and digital tools and government policies and video games. Users matter.

In all the data I have collected, what I have observed is that the talk between players is as important as the games they play. Studies of play show how players construct social organization and maintain relationships through their interactions, and primarily through talk (Goodwin & Kyratzis, 2007; Goodwin, 2006; Kyratzis, 2004). All games, not just video games, are entertaining because we get to comment about them when they are in progress and talk about them when they are over. To exclude or ignore the ongoing talk is to miss a big part of what makes games fun. It is also to miss what makes games *not* fun, because players do get angry, frustrated, and marginalized, either by their fellow players, the game itself, or by other conditions (Varenne, Andrews, Hung, & Wessler, 2013).

Paul Dourish (a computer scientist) and Graham Button (an ethnomethodologist) coined the term "technomethodology" to give equal footing to both disciplines in investigating computer-supported cooperative work environments (Dourish & Button, 1998), where CA is a useful component of their toolkit. In their view, both designers and users have something meaningful to contribute to the dialogue. To the extent that new literacies is about collaboration, design, negotiated meanings, and production, CA can offer unique insights into the how collaboration works, how designs are achieved, how meanings are negotiated, and how encoded texts are produced. CA is one of many tools that can contribute to new literacies studies, and one that should perhaps be brought out of the toolkit more often.

REFERENCES

Abt, C. C. (1970). *Serious games*. New York, NY: The Viking Press.

Bennett, W. L. (2008). Changing citizenship in the digital age. In W. L. Bennett (Ed.), *Civic life online: Learning how digital media can engage youth* (pp. 1–24). Cambridge, MA: The MIT Press.

Bogost, I. (2005). Procedural literacy: Problem solving with programming, systems and play. *Telemedium, Winter/Spr*, 32–36.

boyd, d. (2014). *It's complicated: The social lives of networked teens*. New Haven, CT: Yale University Press.

Crookall, D. (2000). Editorial: Thirty years of interdisciplinarity. *Simulation & Gaming, 31*(1), 5–21.

Dourish, P., & Button, G. (1998). On "technomethodology": Foundational relationships between ethnomethodology and system design. *Human Computer Interaction, 13*(4), 395–432.

Duke, R. (1974). *Gaming: The future's language*. New York, NY: Sage.

Duke, R. (2000). A personal perspective on the evolution of gaming. *Simulation & Gaming, 31*(1), 79–85.

Fullerton, T. (2014). *Game design workshop: A playcentric approach to creating innovative games* (Third). New York, NY: Taylor and Francis.

Garfinkel, H. (1967). *Studies in ethnomethodology*. Upper Saddle River, NJ: Polity Press.

Garfinkel, H., & Sacks, H. (1970). On formal structures of practical actions. In J. C. McKinney & E. A. Tiryakian (Eds.), *Theoretical sociology: Perspectives and developments* (pp. 337–366). New York: Appleton-Century-Crofts.

Gee, J. P. (1996). *Social linguistics and literacies* (2nd ed.). London, UK: Taylor and Francis.

Gee, J. P. (2003). *What video games have to teach us about learning and literacy*. New York, NY: Palgrave Macmillan.

Gee, J. P. (2005). Pleasure, learning, video games, and life: The projective stance. *E-Learning and Digital Media, 2*(1), 95–113.

Goodwin, C. (1980). Restarts, pauses, and the achievement of mutual gaze at turn-beginning. *Sociological Inquiry, 50*(3/4), 272–302.

Goodwin, C. (1981). *Conversational organization: Interaction among speakers and hearers*. New York, NY: Academic Press.

Goodwin, C. (1986). Between and within: Alternative sequential treatment of continuers and assessments. *Human Studies, 9*(2/3), 205–217.

Goodwin, C. (1994). Professional vision. *American Anthropologist, 96*(3), 606–633.

Goodwin, C. (2001). Practices of seeing: Visual analysis: An ethnomethodological approach. In T. van Leeuwen & C. Jewitt (Eds.), *Handbook of Visual Analysis* (pp. 157–182). London, UK: Sage.

Goodwin, C., & Goodwin, M. H. (1996). Seeing as a situated activity: Formulating planes. In Y. Engestrom & D. Middleton (Eds.), *Cognition and communication at work* (pp. 61–95). Cambridge: Cambridge University Press.

Goodwin, M. H. (1995). Assembling a response: Setting and collaboratively constructed work talk. In P. ten Have & G. Psathas (Eds.), *Situated order: Studies in the social organization of talk and embodied activities* (pp. 173–186). Washington, DC: International Institute for Ethnomethodology and Conversation Analysis.

Goodwin, M. H. (2006). *The hidden life of girls: Games of stance, status, and exclusion.* Malden, MA: Blackwell.

Goodwin, M. H., & Kyratzis, A. (2007). Children socializing children: Practices for negotiating the social order among peers. *Research on Language & Social Interaction, 40*(4), 279–289.

Hung, A. C. Y. (2011). *The work of play: Meaning-making in videogames.* New York, NY: Peter Lang.

Hutchby, I., & Wooffitt, R. (2009). *Conversation analysis* (2nd ed.). Cambridge, UK: Polity Press.

Ito, M., Baumer, S., Bittanti, M., boyd, d., Cody, R., Herr-Stephenson, B., Horst, H., Lange, P., Mahendran, D, Martínez, K., Perkel, D., Robinson, L., Sims, C., & Tripp, L. (2010). *Hanging out, messing around, and geeking out: Kids living and learning in new media.* Cambridge, MA: The MIT Press.

Jefferson, G. (2004). Glossary of transcript symbols with an introduction. In G. H. Lerner (Ed.), *Conversation analysis: Studies from the first generation* (pp. 13–31). Amsterdam, The Netherlands: John Benjamins.

Jenkins, H., Ito, M., & boyd, d. (2015). *Participatory culture in a networked era: A conversation on youth, learning, commerce, and politics.* Cambridge, UK: Polity Press.

Kyratzis, A. (2004). Talk and interaction among children and the co-construction of peer groups and peer culture. *Annual Review of Anthropology, 33*, 625–649.

Lankshear, C., & Knobel, M. (2011). *New literacies: Everyday practices and social learning* (3rd ed.). New York, NY: Open University Press.

Lenhart, A. (2015). *Teen, social media and technology overview 2015.* Retrieved from http://www.pewinternet.org/2015/04/09/teens-social-media-technology-2015/

Prensky, M. (2006). *"Don't bother me Mom, I'm learning!": How computer and video games are preparing your kids for twenty-first century success and how you can help!* (1st ed.). St. Paul, MN: Paragon House.

Sacks, H. (1984). Notes on methodology. In J. M. Atkinson & J. Heritage (Eds.), *Structures of social action: Studies in conversation analysis* (pp. 21–27). Cambridge: Cambridge University Press.

Sacks, H. (1995). *Lectures on conversation.* Oxford, UK: Blackwell Publishing.

Sacks, H., Schegloff, E. A., & Jefferson, G. (1974). A simplest systematics for the organization of turn-taking for conversation. *Language, 50*(4), 696–735.

Salen, K., & Zimmerman, E. (2003). *Rules of play: Game design fundamentals.* Cambridge, MA: The MIT Press.

Schegloff, E. A. (1968). Sequencing in conversational openings. *American Anthropologist, 70*, 1075–1095.

Schegloff, E. A. (1979). Identification and recognition in telephone conversation openings. In G. Psathis (Ed.), *Everyday language: Studies in ethnomethodology* (pp. 23–78). New York, NY: Erlbaum.

Schegloff, E. A., Jefferson, G., & Sacks, H. (1977). The preference for self-correction in the organization of repair in conversation. *Language, 53*(2), 361–382.

Schegloff, E. A., & Sacks, H. (1973). Opening up closings. *Semiotica, 8*(4), 289–327.

Shaffer, D. W., Squire, K., Halverson, R., & Gee, J. P. (2005). Video games and the future of learning. *Phi Delta Kappan, 87*(2), 104–111.

Sidnell, J. (2010). *Conversation analysis: An introduction.* Malden, MA: Wiley-Blackwell.

Squire, K. (2006). From content to context: Videogames as designed experience. *Educational Researcher, 35*(8), 19–29.

Squire, K. (2011). *Video games and learning: Teaching and participatory culture in the digital age.* New York, NY: Teachers College Press.

Street, B. (2003). What's "new" in new literacy studies? Critical approaches to literacy in theory and practice. *Current Issues in Comparative Education, 5*(2), 1–14.

Suchman, L. A. (2002). *Human-machine reconfigurations: Plans and situated actions* (2nd ed.). Cambridge: Cambridge University Press.

ten Have, P. (1990). Methodological issues in conversation analysis. *Bulletin de Methodologie Sociologique, 27*, 23–51.

Traverso, V. (2009). The dilemmas of third-party complaints in conversation between friends. *Journal of Pragmatics, 41*(12), 2384–2399.

Varenne, H., Andrews, G., Hung, A. C. Y., & Wessler, S. (2013). Polities and politics of ongoing assessments: Evidence from video-gaming and blogging. In D. Tannen & A. M. Trester (Eds.), *Discourse 2.0: Language and new media* (pp. 27–45). Washington DC: Georgetown University Press.

Watkins, S. C. (2009). *The young and the digital.* Boston, MA: Beacon Press.

Wooffitt, R. (2005). *Conversation analysis and discourse analysis: A comparative and critical introduction.* Thousand Oaks, CA: Sage.

CHAPTER FOUR

Theorizing Context

A design-based analysis of an online affinity space

ALECIA MARIE MAGNIFICO

INTRODUCTION

In the 20 years since the New London Group articulated a new focus on literacies and design (1996), the field of New Literacy Studies has examined and theorized how young people use online and off-line media tools and composition processes to design their own meanings. Additionally, these 20 years have seen massive expansion and change in the tools and settings available for this kind of work. The online creation and distribution of writing, photographs, video, podcasts, and art have come to be common activities for teens and young adults. Wide-ranging access to the Internet in home, school, and mobile environments has granted young writers and artists the ability to distribute their creations, solicit feedback from others, and publish their work in a variety of media. The Pew Internet and American Life project, for instance, has found that 72% of U.S. teens share content with friends on social networks like Instagram or Facebook (Lenhart, 2015). Similarly, OFCOM (2014) research in the United Kingdom shows that 69% of young adults share photos and 44% share videos online.

Although many young people distribute their work on general social networks, several "creative archives" (Magnifico & Curwood, 2012) have arisen to meet the needs of writers. For instance, Fanfiction.net (n.d.) and the Archive of Our Own (n.d.) explicitly gather fan fiction and other transformative works, while Figment.com encourages young writers to write and distribute original fiction in addition to fan fiction. These creative acts, along with remixing videos, creating memes, making machinima, maintaining wikis, and the like, have been studied as social, multimodal, literacy practices that expand the ways in which individuals can design, make, and share meanings. This focus on new literacies and new practices (e.g., Coiro, Knobel, Lankshear, & Leu, 2008; Cope & Kalantzis, 2000; Knobel & Lankshear, 2008) highlights ways in which technical expertise has become both necessary and deeply changeable as new technologies shift from year to year.

Interest-driven and technologically enabled forms of composition work to connect participants across and through such contexts, and the sites that house them serve as repositories for the knowledge that members build over time. New literacies scholars have noted these developing, distributed, mediated actions and have called for new understandings of collaboration and community as a result. James Paul Gee (2004) initially conceptualized communal, topic-driven spaces where such interests are shared as *affinity spaces* where "newbies and masters and everyone else" (p. 85) interact. One challenge for researchers who wish to study these large, sometimes-amorphous sites is how to conceptualize participants' learning and literacies. Many who have theorized them (e.g., Gee, 2004; Hayes & Duncan, 2012; Jenkins et al., 2006; Lammers, Curwood, & Magnifico, 2012) have found that different participants may engage in different kinds of learning because the space itself offers multiple legitimate paths to participation. A network of fan fiction writers, for instance, needs readers, writers, reviewers, art designers, and social media promoters to be successful, and any given participant will play only some of these roles. Some of these roles may seem far more socially oriented than learning oriented (Magnifico, Curwood, & Lammers, 2015), particularly to researchers, but "hanging out," too, is necessary to keep the conversation flowing (Ito et al., 2010).

The development of methods to trace how participants communicate across and through affinity spaces has necessarily followed. Heretofore, attention to connective ethnography (Fields & Kafai, 2009; Leander, 2008), textual tracings (Prior, 2004), and connected learning (Ito, et al. 2010, 2013) has shown how people traverse and cross contexts, and the ways in which their practices "travel" (Leander & McKim, 2003, p. 212). These web-based contexts for participation themselves, however, have seen less intensive analyses, despite the fact that affinity space culture has hit critical mass and corporate concerns have responded by shaping and monetizing spaces for young people. Lionsgate Films, for example, created The Capitol (http://www.thecapitol.pn), a multisited alternative reality/viral marketing game for *The Hunger Games* films (Bissell, Collins, & Ross, 2012), and media properties including Mattel and Viacom have launched children's MMOs replete with microtransactions and tightly controlled consumption messages (Grimes, 2015). Fan-created and fan-built spaces continue to exist, but this movement toward corporate designs suggests the necessity of a new focus, or, at least a new element of ethnographic observation: How the networks that make up spaces coalesce into *contexts for participation*, and how they communicate diverse messages to their users.

This chapter reports on a 2012–2013 study of a multisited fiction writing affinity space, Figment, which is owned by Random House Children's Books. This work centers on Figment.com and extends to associated social networks. To consider what contexts for participation mean within affinity spaces, I seek to describe *not* participants' movements and trajectories through the space (although that could certainly become a further step in this research), but how a variety of databases, profiles, blogs, and media make participation possible. In other words, how can researchers conceptualize and bound an affinity space so that it becomes a workable networked field site for understanding participation (Gerber, Abrams, Curwood, & Magnifico, 2017)? In this descriptive close reading, my aim is to craft a coherent account of how the design of Figment.com and its official social media portals set the context for creative writing and learning to write.

THEORETICAL FRAMEWORK: THE STUDY OF AFFINITY SPACES

In the realm of online interaction, multisited affinity spaces—that is, loose networks of topic-driven root sites, creative archives, and social media—are a relatively new phenomenon. Using sociocultural and New Literacies lenses (e.g., Cope & Kalantzis, 2000; Gee, 2004; Ito et al., 2010; Knobel & Lankshear, 2008) to examine them allows researchers to situate participants' activity in these spaces in wider social, cultural, and political meaning-making ventures. Taking such a view allows researchers to examine how participation in such spaces is not only rooted in and affected by participants' personal histories, but the histories of various media properties as well.

In the recent past, online sites where affinity space members congregated, socialized, and shared their work were usually singular entities that were created and maintained by fans. For instance, players of the massively multiplayer online game, *World of Warcraft*, were typically found playing the game or on the *WoW* wiki (Chen, 2012; Steinkuehler, 2007), while Harry Potter fans chatted about theories and shared their creations on The Leaky Cauldron fan site (Jenkins, 2006). Social networks, however, have changed this landscape. Many young fans and content creators now maintain accounts at sites devoted to their favorite fandoms as well as social media sites like Twitter, YouTube, or Tumblr that allow them to collect information and share news quickly.

Affinity spaces comprise loosely organized arrays of "portals" devoted to a "common endeavor" (Gee, 2004, p. 85) and are connected by such features as topics, links, tags and hashtags. The different portals of affinity spaces allow young users to take advantage of several kinds of online collaboration. Traditional collaborations adapt easily to many online spaces. For instance, small review groups, collaborative author dyads, and "beta-readers" of first drafts productively exist in spaces like Neopets.com and Fanfiction.net (Black, 2008; Curwood, Magnifico, & Lammers, 2013; Magnifico, 2012). At the same time, Yasmin Kafai and Kylie Peppler's (2011) description of broad "collective learning" seems far more apt in situations where young fans send out a call to popularize a Twitter hashtag or make a Tumblr post asking a broad swath of fellow members for response or assistance.

Affinity spaces provide venues for participation and collaboration, but the contexts for participation, particularly in commercial spaces (like Figment, owned by Random House), are deeply affected by the options available within. Particularly in spaces designed for young people, advertisers and corporate media properties have begun to build brand loyalty and desires for consumption, as well as algorithms to control what kinds of content (or advertising) different users see at different times (e.g., Grimes, 2015). Little research in new literacies explores such connections to commercial entities, although some studies have begun to break this ground. For instance, while Rebecca Black, Ksenia Korobkova, and Alexandra Epler (2014) have documented gendered marketing in virtual worlds for children, Karen Wohlwend's (2012) work has shown that children do resist the identities and values that the corporate makers of toys put forth. Similar acts of resistance can be found in the popularity of "slash" and "alternative universe" fan fiction that breaks characters free of their original storylines and intentions (Jamison, 2013; Tosenberger, 2008).

In order to understand *how* such acceptance or resistance occurs within an affinity space, researchers must become familiar with the space itself, learning what its norms are, as well as its boundaries and limitations. Many studies of participation in writing-focused spaces like Figment have centered on young authors, likely as a result of their visibility and willingness to share their experiences (e.g., Black, 2008; Curwood, 2013; Jenkins, 2006; Lam, 2000; Magnifico, 2012). Kevin Leander's (2008) work, however, reminds us that the contexts of such participation are central, too—and, in an affinity space that stretches across a central website and social media accounts, difficult to define. Transforming often-reified constructs including "space" and "site" into opportunities for empirical observation like participants' "spacings" and "sitings" is critical to understanding how young writers use the Internet to write, read, and share their work (Leander & McKim, 2003; Leander, 2008).

This kind of work does not constitute traditional virtual ethnography on its own. It is an early step that seeks to bound the field site in a way that helps researchers to understand the full extent of how learning and writing practices "travel" (cf. Fields & Kafai, 2009; Leander & Lovvorn, 2006), and how contexts like Figment enable this. Researchers who are interested in young people's digital literacies and Internet writings need to understand not only their participants' trajectories, but how a variety of databases, profiles, blogs, and media make possible these various sitings. If an entity like Figment.com builds an affinity space to allow passionate individuals to network around reading and writing, the design choices of the various portals become very significant because they enable or hinder Figs'—that is, the site's participants—connections and trajectories. While some may consider this focus on space (rather than participants) a limitation, this search for structure mirrors participants' interactions and the ways in which *they* navigate online affinity spaces. In many spaces, including Figment, members learn and communicate with complex mixed genres and artifacts (e.g., messages, tweets, Tumblr posts, artwork, videos) instead of speaking face-to-face (e.g., Curwood, 2013; Lammers, 2013). Researchers must become familiar with such compositions and how they circulate.

BACKGROUND: FIGMENT.COM AND THE ORIGINS OF THIS STUDY

Figment was started in 2010 by a former managing editor of *The New Yorker*. The space is aimed at teens and young adult writers, providing an informal place "where writers meet, create, share, and connect" (Figment.com Front Page, n.d.). While Figment is focused on original creative writing and young adult novels, popular forums for fan fiction and role play also exist. As mentioned earlier, Figment is not a fan-designed space. Its funding originated from a combination of angel investors and publishers who market their books to the young adult demographic (Springen, 2011), and, in 2013, Figment was acquired by Random House Children's Books (Reid, 2013).

The space includes many typical features of writing sites, such as the ability to share writings (known as "books" on the site), comment on and review others' written works, and join topic-focused groups. If books win contests or receive enough attention through users' comments and "hearts" (similar to a Facebook "like"), they may be featured in the site's "library" of books. These writing and reading elements are combined with motivational features such as spotlight recommendations, contests, badges, social media "following," and interactions with professional writers and editors.

The Daily Fig, the site's regularly updated blog (Figment.com, n.d.), provides news for Figs—site participants—in several categories including "books and authors" (e.g., author chats, YA book news), "the writing life" (e.g., writing tips, features about individual Figs), and "diversions" (e.g., contests, quizzes, articles about various fandoms). Young writers who frequent the site interact with each other in chats on their profiles, in topic-oriented "groups," or in the public forums that are devoted to many aspects of reading and writing (e.g., recommended reading, feedback requests, fandom activities, writing in various genres). This news spreads further to social media networks through official and affiliated social media accounts. While user profiles are public, individual writings may be shared with a public or limited readership, and teachers may create restricted communities for their classrooms.

In short, the space, on the whole, is a mixture of a virtual writers' workshop, an educational venture focused on writing, and a tool for marketing young adult fiction to teen fans—a group of people who tend to read and write voraciously. These split purposes become evident particularly through close readings and content analyses of the diverse sites that comprise the Figment affinity space.

When I began this study, I had intended to interview Figs about what it was like to share writing on a site that is dedicated to writing and writers, unlike my earlier work in *Neopets*, where writing represented the passions of a much smaller niche group (Magnifico, 2012). Six months of preliminary work, however, engaged me in observation of Figment's public face, including its rotating front page, book and profile templates, communications with readers and writers, and explicitly multiple spaces for interaction. By examining this "official" site language and layout, I quickly became fascinated by the very different, sometimes contradictory messages and interactions that traveled across the public communications of Figment.com and its social media. Instead of framing the study as one of Figment's participating writers, I began to frame it as a study of Figment's *design*—and how I might use that design to think about theorizing the context of affinity spaces that have multiple portals, goals, and audiences for communications.

RESEARCH QUESTIONS

To shed light on the challenges of doing affinity space research in a fully online environment where technologies and participation sites change rapidly, this chapter reports on a 2012–2013 study of the fiction writing affinity space that centers on Figment.com and extends to associated social networks. As many large online sites have come to do, Figment maintains an active presence on Instagram, Twitter, Tumblr, Facebook, and Pinterest.

While Figs' writing may focus on a particular subject or fandom, their work often spans a variety of media and venues for sharing and distribution. I examine the ways in which Figment, along with its official Twitter and Tumblr accounts, provides a context for participants to interact. A primary goal of this study is to open up methodological conversations about online writing, content creation, and literacy learning in light of such changing, multisited opportunities. To focus this inquiry into Figment and its affiliated media spaces, I examined these research questions: How is Figment's writing community structured or designed, and which structures seem especially salient to participants? Are sites that are affiliated with Figment linked together in an affinity space? How so?

METHODS

Figment caters to readers and writers of young adult fiction and is representative of the online creative opportunities that are available to youth who have regular Internet access. In its design, Figment engages its users through social media, sharing links to content from the main site (Figment.com and its *The Daily Fig* blog), promoting authors and contests, and responding to Figs' tweets. Its designers include explicit spaces on users' profiles for links to their blogs and other social media spaces, and they maintain official site accounts across several social networks. The implication seems to be that published authors promote their work and gain readers across all of these social networks—and young authors can take advantage of these possibilities as well. As such, Figment takes the form of a deliberately designed, multisited affinity space, hosting conversations about its content on its own site and through several official social media "portals" (cf. Gee, 2004).

In this chapter, I discuss six months of observations, close reading, field notes, and thematic content analyses that center on the design of and the public data affiliated with Figment.com. In this interpretive and descriptive work, my aim was to craft a coherent account of how the design of Figment.com and its associated official social media portals functioned to create a sense of writerly community and set the context for creative writing and learning to write. To do so, I employed two primary methods for this exploration of Figment's designed writing and social media environment.

First, I present a descriptive account of Figment's design, comprising a close reading (Davidson, 2009; Griffin, 2005) of the discourse and design of its self-presentation and writing spaces. To develop an accurate sense of an online culture, Jannis Androutsopoulous (2008) recommends documentation of participants' practices across the space and examination of researchers' own movements from the "core" to the "periphery" (p. 6). Because Figment comprises many portals, these observations are complex, primarily employing screenshots and field notes to capture events for interpretation. Such tools have helped me to trace various legitimate ways of participating in this affinity space (Gee, 2004).

Second, to understand how Figment uses its multiple portals to maintain contact with members, I conducted a thematic content analysis (Boyatzis, 1998; Saldaña, 2009). I focused on Figment's highest-traffic portals: Twitter, Tumblr, and *The Daily Fig* site blog. I began with descriptive coding of the official site's communications with users, refining and triangulating codes across the content from different portals. The first codes were very specific (e.g., "harry potter fandom, graphic mashup," "retweet of literary content"), and then I gradually refined them into general categories that crossed portals (e.g., "figment poll," "conversation with follower"). For this chapter, I examined all the posts from the Twitter, Tumblr, and blog portals that occurred in the first two weeks of February 2013. This timeline was somewhat arbitrary; I aimed for a manageable sample that cross-cut portals so that I could examine how information repeated and spread in three social media portals with each having diverging communication norms and audiences.

Taken together, these qualitative analyses present a complex, conflicted picture of the context (or *contexts*) in which writing—and learning about writing—occurs on Figment.com and its associated social media. The following results map Figment's features, document its communications with users, follow connections to social media accounts, and report on major participation trends.

RESULTS

Looking In: Close Reading and Design Analysis

Figment User Profiles: Encouragement to Network. Figment user profiles are laid out much like blogs with right-hand sidebars. This standard design allows writers and visitors to quickly navigate several facets of users' writing and site activity. In this design, writing, personal information, and public, Facebook-style "wall" chat (which Figs can choose to disable) are given similar amounts of space. As in most social networks, the author's personal information and links are available at the top left of the profile's main pane, while Figment displays achievement badges in the top right (shown in Figure 4.1). Users' "books" (writings) and wall chat primarily appear further down in the main pane, and their groups in the right sidebar (Figure 4.1).

User profiles allow little customization. The profile editor includes space for Figs to enter a real or false name, post a picture, and answer several questions about themselves. Some questions are open-ended questions (e.g., "a little about me"), while others are directive (e.g., "my favorite place to read is …," "favorite movies"). These questions focus on reading and media consumption, perhaps encouraging discovery of media properties through friends' profiles. Figs are further encouraged to "follow" fellow Figs. This language borrows from Twitter's description of social media tracking, but this feature does something quite different. Instead of allowing users to write broadcast messages to their "follows," Figment creates updated links to friends' writings and activity on the site. Finally, the digital profile editor asks Figs whether they want to link their Figment accounts to offsite blogs and social media profiles, like Twitter, Tumblr, or Facebook. Through these connections, Figment widens the number of portals in the affinity space, the number

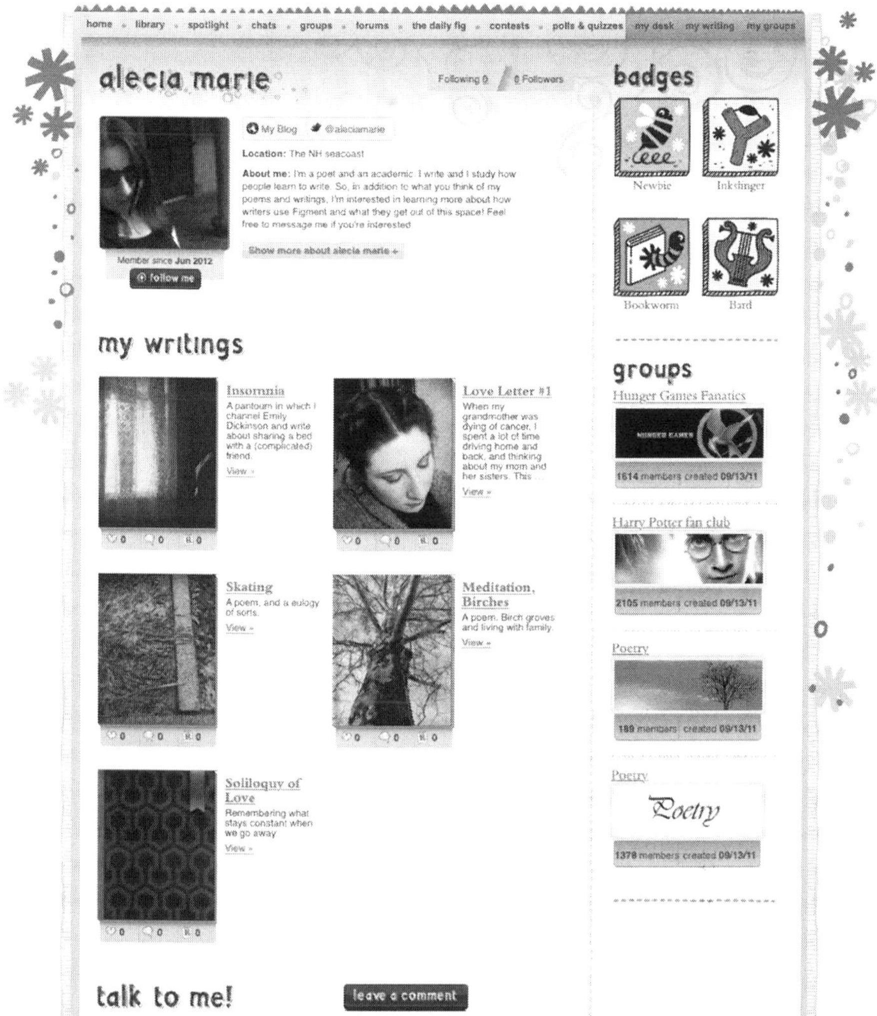

Fig. 4.1. Screenshot of the author's Figment profile.

of ways that Figs can interact with each other, and the number of possibilities for their activity to mention or promote the main site.

As shown in Figure 4.1, there is a space for Figs to list their social media connections. My profile lists these contact methods because I want others who are interested in my research to be able to contact me. Many Figs do not list such connections in their profiles, however, perhaps because all profiles are public. Even fewer Figs seem to actively promote their writing work across social networks by using the site's built-in scripts to push story updates to Twitter, Facebook, or

Tumblr. In my six months of affinity-space-wide explorations, I discovered only two Figs who engaged in this behavior regularly. Of members who do list social media accounts, their posts often mention writing or literature fandom activities, but they engage in diverse personal content sharing—rather than presenting a marketing-style focus on their reading, writing, or fandom activities. Even though social networking content receives headline-level space in the profile design (which pushes writing, nominally the core of the site, further down), social media features appear to be much less popular with Figment's writers.

Figs' badges for on-site reading and writing appear in the right sidebar and reward behaviors such as reading others' books, writing reviews, and posting books. Badges tie into internal and external social media features as well. For example, the "bookworm" badge shown in Figure 4.1 is awarded when a user reads others' writings. "Cardiologist" (not pictured here) is awarded when a Fig receives 5 hearts on a story, and "shares nicely" is awarded to users who push ten writing updates to Facebook or Twitter. While all users who engage in the core site activities of reading, writing, and reviewing receive badges, few forum discussions or groups are devoted to winning these achievements. At the time of this study, I counted only five (of 15,384 total) site-wide groups devoted to badges, each had only a small number of members (54 figs across the five groups).

Site-wide group membership completes the suite of social features on the right-hand side of each Fig's profile page (see Figure 4.1). Each group listing includes a cover image, the number of members, and date that the group was founded. Many Figs belong to several groups that reflect their writerly or readerly interests—including writing topics, genres, fandoms, and reviewing styles. Popular groups at the time of my data collection included those devoted to writing specifically for girls (e.g., Girls Who Write, 2051 members), fandom-based readers and writers (e.g., Hunger Games Fanatics, 1472 members; The Whovian, 1158 members), and critique circles (e.g., Critics Group, 1351 members). In addition, some groups support site practices like designing book covers (e.g., Cover Designs, 705 members) or site-wide contests (e.g., Exciting Contests, 1495 members). Differently from the wide-open public forums (linked in the top navigation bar on a user's profile page), groups can be public or private. They allow Figs to build smaller discussions where conversation and writing is shared with a more focused group of people about more specific topics.

Figment Book Profiles: Encouragement to Write. Depending on the amount of personal information that Figs choose to share, members' writings—in many ways, the core of the site's mission—appear in the second major section of users' profiles. While a few "books" (site parlance for writings) may appear on the main profile screen, as in Figure 4.1, many of these writings appear just "below the fold" of a typical laptop screen, requiring some scrolling. Books may be sorted according to profile owners' preferences and are presented with titles, short pitches to entice readers, and graphic "covers" (users may design covers themselves, although many trade designs on the forums). In addition, the bottom edge of the book cover displays popularity statistics about the piece, including its numbers of hearts, comments, and full reviews from other Figs.

Each book or draft additionally receives a book profile page, which shows the length of a work in chapters, words, "minutes" of approximate reading time, and a short preview. Figure 4.2 displays the profile of a highly "hearted" book in the short story category on Figment. This figure shows the 2,583 hearts, 551 comments, and 176 reviews that it has received from fellow Figs. Heart and comment statistics this high are rare, and at the time of this data collection, these statistics had earned this story a place in the main site "library," where Figment members are even more likely to see and read it.

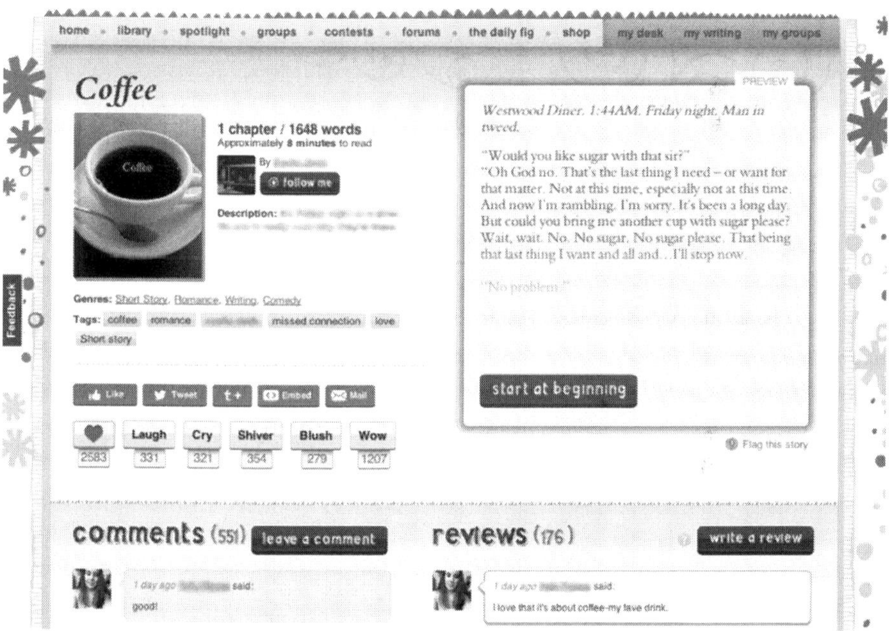

Fig. 4.2. A book profile, showing previews, social reactions, comments, and reviews (authors and reviewers blinded).

In this way, books, and by extension, creative writing of all kinds, are given a central place in the Figment site design. While some groups may privilege different genres of writing, no genre hierarchy is built into this design. Everything from novel-length fiction to fan fiction to poetry is classified as a "book" and presented with equivalent discourse, including opportunities to request or give feedback, to share "books" via social media, and the like.

Figs' main source of interactions around their writing—that is, comments and reviews—reside here, although users' profiles additionally list two recent reviews that they have contributed to others' writing. In addition to writing comments (often shorter and more specific) or reviews (often longer and more global), Figs who come to a book's page have the opportunity to react quickly by pressing buttons—"heart," "cry," "wow," etc.—or to share the story on social media using the site's built in scripts (see buttons in the bottom left-hand corner of Figure 4.2). One perennial conflict in Figment's groups and forums comes from what many Figs believe to be the misuse or overuse of these reaction buttons. Some achievement badges, as well as some site writing contests, require authors to quickly gain hearts on their books. These contests lead to "heart swap" threads on the forums and "heart requests" on walls, where writers ask others to click their reaction buttons in exchange for clicks in return. While Figs who are interested in contest writing engage in this "swapping" behavior, others—some of whom label themselves as "real writers" or "anti-swappers"—decry these practices. Instead, they prefer critical comments, detailed "honest reviews," and hearts that were granted from readers' genuine reaction to their writing.

Overall, writerly activities sit at the core of the site's design and layout. Creative writing and forming writing and review partnerships are central behaviors for Figs, as are finding ways to share writing and receive feedback through social networking, forum swapping, review swapping, heart swapping, and the like.

This section of descriptive results has sought to look inward at the design, layout, and standardized site discourse that enables these social and writing practices, examining how the Figment site supports Figs as they write and share books, reviews, forum or group posts, and social networking posts.

Looking Out: Content Analysis of Official Site Content

A view of Figment's core discourse practices that privileges talk about writing and books, however, does not consistently appear across portals. In the next results section, I report on a thematic content analysis that examines Figment's official social media accounts and how the staff members who manage these accounts interact with a perhaps broader sphere of young writers and young adult fiction aficionados than those found solely on Figment.com.

In this section, I take up the second research question: How are sites that are affiliated with Figment linked together in an affinity space? While the core design elements of Figment are devoted to its young adult writers and readers, enabling them to share creative writing and comment on reading of all kinds, Figment also maintains an active presence across its own blog and social networks including Twitter and Tumblr. This presence reaches out to (and is hosted on) several affiliated portals. Much of the content that is disseminated in these ways begins with events and articles on Figment that are then shared much more broadly.

The Daily Fig: Site Blog. Members of the Figment staff post a wide variety of content on *The Daily Fig*, the Figment.com site blog. Blog posts appear one to four times per day, and content in these posts is aggregated along with site announcements in a regular newsletter that provides event details (e.g., author chats, polls), contest promotions (e.g., writing contests, raffles for Advance Reader Copies of books), and staff reading recommendations (e.g., popular Figment books, newly published novels that include Figment previews).

The Daily Fig focuses on a variety of interests, only one of which is writing. As shown in Table 4.1, across the articles that were posted in the timeframe of this data collection (n = 34), only two of these had writers or writing as their main theme, with another three outlining details or results from writing contests.

Table 4.1. *The Daily Fig* Article Theme Percentages (Greatest to Least).

Category	Article Examples	Number (n = 34)	Percentage
Odds and Ends	"Links You'll Like" link roundup; "Oddball Love Songs" music mix	9	26.47%
Fandom	"Vampire Diaries" episode recaps; Geeky Valentines (e.g., Harry Potter, Dr. Who)	6	17.65%
Figment Poll	"Favorite Forbidden Romance" site poll; "Nerd Crush Showdown" site poll	6	17.65%
Figment Quiz	"Tragedy Paper" quiz; "Hysteria" dream interpretation quiz	5	14.71%
Writing Contest	"Writing Characters with Accountability" writing challenge; winner of the SMITHTeen/Figment contest	3	8.82%
Books/ Literary	"Dates with Fictional Men" article (e.g., Romeo); "Literary Love Quotations"	2	5.88%
Contest (not writing)	"Beautiful Creatures" movie raffle	1	2.94%
Writers	"Featured Fig" writer profile	1	2.94%
Writing	"Figment Daily Theme" writing prompt	1	2.94%

Although *The Daily Fig* includes literary content across the categories, in that many of the poll and fandom posts require readers to have deep knowledge of various literary and media references in order to understand the articles fully, writing appeared as a relatively minor interest in these weeks of *The Daily Fig*. Figment additionally provides a separate email newsletter, "Figment

Daily Themes," that mails all recipients a story, character, or poem prompt each day, but this kind of writing content makes it to the main blog relatively rarely. Instead, it is much more common for Figment writers to post a humorous "odds and ends" article or an activity requiring only surface-level interaction (such as a novel-based personality quiz), and for readers to comment saying how much they enjoyed this content.

It is possible, too, that the specific timeline chosen for this analysis (the first half of February, 2013) may have led to an unusual amount of "odds and ends" diversionary content across all of these content analyses due to the Valentine's Day holiday occurring during this period.

Figment's Tumblr: Reblogging and Image Sharing. Many of the articles that Figment staff post on *The Daily Fig* are re-posted on the site's microblog collection of articles, conversations with Figs, links, and images, which is hosted on Tumblr. Over the course of the two weeks under analysis, the corpus built from the Figment tumblr included 67 posts, approximately half (n = 34) of which were re-blogs from other Tumblr users (a common use of this medium). The other half of these posts (n = 33) were original posts, most of which provided links and summaries of *The Daily Fig* site articles, as well as teasers that led to other diversionary content like quizzes and site polls. Table 4.2 shows a breakdown of the themes of these posts, as well as a breakdown of whether these posts were original content or reblogged from a different source:

The most striking finding expressed in this table is that while *The Daily Fig* contains content that is original to Figment, approximately half of the posts on the Figment Tumblr are reblogs of other people's content. While much of this content is literary—for instance, Harry Potter valentine puns, Lord of the Rings jokes, and artfully rendered quotations from books—little of it bears a direct connection to writing. Instead, Figment seems to be making connections between young writers and the "geekiness" frequently associated with fan fiction writers or fantasy/sci-fi fans (cf. Jenkins, 2006 for further discussion). Reposting graphics and articles that are loved by fans of the Tolkien or *Hunger Games* books, then, continues to circulate a particular artifact and potentially widens a particular conversation, and it makes Figment a part of that conversation.

Figment's original posts have received far fewer likes and shares than many of its reblogging posts. During the data collection period, only five Figment original posts reached 100 likes or shares, whereas 23 of the posts that Figment reblogged have reached 100 likes or shares (one popular *Lord of the Rings* meme that the Figment Tumblr reblogged was liked or shared 25,000 times). It is, unfortunately, difficult to discern how Figs further reblog, like, or share the content that Figment posts on Tumblr because it is uncommon for microblog designs to include personal information about their curator. Few Tumblr users add their names, Figment usernames, or contact information that enables others to identify them as Figs,

Table 4.2. Figment Tumblr Article Theme Percentages (Greatest to Least).

Category	Article Examples	Number (n = 67)	Reblog/ Original	Percentage of Total
Books/Literary	Little Prince book covers; animated quotations	15	13 Reblog; 2 Original	22.39%
Fandom/Media	Reactions to SuperBowl commercials; Harry Potter punny valentines	13	11 Reblog; 2 Original	19.4%
Daily Fig Article	"6 Possible Reasons Valentine's Day Exists;" "6 Ways to Avoid Spending Money on V-Day"	9	9 Original	13.43%
Conversations	"Will you be my valentine" question; "Figment emails are awesome" comment	5	5 Reblog	7.46%
Figment Daily Theme	"Write a story or poem inspired by this photograph"	4	4 Original	5.97%
Figment Writing Contest	"Out of the Easy" essay contest; "Write a story about forbidden love" contest	4	4 Original	5.97%
Art	Image of books bursting through a wall	3	3 Reblog	4.48%
Daily Fig Odds & Ends	Geeky Valentines (e.g., Harry Potter, Dr. Who)	2	2 Original	2.99%
Figment Contest	Beautiful Creatures movie raffle	2	2 Original	2.99%
Figment Quiz	"What's Your Destiny" quiz; "8 Love Quizzes"	2	2 Original	2.99%
Daily Fig Fandom	Modern Family recap	1	1 Original	1.49%
Affiliated Site	Figfinds, a tumblr that posts lines from Figment stories	1	1 Reblog	1.49%
Writing	Paris Review Roberto Bolano writing tips	1	1 Reblog	1.49%

and, as discussed in the first section of results, few Figs link social media accounts to their Figment profiles.

At the same time, Table 4.2 shows there are few posts directly related to writing, and only one post that shares Figment-hosted stories through a link to an affiliate Tumblr called figfinds. As the official account of a social network devoted to writing, writers, and readers, Figment's decision to share little of its young writers' work raises questions. At the very least, these Tumblr numbers seem to imply that little correlation exists between prolific writing and the wry puns, quotation-sharing, or fandom-based images that become common knowledge in the social media spheres that surround this writing space.

Figment's Twitter: Contest Retweets. Figment's Twitter account offers yet another view of how content from Figment and *The Daily Fig* is broadcasted into the associated spaces of social media. Over the course of the two weeks under analysis, the corpus built from the Figment Twitter account included 114 tweets, 27 of which were retweets from other Twitter users. The remainder of the tweets included 33 replies to an individual or conversation, as well as 59 original posts, many of which refer back to *Daily Fig* content or are part of Figment's Twitter contests. Table 4.3 shows a breakdown of the themes of these posts, as well as a breakdown of whether these posts were original content or retweeted from a different source. It should be noted that on Twitter (unlike Tumblr), "retweet," "original," and "reply" are not mutually exclusive; a tweet can be both a retweet (an attributed copy of another tweet) and a reply (a tweet tagging or directed to a user), or a reply and original content.

Because Twitter allows for 140-character communication, and, with retweets, 1-click responses, this medium can quickly generate content and enthusiasm around a particular event or idea. In the two weeks covered by this corpus of data, Figment used Twitter in two key ways: to host retweet contests, and to converse with other Twitter users (see "Figment Contest" and "Conversation" cells in Table 4.3, for example). The majority of the contest tweets, which overall represented more than one third of this corpus, occurred within a few hours on each of two separate occasions during these weeks. Figment began a "Twitter contest" in which the account administrator would tweet facts about angels (on one occasion) and urban legends (on another occasion). In order to be entered into a raffle to win an Advanced Reader Copy of a novel, followers needed to retweet these facts. While many of Figment's tweets over the course of the month received one or two retweets, each of these contest tweets received many retweets. Tweets announcing the contests received between 7 and 15 retweets, while each of the 23 facts that counted for the raffle received between 41 and 72 retweets. Although each of these facts was literary, it required no transformation, writing, or creativity. It seems that this contest was most likely better marketing for the publishers investing in Figment than anything else, in that it produced many people tweeting about their books.

It is more possible to trace retweets than Tumblr likes because Twitter stores information about who retweeted or favorited (now "liked") a particular post. To claim a contest prize, several contests asked Figs to enter their Figment name and/or link in their tweets as well, which made it easier for me to trace solid connections across accounts. Still, few Figs seemed to participate in these Twitter contests. Of

Table 4.3. Figment Twitter Tweet Theme Percentages (Greatest to Least).

Category	Example Tweet	Number (n = 114)	% of Total
Figment Contest	"In ONE HOUR we'll be tweeting urban legend facts. RT each for more chances to win #HYSTERIA …"	39	34.21%
Conversations	"*socialmediasquee* RT @syntactics: When I grow up, I want to write social media …"	28	24.56%
Daily Fig Article	"Amazing pics inspired by your favorite YA books! …"	10	8.77%
Fandom/Media	"The Lizzie Bennet Diaries needs to stop making me cry at work …"	8	7.02%
Conference	"Our CEO @jacoblewism is moderating a panel at #TOCcon's #ARDay right now! …"	6	5.26%
Figment Writing Contest	"Ever dream of writing for http://Teen.com ? Our contest with @figment & @harperteen …"	6	5.26%
Figment Poll	"Nerd Crush Showdown: Save Sherlock or Stewart? Weasley or Whedon? http://bit.ly/156txuy …"	5	4.39%
Books/Literary	"NEW HARRY POTTER COVER …"	2	1.75%
Figment Events	"Valentine's Day storytelling at @92YTribeca w/ @OphiraE, @ajjacobs, @catielazarus - 2/14 w/@Figment …"	2	1.75%
Figment Odds & Ends	"Geek Love: Send a dorky #Valentine to your love! http://bit.ly/156j2r0 …"	2	1.75%
Figment Quiz	"Took the quiz "Which Panem District Are You From?" & got "District 2" …"	2	1.75%
Figment General	"figment <--- One of the the best things that EVER happened to me!!!! :) <3 Love this"	2	1.75%
Affiliated Site	"YA under $3.99—check out the YA ebooks …"	1	0.88%
Writing	"Neil Gaiman (@neilhimself) is writing stories with his fans TODAY, including you! …"	1	0.88%

the approximately 50 retweets and responses that each contest received, only an average of two could be traced back to a Fig with any certainty. I even found a set of Twitter accounts that were explicitly labeled "contest account," suggesting that some Twitter users create and maintain separate identities for the purpose of participating in viral marketing in hopes of winning books or other paraphernalia.

Again, similarly to the Figment Tumblr, little explicit writing content appeared in the Figment Twitter account (as indicated by the bottom row of Table 4.3) during the time of explicit observation and coding. While its administrator frequently talked with other tweeters, the conversation usually revolved around a Figment question, tech support, or Internet diversions like quiz results or site poll results. Here, the corporate side of Figment, and its job to create buzz around new young adult novels, seemed to take center stage.

DISCUSSION

Within Figment, the difference in situated practices and online writing across these various portals presents an interesting conundrum about how to understand participation in the broader affinity space. Much of the design of the Figment.com site is devoted to creative production and young creative writers. Its social network and book network design allows users space to write, share, and publish works in many genres; to build an audience for their work; to create public or private critique groups; and to talk about popular published fiction. All of these social practices are valued and supported in various design features, and it is impossible to fully separate these activities from elements of user interface and design that provide particular contexts for creative writing.

At the same time, much as danah boyd (2014) has found among young users of Facebook who manage their shared content and audience members carefully, many Figs avoid or subvert the networking norms that are built into the site. Figs do use the internal features of the site pervasively, collecting reviews, providing critical and praising feedback, and swapping reactions (e.g., hearts). Similar to studies of gamers (see Hayes & Duncan, 2012), Harry Potter fans (Ito et al, 2013; Jenkins, 2012), and Sims writers (Lammers, 2013), Figs are clearly participating in discussions surrounding their own creations, as well as favorite books and media properties. Even as external social networking receives headline-level space in users' profiles, though, my observations revealed few "sitings" (Leander & McKim, 2003; Leander, 2008) of Figs who made active use of these features to traverse connections and market their writing in spaces like Facebook or Twitter.

On Figment's associated Twitter and Tumblr portals, legitimate participation appears to involve little sharing of original writing to audiences external to Figment. *The Daily Fig* blog and Figment's Tumblr feed suggest that the affinity space values geeky fandom-based diversions *from* writing at least as often as it values writing. In these portals, blogging about Internet quizzes and sharing images of *The Hunger Games* or *Lord of the Rings* art are welcomed forms of interaction, whereas sharing original art or writing is much rarer. Readers make comments, retweet, or reblog content, but such sharing tends to be brief and affirmative.

Such contexts for participation have a much thinner, surface-oriented feel, so one might question the creativity or richness of ongoing *learning* that is possible in these activities, particularly compared to the reviews and critique groups that are encouraged on the main site. At the same time, studies have pointed out the value of this "hanging out" social interaction—it provides an entrance point for new members, allows a variety of readers to establish their presence and ethos, and shares content beyond the core participants (Ito, et al., 2010; Magnifico, Curwood, & Lammers, 2015).

These questions are particularly salient with reference to the Figment Twitter feed, which seems to serve largely as a tool for publisher marketing and news generation rather than a tool for Figs' creative engagement or conversation (Grimes, 2015). Twitter contests that are based on retweets may get the names of books out to a wide array of readers, thus serving the publishers who fund Figment's free creative space without much direct benefit to Figs. Such interactions are made legitimate by Figment's generation of these contests—they are clearly an active context for participation, at least for some users of the affinity space—but again, these facets of participation seem to carry little weight in the realm of participants' deeper writing. Still, as those who have theorized affinity spaces point out, it takes many kinds of activities, from deep critique to social discussion to active marketing, to maintain a participatory space (e.g., Gee, 2004; Hayes & Duncan, 2012; Jenkins et al., 2006; Lammers, Curwood, & Magnifico, 2012).

As educational and social venues increasingly move to online settings, researchers must develop new methods of understanding such root concepts as context, literacies, learning, and interaction in these spaces. In many online writing spaces, researchers have documented evidence of digital versions of more traditional collaborative groups (Black, 2008; Lammers, 2013; Magnifico, 2012). But, at the same time, we must observe the activity of collective online worlds, as well. Differently from blog content and, indeed, typical creative writing, the hypothesis for Figment's Tumblr and Twitter administrators seems to be that social media works best when a user shares and reshares many thematic—in this case, literary—posts, regardless of whether those posts are composed from original content or not. Individual interactions are downplayed, and the value is in the full collection of images, texts, and relationships to larger interest groups.

As such, Figment calls for continued study and conceptualization of the social media collective (Kafai & Peppler, 2011) *as well as* individual participants' artifacts and collaborative traveling practices. Such insight, combined with continued observation and participation, might help to explain why the context for participation and learning seems so significantly different among Figment's creative-writing-driven website design and discourse, Internet-diversion-driven blog and Tumblr, and contest-marketing-driven Twitter portals.

Overall, this analysis raises questions about what the context for participation looks like in diverse, multisited, online creative spaces, and how it is influenced by a myriad of factors. Additionally, this work queries whether or not it is possible to pin down one particular understanding of this learning and participation, or whether it would be desirable to do so. Completing this study certainly revealed much about how a space like Figment looks when viewed from the diverse angles of various portals—not all of them comfortable for this literacy researcher who might want to believe that the end-game of a site like Figment is "pure" writing and reading. As boyd (2014) and Sara Grimes (2015) remind us, though, the truth of such spaces is a complex mix of participants' desires, creative impulses, and corporate design and viability. This multisited content analysis helps researchers to take critical steps towards understanding the complications of affinity space design and context.

Still, though, what is absent here is specific, case-based understandings of how and why Figment users choose to interact with Figment, Twitter, and Tumblr. The observations and analyses presented here have underlined a set of practices and contradictions that can only be resolved through further observation, participation, and interaction with Figs, who are the lifeblood of the site. Future research would do well to take these observations as an early, critical step that highlights contradictions and provides invaluable guidance in future attempts to understand how users make sense of, learn from, and interact with various site discourses, ideologies, and portals.

REFERENCES

Androutsopoulos, J. (2008). Potentials and limitations of discourse-centered online ethnography. *Language@Internet, 5*, Article 8. Available from http://www.languageatinternet.org/articles/2008/1610

Archive of Our Own Front Page. (n.d.). Available from: https://archiveofourown.org/.

Bissell, R. (Executive Producer), Collins, S. (Executive Producer), & Ross, G. (Director). (2012). *The Hunger Games* (motion picture). United States: Lionsgate Films.

Black, R. (2008). *Adolescents and online fan fiction.* New York: Peter Lang.

Black, R., Korobkova, K., & Epler, A. (2014). Barbie Girls and Xtractaurs: Discourse and identity in virtual worlds for young children. *Journal of Early Childhood Literacy.* 14(2), 265–285.

Boyatzis, R. (1998). *Transforming qualitative information: Thematic analysis and code development.* Thousand Oaks, CA: Sage.

boyd, d. (2014). *It's complicated: The social lives of networked teens.* New Haven, CT: Yale University Press.

Chen, M. (2012). *Leet noobs: The life and death of an expert player group in World of Warcraft.* New York: Peter Lang.

Coiro, J., Knobel, M., Lankshear, C., & Leu, D. J. (2008). Central issues in new literacies and new literacies research. In J. Coiro, M. Knobel, C. Lankshear, & D. Leu (Eds), *Handbook of research on new literacies* (pp. 1–21). New York: Routledge.

Cope, B., & Kalantzis, M. (Eds.). (2000). *Multiliteracies: Literacy learning and the design of social futures.* New York: Routledge.

Curwood, J. (2013). Fan fiction, remix culture, and *The Potter Games.* In V. Frankel (Ed.), *Teaching with Harry Potter* (pp. 81–92). Jefferson, NC: McFarland.

Curwood, J., Magnifico, A., & Lammers, J. (2013). Writing in the wild: Writers' motivations in fan-based affinity spaces. *Journal of Adolescent & Adult Literacy*, 56(8), 667–685.

Davidson, D. (Ed.) (2009). *Well played 1.0: Video games, value, and meaning*. Pittsburgh, PA: ETC Press.

Fields, D., & Kafai, Y. (2009). A connective ethnography of peer knowledge sharing and diffusion in a tween virtual world. *International Journal of Computer Supported Learning*, 4, 47–68.

Fanfiction.net Front Page. (n.d.) Available from: https://www.fanfiction.net

Figment.com Front Page. (n.d.). Available from: http://figment.com

Gee, J. (2004). *Situated language and learning: A critique of traditional schooling*. New York: Routledge.

Gerber, H., Abrams, S., Curwood, J., & Magnifico, A. (2017). *Conducting qualitative research of learning in online spaces*. Thousand Oaks, CA: Sage.

Griffin, G. (Ed.) (2005). *Research methods for English studies*. Edinburgh, UK: Edinburgh University Press.

Grimes, S. (2015). Playing by the market rules: Promotional priorities and commercialization in children's virtual worlds. *Journal of Consumer Culture*, 15(1), 110–134.

Hayes, E., & Duncan, S. (Eds.) (2012). *Learning in video game affinity spaces*. New York: Peter Lang.

Ito, M., Baumer, S., Bittanti, M., boyd, d., Cody, R., Herr-Stevenson, B., Horst, H., Lange, P., Mahendran, D, Martínez, K., Perkel, D., Robinson, L., Sims, C., & Tripp, L. (2010). *Hanging out, messing around, and geeking out: Kids living and learning with new media*. Cambridge, MA: MIT Press.

Ito, M., Gutierrez, K., Livingstone, S., Penuel, B., Rhodes, J., Salen, K., Schor, J., Sefton-Green, J., & Watkins, S. (2013). *Connected learning: An agenda for research and design*. Digital Media and Learning Research Hub: Irvine, CA. Available from: http://dmlhub.net

Jamison, A. (2013). *Fic: Why fanfiction is taking over the world*. Dallas, TX: BenBella Books.

Jenkins, H. (2006). *Convergence culture: Where old and new media collide*. New York, NY: New York University Press.

Jenkins, H. (2012). "Cultural acupuncture:" Fan activism and the Harry Potter Alliance. *Transformative Works and Culture*, 10. Available from: http://journal.transformativeworks.org/index. php/twc/article/view/305. doi: 10.3983/twc.2012.0305.

Jenkins, H., Purushotma, R., Clinton, K., Weigel, M., & Robison, A. (2006). *Confronting the challenges of participatory culture: Media education for the 21st century*. Available from: http://newmedialiteracies.org/files/ working/NMLWhitePaper.pdf

Kafai, Y., & Peppler, K. (2011). Beyond small groups: New opportunities for research in computer-supported collective learning. In H. Spada, G. Stahl, N. Miyake, & N. Law (Eds.), *Computer-supported collaborative learning (CSCL) conference proceedings. Volume 1: Long papers* (pp. 17–24). International Society of the Learning Sciences. Available from: http://www.lulu.com/shop/international-society-of-the-learning-sciences/the-computer-supported-collaborative-learning-cscl-conference-2011-volume-1/ebook/product-17487590.html

Knobel, M., & Lankshear, C. (2008). Remix: The art and craft of endless hybridization. *Journal of Adolescent & Adult Literacy*, 52(1), 22–33.

Lam, W. S. E. (2000). Second language literacy and the design of the self: A case study of a teenager writing on the Internet. *TESOL Quarterly*, 34(3), 457–483.

Lammers, J. (2013). Fangirls as teachers: Examining pedagogic discourse in an online fan community. *Learning, Media, and Technology*, 38(4), 368–386.

Lammers, J., Curwood, J., & Magnifico, A. (2012). Toward an affinity space methodology: Considerations for literacy research. *English Teaching: Practice and Critique*, 11(2), 44–58.

Leander, K. (2008). Toward a connective ethnography of online/offline literacy networks. In J. Coiro, M. Knobel, C. Lankshear, & D. Leu (Eds.), *Handbook of research on new literacies* (pp. 33–64). New York: Routledge.

Leander, K., & Lovvorn, J. (2006). Literacy networks: Following the circulation of texts, bodies, and objects in the schooling and online gaming of one youth. *Cognition and Instruction,* 24(3), 291–340.

Leander, K., & McKim, K. (2003). Tracing the everyday "sitings" of adolescents on the Internet: A strategic adaptation of ethnography across spaces. *Education, Communication, Information,* 3(2), 211–240.

Lenhart, A. (2015). *Teens, technology, and friendships.* Washington, DC: Pew Internet & American Life Project. Available from: http://www.pewinternet.org.

Magnifico, A. (2012). The game of Neopian writing. In E. Hayes & S. Duncan (Eds), *Learning in video game affinity spaces* (pp. 212–234). New York: Peter Lang.

Magnifico, A., & Curwood, J. (2012, July). Affinity space ethnography: Qualitative research in online spaces. Invited poster presented at the Early Career Workshop at the International Conference of the Learning Sciences. Sydney, NSW, Australia.

Magnifico, A, Curwood, J., & Lammers, J. (2015). Words on the screen: Broadening analyses of interactions between fanfiction writers and reviewers. *Literacy,* 49, 158–166. DOI: 10.1111/lit.12061.

New London Group. (1996). A pedagogy of multiliteracies: Designing social futures. *Harvard Education Review,* 66(1), 60–93.

OFCOM (2014) Children's media use and attitudes report. Available from: http://stakeholders.ofcom.org.uk/binaries/research/media-literacy/media-use-attitudes-14/Charts_Section_4.pdf

Prior, P. (2004). Tracing processes: How texts come into being. In C. Bazerman & P. Prior (Eds.), *What writing does and how it does it* (pp. 167–200). Mahwah, NJ: Lawrence Erlbaum.

Reid, C. (2013, October 29). Random House acquires Figment. *Publishers Weekly.* Available from: http://www.publishersweekly.com/pw/by-topic/childrens/childrens-industry-news/article/59745-random-house-acquires-figment.html

Saldaña, J. (2009). *The coding manual for qualitative researchers.* Thousand Oaks, CA: Sage.

Springen, K. (2011, May 19). $1 Million to a literary site called Figment—and it's not imaginary. *Publishers Weekly.* Available from: http://www.publishersweekly.com/pw/by-topic/childrens/childrens-industry-news/article/47337-1-million-to-a-literary-site-called-figment-and-it-s-not-imaginary.html

Steinkuehler, C. (2007). Massively multiplayer online gaming as a constellation of literacy practices. In B. Shelton & D. Wiley (Eds.), *The design and use of simulation computer games in education* (pp. 187–212). Rotterdam: Sense Publishers.

Tosenberger, C. (2008). "Oh my god, the fanfiction!": Dumbledore's outing and the online Harry Potter fandom. *Children's Literature Association Quarterly,* 33(2), 200–206.

Wohlwend, K. (2012). The boys who would be princesses: Playing with gender identity intertexts in Disney Princess transmedia. *Gender and Education,* 24(6), 593–610.

CHAPTER FIVE

Understanding Twitter as a Networked Field Site

Implications for Research on Teacher Professional Learning

JEN SCOTT CURWOOD AND CARLY BIDDOLPH

INTRODUCTION

There are more than 360,000 teachers in Australian schools, all of whom are required to meet and maintain national standards for the profession through postqualification and in-service learning. However, a significant body of research has questioned the efficacy of traditional, top-down approaches to teacher professional development (Hammerness et al., 2005; Walshe & Hirsch, 1998; Wilson & Berne, 1999). Prior work suggests that effective professional development involves a content area focus, opportunities for hands-on and active learning, collective participation with colleagues, a substantial duration of contact hours, and consistency with teachers' knowledge and beliefs as well as educational reforms and policies (Cohen & Hill, 2001; Curwood 2014a, 2014b; Desimone, 2009; Garet, Porter, Desimone, Birman, & Yoon 2001; Little, 2012; Penuel, Fishman, Yamaguchi, & Gallagher 2007). Due to issues with time and cost, however, formal professional development available to teachers remains "woefully inadequate" (Borko, 2004).

Outside of school contexts, a growing number of teachers are engaging with new literacies, using social media tools, accessing online resources, and participating in local teacher-led groups in an effort to improve their teaching and support their students' learning (e.g., Carpenter & Krutka, 2015; Chapman & Ortlieb, 2015; Esterman, 2013; Lu & Curwood, 2015). As Cynthia Coburn (2001) stated, "Informal networks among teachers are largely unacknowledged by the policy world. Yet they have enormous potential to play an influential role in teacher sense-making" (p. 163). Despite the potential of such networks, particularly in rural and remote areas, there is a lack of research in this area. We argue that professional learning extends beyond government-endorsed workshops and school-based initiatives to include self-directed and self-regulated activities, which are often invisible to accrediting organizations and school administrators. Informal networks are part of teachers' wider social systems, and they offer teachers mentorship opportunities outside of their local schools. Not only does this give teachers access to new strategies, activities, and perspectives, it provides them with a way to engage in new literacy practices, explore new digital tools, and participate in personally meaningful professional learning.

In this study, we sought to gain insight into how Australian English teachers use Twitter as part of their professional learning and how this impacts their knowledge of content and pedagogy. As part of their daily lives, teachers traverse home, school, and community contexts, and they move across digital and physical environments—all of which have the potential to shape their beliefs, understanding, and practices. Consequently, research into teachers' professional learning must value the complex ways in which they access information and engage in dialogue in order to support their professional development and improve student learning outcomes. For researchers, this line of inquiry poses methodological challenges as well as opportunities, particularly in terms of establishing the boundaries of the field sites, deciding upon data sources, and drawing upon analytical tools. In this chapter, we consider: In what ways are new literacy practices evident on Twitter? How can Twitter be understood as a networked field site? What approaches to data collection and data analysis can capture how teachers use Twitter as part of their informal, self-sponsored professional learning?

CONCEPTUALIZING PROFESSIONAL LEARNING: NEW LITERACIES, NEW PRACTICES

Teachers' professional learning is situated in specific contexts, social in nature, and distributed across people, tools, and resources (Putnam & Borko, 2000). Prior studies demonstrate that there is often a disconnect between sociocultural theory, which conceptualizes learning as social and contextual, and the professional development offered in schools, much of which implicitly follows a transmissionist model (Cochran-Smith & Zeichner, 2005; Webster-Wright, 2009). These studies emphasize the importance of rethinking the way professional development is approached, so that it is more relevant and tailored to the needs of individual teachers and local schools (Borko, 2004). Even in professional learning communities, a model of school-based professional development that seeks to move away from a top-down, prescribed approach, the end result can be restrictive for teachers (DuFour, 2004).

Professional learning supports teachers in adapting their pedagogy in response to the rapidly changing social, cultural, and economic environments in which they live and work. For this reason, it is essential that teachers update their skills and innovate their practices in order to meet students' complex and evolving learning needs (Avalos, 2011; Curwood, 2011; Desimone, Smith, & Phillips, 2013). Despite significant financial investments at local, national, and international levels, a substantial body of research challenges the effectiveness of traditional approaches to teacher *professional development*, which understands learning as a progression through stages and a series of learning opportunities that are frequently designed and administered by an outside expert (Little, 2002; Walshe & Hirsch, 1998). It instead emphasizes the importance of *professional learning*, which involves an active, collaborative, iterative, and ongoing process based on a teacher's personal interests, professional goals, and sociocultural contexts (Darling-Hammond & Sykes, 1999; Desimone, 2009). As Hilda Borko (2004) argued, "To understand teacher learning, we must study it within these multiple contexts, taking into account both the individual teacher-learners and the social systems in which they are participants" (p. 4).

Compared to passive forms of learning, such as attending a lecture, active learning is linked to more positive outcomes for teachers (Desimone et al., 2002). Active professional learning allows teachers to develop their knowledge of specific subject content, to engage in dialogue with other educators, to share resources and ideas, and to try out new strategies and materials in the classroom (Curwood, 2013). With the growing accessibility of social media tools and online spaces, and the recent popularity of informal, community-based meetings, teachers around the world are engaging in professional learning in new ways. These approaches are rapidly gaining momentum at a grassroots level, but have not yet been subjected to systematic study. To date, large-scale studies of professional learning have only touched on this area, such as Darleen Opfer and David Pedder's (2011) survey in the United Kingdom, which included one broad item: "I use the web as one source of useful ideas for improving my practice" (p. 10). Recent studies in Australia, the United States, and other countries have offered case studies of teachers within specific online contexts, including Facebook (Lu & Curwood, 2015), Twitter (Biddolph & Curwood, 2016; Britt, 2015; Carpenter, 2015; Carpenter & Krutka, 2015; Visser, Evering, & Barrett, 2014), Instagram (Billen, 2015) and Pinterest (Chapman & Ortlieb, 2015), as well as within community-based meetings, such as TeachMeets (Esterman, 2013).

Research on new literacies can help frame investigation into how teachers are engaging in professional learning in online spaces. Julie Coiro, Michele Knobel, Colin Lankshear, and Don Leu (2008) argue that: (1) new technologies create new spaces for literacy and learning; (2) new literacies are vital to full participation in a global community; (3) new literacies are deictic and rapidly evolve as new tools and spaces emerge; (4) new literacies are multiple, multimodal, and multifaceted. Consequently, teachers' engagement in professional learning in online spaces can be understood through a new literacies framework. Today, digital technologies are rapidly changing and expanding; for example, while a social media tool like Facebook might seem like part of the fabric of our daily lives, it was only launched in 2004. Within a dozen years, it grew to 1.59 billion users and counting. Social media tools like Facebook and Twitter can serve as potential professional learning contexts for teachers as well as field sites for researchers. As we see it, in order to access and participate within online, informal networks to advance their professional learning, teachers must engage in new literacy practices. Not only do new literacies involve exploring new technologies and utilizing multiple modes of representation, they enable teachers to readily connect to a global community of educators.

New literacies reflect a sociocultural and situated approach to professional learning. At its core, professional learning is rooted in specific social and cultural contexts. While teachers previously may have been restricted to learning in and through physical contexts, the accessibility of Internet-connected devices means that online contexts are now readily available to them. From Instagram to ReadWriteThink.org, these new spaces give both "new potentials to literacy tasks" (Coiro et al., 2008, p. 14) and new potentials for professional learning. In order to access these spaces, teachers need to be able to understand, interpret, and communicate across a variety of modes and semiotic resources. At the same time, they must embrace (or at least tolerate) the fact that online spaces will evolve due to a variety of reasons, from technological advances to community demands. By drawing on a sociocultural, situated perspective of teacher learning that values dialogue in an online context, our study aimed to offer an innovative theoretical perspective and methodological approach (see also Biddolph & Curwood, 2016).

PUSHING THE BOUNDARIES: TWITTER AS A NETWORKED FIELD SITE

Prior research on Twitter and professional learning has demonstrated that it encourages preservice and in-service teachers to share resources and connect with other educators in a way that is both time- and cost-effective. Jeffrey Carpenter and Daniel Krutka's (2015) survey found that teachers appreciated the personalization and differentiation offered by Twitter-driven professional learning. Their survey collected quantitative and qualitative data, and their subsequent analysis of 494 responses provided insight into how classroom teachers, school administrators, and university professors used and perceived Twitter. In Carpenter's (2015) study of Twitter within his own teacher education program, he found that it helped preservice teachers to feel empowered and to see themselves as valued members of the teaching profession. He argued, "Twitter's concise, open, and ubiquitous nature potentially provides opportunities to increase teacher-student and student-student interactions, both inside and outside of the physical classroom" (p. 210). In addition to surveys and Twitter content, Carpenter (2015) also generated field notes and analytic memos. The approach to data collection within these studies highlights how Twitter can be used as part of informal professional learning as well as formal professional development. Moreover, they also show that researchers' methodological choices can position Twitter as one of multiple field sites within a study.

Traditionally, researchers have focused on a specific physical site in an effort to understand people's values, beliefs, cultural expectations, and social practices. With the growing availability and accessibility of digital technologies, however, today's online spaces challenge this narrow conceptualization of field sites. In many ways, researchers are no longer geographically or temporally restricted in terms of their access to potential participants and data sources (Lammers, Curwood, & Magnifico, 2012). Research, in this sense, is increasingly digitally mediated, and literacy researchers must consider how digital tools and online contexts shape their research questions, the design and implementation of their study, and their process of data analysis.

A field site can be understood as a "network composed of fixed and moving points including spaces, people, and objects" (Burrell, 2009, p. 189). In this light, field sites do not necessarily have established borders, which can present theoretical and methodological challenges to researchers at each step in the research process. Instead of defining a field site by physical contexts and boundaries, the concept of a network offers a way to understand the complex interactions between and among individuals, tools, and contexts across time and space. By their nature, networks are often multifaceted and malleable, subject to internal and external forces, and able to adapt and evolve. In addition, as danah boyd (2008) noted, "Networked technologies have completely disrupted any simple construction of a field site" (p. 27). In terms of new literacies, Julia Davies (2012) proposed that new technologies can facilitate new social literacy practices, which in turn allows people to perform new social acts that were not previously possible. Before the advent of digital tools and online spaces, teacher professional development was primarily studied within physical field sites driven by paper-based materials and face-to-face interactions. Today, Twitter and other social media offer researchers diverse and *dispersed* field sites.

Networked field sites are dynamic spaces that are user-driven, social, and collaborative (Gerber, Abrams, Curwood, & Magnifico, 2017) and promote "meaningful human interactions" (Markham, 2003, p. 8). For researchers interested in teachers' professional learning within informal, online networks, this means that they may need to leverage available technologies, access online traces of activity and participation, and engage with participants both near and far throughout their study. As a result, researchers need to be able to successfully navigate networked field sites at the same time that they reflect on what the various links, pathways, and intersections mean for individuals and communities (Hine, 2008). We argue that Twitter, as a networked field site, is a sociocultural context that involves new literacies, promotes meaningful interactions, and encourages self-directed, readily accessible, and personally relevant professional learning opportunities for teachers.

As a networked field site, Twitter encourages teachers to share resources and links from other online spaces, allows them to distribute their tweets across multiple social media platforms, and supports their engagement in ongoing discussion, such as through weekly chats on specific hashtags. To study Twitter as a networked field site, multimethod research (Creswell, 2015; Gerber et al., 2017) can examine professional learning in terms of both individual teacher-learners and wider social systems (Borko, 2004). In terms of methodologies, researchers can ask teachers (through surveys, interviews, and focus groups) how, where, and why they engage in professional learning in informal networks; they can also look at the networks themselves (through the online content) to understand the types of contributions and interactions that shape these professional learning experiences. In our study, we decided to conduct surveys and interviews to obtain teachers' self-reports of professional learning on Twitter, as well as to examine Twitter content, in order to access teachers' interactions within the network.

METHODOLOGY

Twitter as a Research Context

As a form of social media, microblogs allow individuals to generate their own online content, add hyperlinks and tags, and reach a global audience. Founded in 2006, Twitter allows users to read and write 140-character messages, called tweets, to communicate synchronously and asynchronously. Within a decade, Twitter has grown to over 310 million users worldwide. Tweets can contain text, images, and links to external pages, articles, and websites (Greenhow & Gleason, 2012). Through the use of hashtags, tweets can be part of larger conversations on Twitter, and tweets can be linked to or shared on other social networking sites and through e-mail. In 2015, at the time of our study, the standard website interface of Twitter included a navigation bar running across the top of the window that displayed icons for Home, Notifications, Messages, and Discover as well as a search box. This latter function can be used to search for keywords, usernames, and hashtags.

The top left-hand corner of the screen displays the profile information of the user, including their name, profile picture, number of tweets, number of followers, and amount of people they are following. Hashtags are created by including the # symbol before a word or phrase. They are searchable within Twitter, and, as such, can be used to broaden the scope of a tweet by reaching a larger audience that extends beyond one's "followers" and can serve to highlight a particular topic, and also turn a topic into a "trend" (a topic that is popular at a particular time). Some popular education-themed hashtags include #engchat, #edchat, #pstchat, and #ozedchat. Our study focused on #ozengchat, which was created in 2012 for Australian English teachers to discuss and share ideas and resources related to the subject area. The chat is moderated by several members of the community, who tweet questions about previously agreed-upon topics, which assists in maintaining #ozengchat as a space for professional learning that is relevant to English teaching. While the hashtag can be used and accessed publically at any time, a live chat occurs fortnightly on Tuesday evenings.

Research suggests people regularly use Twitter to develop and maintain relationships through conversation (Marwick & boyd, 2011). The use of hashtags can bring individuals together around a shared interest or topic; for instance, Australian educators may use #aussieED to engage in ongoing conversation around education in general. Tweets appear as a constantly updating list down the center of the interface, and can be replied to, favorited, or retweeted (Cho, Ro, & Littenberg-Tobias, 2013). In this sense, "a tweet stream is a constantly evolving, co-constructed conversation" (Greenhow & Gleason, 2012, p. 472). A favorite is used to like or praise another user's tweet, and can also save the tweet to the user's account for access at a later time. Individuals can also retweet, which involves reposting another user's tweet to show agreement with or provide validation (Khan, 2012) as well as distribute information and encourage participation in public discourse (boyd, Golder, & Lotan, 2010). All of these actions, and opportunities for interaction, allow individuals to build and maintain relationships through Twitter.

It is important to acknowledge that the Twitter interface has updated substantially since our data were collected in 2015. This speaks to the fact that digital tools and networked spaces are in a perpetual state of flux, which can present challenges to researchers studying these spaces. For instance, researchers face the problem of maintaining relevance when their field site is constantly shifting and updating, both aesthetically and functionally. Perhaps more significantly, when a networked field site is updated, it may impact the way participants use and interact within the space as well as how data are stored and archived. We suggest that this may have implications for how data are accessed and interpreted, and ultimately, for how the findings of the study are created and disseminated. Researchers' data collection tools may need to adapt to changing interfaces, and their research questions may need to evolve concomitantly with the field site.

Designing Our Study

Each study must have a *logic of inquiry* (Gee & Green, 1998) that links the research questions, theory, methodology, and findings. Research questions aren't necessarily set in stone, however. John Creswell (2013) posited, for example: "Qualitative research questions are open-ended, evolving, and nondirectional" (p. 138). Our study was driven by the following questions: How and why are English teachers using Twitter for professional learning? In what ways does participating in professional learning through Twitter influence teachers' professional practices? In framing our questions this way, we strove to keep them open and allow for multiple possibilities to emerge.

Building on prior research into teacher professional learning, we took a sociocultural and situated theoretical perspective. Because we wanted to know both *how* and *why* teachers were using Twitter, we decided to collect multiple forms of data. While surveys and interviews would allow teachers to tell us, in their own words, about their experiences with using Twitter, a content analysis of their actual tweets would offer a more nuanced perspective. In addition, multiple sources of data provide for triangulation and increase the trustworthiness of the research findings. Trustworthiness is also tied to the explicitness of a study's data collection and analysis process. As Mark Constas (1992) noted almost 25 years ago and still relevant today: "Since we are committed to opening the private lives of participants to the public, it is ironic that our methods of data collection and analysis often remain private and unavailable for public inspection" (p. 254). In what follows, then, we share our approach to data collection and analysis in this study for inspection, in order to move the field's understanding of methodologies forward and to support research into new literacies and professional learning.

Participants

Participant recruitment for this study involved posting links to educational-related hashtags #engchat and #ozengchat, as well as to the Facebook pages of the English Teachers Association of New South Wales, National Council of Teachers of English, and Australian Association for the Teaching of English. Guided by the study's research questions, these venues or channels were chosen in a deliberate manner (Gerber et al., 2017). Interestingly, and despite the global reach of Twitter and Facebook, the 64 survey respondents were primarily from an Australian context (see Table 5.1). This was possibly due to the differences in time between countries and when we posted our calls for participants, which was an issue concerning

Table 5.1. Survey Demographics.

		Number of participants
Country	Australia	49
	USA	12
	New Zealand	1
	Singapore	1
	Ireland	1
Age	20–24	5
	25–30	8
	31–35	5
	36–40	14
	41–45	10
	46–50	7
	51–55	8
	56–60	6
	61–65	1
Years Teaching Experience	Preservice	3
	1–5	8
	6–10	15
	11–15	16
	16–20	7
	21–25	7
	26–30	2
	31–35	6

researching in online spaces that we initially failed to consider. The recruitment tweets were posted during the evening, when the Australian-based chats are most active, while the global-based #edchat had less traffic at this time. This prompted us to narrow the focus of our study to provide an Australian perspective, and all interviews were conducted with Australian educators who had participated in the #ozengchat discussion. Future studies could actively seek more global representation and higher survey participation, driven by their research questions, aims, and scope.

At the end of the survey, respondents were given the opportunity to express their interest in participating in an interview. These self-nominated participants were all users of #ozengchat, the Australian English teacher hashtag, and they were varied in terms of their years of teaching experience and their activity on Twitter. For this reason, they were selected as representative of the teachers that participate in #ozengchat. Our use of purposeful sampling was based on "the assumption that the investigator wants to discover, understand, and gain insight and therefore must select a sample from which the most can be learned" (Merriam, 2009, p. 77). All interview participants taught in secondary schools, with the exception of Leah, who worked as a university lecturer. All were Australian and based in New South Wales, with the exception of Hannah, who taught in South Australia, and Leah, who taught in Queensland (see Table 5.2).

Table 5.2. Interview Participants.

Name*	Role	Age	Years of teaching experience	Years using Twitter	Number of tweets posted	Number of followers	Number following
Jackson	English teacher	25–30	4	6	37K	1,495	1,259
Whitney	English and ESL teacher	36–40	16	3	21K	1,885	1,461
Kat	English teacher and Head of Professional Learning	31–35	10	6	49.9K	4,428	1,316
Hannah	Head of Library, and an English teacher prior to this study	36–40	13	3	8,585	413	213
Elise	Head of English	36–40	11	3	2,726	1,036	1,722
Jill	Head of English	51–55	30	5	12.8K	1,627	1,132
Ryan	Head of English	31–35	10	6	570	104	444
Leah	University lecturer of English curriculum, and an English teacher prior to this study	31–35	10	6	10.7K	3,044	2,633

* All names are pseudonyms

Data Collection

To answer our research questions concerning English teachers and their use of Twitter for professional learning, we collected multiple sources of data, including: (1) an online survey (see Figure 5.1) of 64 teachers about their professional learning and Twitter use, which included Likert scale and open-ended questions; (2) hour-long semi-structured interviews (see Figure 5.2) with eight focal participants, and

Survey items

1. What is your current country of residence?
2. Please indicate your age.
   Under 20
   20–24
   25–30
   31–35
   36–40
   41–45
   46–50
   51–55
   56–60
   61–65
   66–70
   over 70
3. What is your full time equivalent teaching experience?
   Preservice teacher
   1–5 years
   6–10 years
   11–15 years
   16–20 years
   21–25 year
   26–30 years
   31–35 years
   more than 35 years
4. How long have you been using Twitter for professional development purposes?
   Less than a year
   1 year
   2 years
   3 years
   4 years
   5 years
   6 years
   7 years
   8 years or more
5. How often do you READ tweets related to your professional practice?
   Daily
   Several times a week
   Once a week
   Several times a month
   Rarely
6. How often do you RETWEET related to your professional practice?
   Daily
   Several times a week

(*Continued*)

(*Continued*)

Once a week
Several times a month
Rarely

7. **How often do you POST original tweets related to your professional practice?**
   Daily
   Several times a week
   Once a week
   Several times a month
   Rarely
8. **How often do you use Twitter completely UNRELATED to your professional practice?**
   Daily
   Several times a week
   Once a week
   Several times a month
   Rarely
9. **What educational hashtags do you use on Twitter?**
   #edchat
   #aussieED
   #engchat
   #ozengchat
   #pstchat
   #edtech
   other (please specify)
8. **Describe the types of professional training and development you have engaged with throughout your career (e.g., school in-services, graduate classes, conferences, online seminars). Please indicate if they were compulsory or voluntary.**

9. **Describe at least one professional development experience that you found highly valuable. Explain why.**
10. **Read the following statements and indicate the degree to which you agree or disagree using the scale from 1 to 5, with 1 being strongly disagree, 2 is disagree, 3 is neutral, 4 is agree, and 5 is strongly agree.**
    The professional development opportunities offered by my school are relevant to my classroom practice.

    Professional development offered by my school is tailored to my individual needs.

    Professional development offered by my school is tailored to my individual interests.

    Participating in live and synchronous Twitter chats is a meaningful form of professional development.

Participating in asynchronous Twitter chats is a meaningful form of professional development.

My level of participation in Twitter chats depends on my interest in the topic.

My participation in Twitter chats fluctuates.

If I need help or advice then I am active in Twitter chats, otherwise I do not participate.

My participation in Twitter chats is not limited to my own needs; I try to participate in most discussions.

Reading Twitter chats related to teaching has influenced my classroom practice.
Reading Twitter chats related to teaching has significantly changed my classroom practice.
Contributing to Twitter chats has influenced my classroom practice.
Contributing to Twitter chats has significantly changed my classroom practice.

11. **Please indicate if you are willing to participate in a 30- to 60-minute interview about your use of Twitter for professional development.**
No, I do not wish to participate in an interview.
Yes, I am happy to be interviewed.
If "yes," please provide your name and contact details in the box (Your personal details will remain confidential, they will only be used to get in touch with you. Please see Participant Information Statement for more information):

Name:
Contact number:
Email:
Twitter handle:

Fig. 5.1. Survey questions.

conducted via Skype; and (3) 530 tweets that included the #ozengchat hashtag. These tweets were taken from four separate #ozengchat weekly chats, and were selected as representative of the hashtag based on recommendations by the creator of #ozengchat, who we interviewed as part of the study, and who assisted us in accessing the #ozengchat archives. We collected tweets that used this hashtag because of its Australian focus, and because all of the participants had previously contributed to this hashtag. Our decision to collect these data sources was in direct response to our research questions. For example, the tweets themselves offered insight into how teachers use Twitter as part of their professional learning, but the interviews and surveys gave us a robust understanding of why. Similarly, we included specific questions in the interviews to uncover how Twitter participation shaped teachers' knowledge of content and pedagogy.

According to Catherine Marshall and Gretchen Rossman (2006), "In deciding to survey a group of people, researchers make one critical assumption—that

Interview questions

- Where do you teach? What subjects do you teach? How long have you been teaching?
- Describe your experiences of professional development. What activities does it typically involve? Is the experience mostly positive or negative? Do you think it is important?
- Why did you start using Twitter? Was it initially for professional purposes?
- What Twitter chats do you regularly participate in? Participation includes reading other users' tweets, and contributing your own.
- How did you hear about the Twitter chats you participate in?
- What are the most important characteristics of Twitter chats for you? What do you get out of participation? (For example, sense of belonging, emotional support, resources, advice, guidance, inspiration, and networking).
- What are the advantages of Twitter chats over other forms of professional development?
- What are the disadvantages of Twitter chats in comparison to other forms of professional development?
- Please provide one or two examples of something you learnt in the last Twitter chat you participated in. (For example, content, pedagogy, or skill).
- How are weekly topics for discussion decided? Are there any topics that are off-limits? Do you think the public nature of Twitter influences the types of content and information you share? In what ways?
- Are there any restrictions or rules when participating in Twitter chats (types of information or content posted)? How are these rules conveyed? Is it implicit or explicit? How are breaches in these rules addressed?
- Have you been able to convince other people you work with to participate in Twitter chats? If yes, how many? If no, what do you think is causing the resistance?
- Do you communicate with participants outside of the chat session hours? If yes, how do you communicate, and why? What limitation of Twitter are you addressing? (For example, Twitter, face-to-face, phone conversations, e-mails, etc.).
- What were your initial goals of participating in Twitter chats?
- Describe the first time you participated in a Twitter chat. Was it a positive, challenging, overwhelming, or exciting experience?
- What motivates you to regularly participate in Twitter chats?
- What are the biggest challenges of participating in Twitter chats? How do you overcome these?
- How has your experience of engaging in Twitter chats developed or changed over time?
- How could the quality of discussion in Twitter chats be improved?
- How has Twitter influenced your practice as an English teacher?
- What direction would you like to see professional development move toward in the future? Explain your answer.

Fig. 5.2. Interview questions.

a characteristic or belief can be described or measured accurately through self-reporting. In using questionnaires, researchers rely totally on the honesty and accuracy of participants' responses" (p. 125). As researchers, we recognized that both our survey and our interviews involved teachers' self-reporting of their professional learning that involved Twitter. In order to offer a more nuanced perspective, we also looked at their tweets as part of a specific hashtag. Consequently, this allowed us to ask participants about their new literacy practices that shaped their professional learning as well as to examine the specific digital tools that supported this process. One of our research questions specifically asked how Twitter participation shaped teachers' professional practices; additional data sources could have included classroom observations, lesson plans, and even student work. However, we decided that this was beyond the scope of the present study, but that it would offer opportunities for future research. We continue the discussion of our methodological decisions in the following sections.

Data Analysis

For the surveys, we interpreted multiple choice and Likert scale data quantitatively, and we identified frequently used terms in the open-ended question responses. The interviews and tweets were interpreted through a process of thematic analysis. This involved closely reading the data line by line and separating it into salient fragments or themes, which were then used to infer meaning (Saldaña, 2012). This is an inherently subjective process, as meaning is shaped by the interpretations of the researcher, the theoretical framing of a study, and the social and cultural context in which the analysis of data takes place (Mason, 2002). The data from interviews and tweets were analyzed concurrently using first cycle and second cycle coding methods (Miles, Huberman, & Saldaña, 2014). During the first cycle, meaningful fragments in the data were labeled using *in vivo* coding, which uses terms and phrases from the participants' own language as codes, thereby allowing us to consider the data from their perspective. "On your own" is an example of an *in vivo* code we used to label data that described a reported lack of support for formal professional learning and instances of self-initiated or independent learning. The tweets were analyzed using process codes, which imply observable action, to help capture the ways in which Twitter is used by educators (Saldaña, 2012). Only one code was applied to each tweet, and sample codes are described in Table 5.3.

During the second cycle of coding interviews and tweets, we identified patterns across both data sources and reduced the number of codes by removing those that occurred less frequently, as well as those that shared the same meaning with another code. During this stage we also changed the *in vivo* codes that used the participants' own language, to descriptive codes that summarized a primary theme. For example, the *in vivo* code "on your own" became the descriptive code "self-directed learning." This clarified the meanings of the codes (see also Table 5.3), which were then cross-referenced with the quantitative data from the survey to highlight salient themes and assist with triangulation (Denzin & Lincoln, 2000).

Table 5.3. Tweet codes.

Code	Description	No. of times code occurred
SHARING RESOURCES	Links to external resources such as websites and articles that inform teaching practice, or can be used in the classroom. Example: "OK, straight off the bat is the top two Shakespeare links I give to my students: nfs.sparknotes.com & shmoop.com/shakespeare/ #ozengchat"	122
REFLECTING ON EXPERIENCES	Reflecting on personal experiences they have had as a teacher. This can include sharing successes and failures, and reflecting on their teaching philosophy. Example: "Hurley is interesting for me personally. I feel it's a bit dry for students. Lots of interesting idea of disc. though #ozengchat"	77
DESCRIBING PRACTICE	Tweets that describe strategies that have been implemented in the classroom. Example: "#ozengchat I did a Macbeth/GoT lesson re: regicide + kingslayer, doubletrust + red wedding, and Lady Macbeth + Cersei …"	75
ASKING A QUESTION	These were in the form of open questions that were directed toward everyone, as well as direct questions that were specifically targeted toward individual users. Example: "#ozengchat I need some help Language, Learning and Literacy Does anyone have any information that's not on the intranet?"	71
OFFERING IDEAS	Suggestions and inspiration for classroom practice. Example: "Engaging with poetry—get students to illustrate a selected poem #ozengchat"	70
RESPONDING TO QUESTION	Directly responding to or answering a question posed by another user. Example: "we do insults as well! And idioms that we use today from Shakespeare #ozengchat #greatminds"	51
NETWORKING	Networking includes making plans to collaborate with other users, and personal conversations unrelated to professional practice. Example: "We should do some collaborative projects w my ESL classes then! :) #sokeen #ozengchat #authenticlearning"	47

TRACING THE ANALYTICAL PROCESS: DECISIONS, EXAMPLES, AND CONCLUSIONS

Developing Codes for Online Thematic Analysis

In our analysis of the content of 530 tweets from the #ozengchat hashtag, we drew from four separate and representative #ozengchat weekly archived chats involving English teachers from across Australia. While our interviews and surveys offered insight into *why* teachers used Twitter as part of their professional learning, our content analysis showed *how* teachers drew on new literacies and actively engaged with this particular networked field site. As noted earlier, we decided to use process codes as part of our thematic analysis. Because process codes focus on observable action, and our aim was to clearly and succinctly describe the purpose of each tweet, this approach was in line with both our research questions and our theoretical framework. Our analysis revealed that teachers most commonly contributed to the #ozengchat hashtag by sharing resources, reflecting on their experiences, and describing their classroom practice. Notably, this resonated with survey data that indicated that responding teachers use Twitter predominantly for professional purposes.

In creating the process codes to apply to the Twitter chats, we asked ourselves: What is the primary purpose of this Tweet? In considering this question, we looked at the structure of the tweet itself: Was it a question, a statement, or a reflection? Who was the targeted audience, and did it extend beyond the #ozengchat discussion, as evidenced by the use of other hashtags or mentions? Did it contain hyperlinks, or include photos, videos, or other potential resources? Was the tweet in direct response to the topic of the weekly discussion, or was it a reply to another person's tweet? In order to capture both the spirit of process codes, and the nature of the tweets, our codes began with gerunds, or verb forms that function as nouns. Through a process of creating, refining, and defining our process codes, the final codes included: (1) sharing resources; (2) reflecting on experiences; (3) describing practice; (4) asking a question; (5) offering ideas; (6) responding to a question; and (7) networking (see Table 5.3).

In analyzing the 530 tweets, we applied one code to each, in order to gain a deeper understanding of how Australian English teachers used Twitter as part of their professional learning. We found it instrumental to develop a working definition of each code, which we refined over time, and to include several example tweets, which we repeatedly referred back to throughout the coding process. While the *sharing resources* code appeared most frequently, 57 of 122 of these instances occurred outside of the designated time of #ozengchat. In terms of new literacies, this suggests that asynchronous participation in Twitter chats may be more about sharing ideas and resources while synchronous participation may focus more on seeking advice and reflecting on experiences. Our analysis of the tweets was complemented by a simple quantitative analysis, which revealed 228 favorites, 143 retweets, and 12 instances of direct praise. Similar to our interview and survey data, these outcomes reinforced our interpretation that teachers' Twitter use entailed contributing to and engaging in a supportive professional learning network.

Interpreting Emergent Findings, Drawing on Theoretical Perspectives

In conceptualizing Twitter as a networked field site, our analysis of #ozengchat showed how it encouraged teachers to share resources and hyperlinks, and how it offered them an opportunity to engage in both synchronous and asynchronous discussion to advance their professional learning. Our theoretical understanding of professional learning was instrumental in shaping both our data collection and data analysis. Because we take a sociocultural and situated approach in our research, we believe that professional learning can only be understood within specific social and cultural contexts. By electing to draw on Twitter content as a data source, we were able to directly examine interactions within the context of an online, informal professional learning network. While this offered us insight into how teachers use Twitter, we knew that we needed to directly ask teachers why they used this tool as part of their self-sponsored professional learning.

In designing our survey and interview questions, we asked participants to share details about their practices, habits, beliefs, and challenges. Notably, this also allowed us to understand Twitter as a networked field site. For instance, our survey asked respondents about other education-related hashtags that they used as well as about available professional development at their school. Because we recognized that professional learning takes place across multiple sociocultural contexts, this approach to data collection offered us a more nuanced perspective on how teachers engage in professional learning. We felt that it was important for our data collection instruments to include open-ended questions, and consequently allow for multiple accounts of experiences and different perspectives to emerge.

As researchers, we know that *inquiry* and *possibility* are vital components of any study. In our Twitter research, we were surprised by the degree to which teachers wanted to have their learning and their knowledge both recognized and valued by their peers. As one teacher reflected, "Twitter was about establishing myself within a community of educators who value me." While we did not specifically ask them about the ways in which their professional learning was officially (by schools or accrediting organizations) or unofficially (by peers or other educators) acknowledged, this emerged in a number of interviews. By drawing on our theoretical framework, we were able to understand that teachers wanted professional learning that occurred within one context to be valued and validated by other contexts. As one teacher pointed out about his colleagues, "They have got no idea [what Twitter can offer]."

MOVING FORWARD

To understand the professional learning of teachers, we must study it within and across the multiple personal and professional contexts in which learning occurs (Borko 2004), and our study sought to address a critical gap in the research. To that end, we drew on multiple forms of data, including a survey, interviews, and tweets, to investigate how and why these particular English teachers used new literacies to participate in Twitter and, in turn, to gain insight into how this shapes their professional learning. This chapter addressed questions about how researchers can approach the study of learning within these multiple contexts, when digital tools and networked spaces have redefined the very notion of field sites. While traditionally research was confined to physical field sites with established boundaries, the permeation of social media and digital technologies into our day-to-day lives has opened up new spaces and opportunities for inquiry. This has prompted researchers to reconceptualize field sites as evolving, networked, and dynamic (Burrell, 2009; Gerber et al., 2017).

Paramount to our study was the understanding of Twitter as a networked field site; a constantly evolving, participatory, and multifaceted space where teachers share ideas and resources and participate in a professional dialogue. In conducting our study within this unique digital context, we faced a variety of theoretical and methodological challenges that shaped the design and implementation of the study as well as the process of data analysis. Our research questions allowed for unexpected findings and multiple perspectives, by asking *how* and *why*, and the multidimensional interactions between and among individual participants within the space were explored through the collection of multiple data sources. Each data source allowed us to consider a different dimension of the research questions, creating a more nuanced understanding of individuals and their interactions within this particular networked field site. The survey provided a broad understanding of *why* teachers use Twitter for professional learning, the interviews conveyed the diverse experiences of individual teachers within a particular online learning community, and the analysis of tweets from #ozengchat archives showcased *how* teachers used Twitter.

Future research on Twitter and teacher professional learning can draw from established approaches to big data. For example, public Twitter data, such as through popular hashtags like #ozedchat or #ozengchat, is easily accessible through Twitter's Application Programming Interface (API). Data collection for

Twitter will include: (1) content (e.g., keywords, language) as well as associated metadata, such as (2) sender (e.g., Twitter username and numerical ID); (3) recipients (e.g., @mentioned usernames in the tweet); (4) timestamp; (5) tweet type (e.g., retweet, reply, or original tweet); (6) hashtags; (7) URLs (Bruns & Steiglitz, 2014). A number of open source tools have been developed through the Digital Media Initiative, including Twitter Capture and Analysis Toolset (T-CAT), and these can be customized by individual researchers.

Social media network analysis examines both network and social structures to "specifically determine how individual influence operates within a complex, interwoven collection of networked individuals" (Hutchinson, 2015, p. 24). Using Gephi, an open-source visualization and exploration software package, Jonathon Hutchinson ran his Twitter through a combination of the Force Atlas 2 and Fruchterman Rheingold spatialization algorithms to indicate which users and topics are more relevant to users' conversation by placing them in the center of the graph. The nodes can then be adjusted by their size according to the amount of outward edges or connections to other nodes. The resulting visualization, using metrics such as between-ness, centrality and connectivity, can represent how teachers within this specific informal online network are engaging with specific education topics.

Diverse methodological approaches can offer insight into how teachers use specific social media tools, such as Twitter, to share their practices, connect with others, and access available resources. By detailing the considerations and challenges within our study, we have provided insight into how research can be conducted within digitally mediated spaces and networked field sites. To move the field of literacy research forward, we argue that researchers need to make their methodological choices, data collection tools, and analytical processes transparent. Not only will this promote the trustworthiness of the findings, it will encourage rich dialogue around the process, product, and impact of new literacies research.

REFERENCES

Avalos, B. (2011). Teacher professional development in teaching and teacher education over ten years. *Teaching and Teacher Education*, 27(1), 10–20.

Biddolph, C., & Curwood, J. S (2016). #PD: Examining the intersection of Twitter and professional learning. In M. Knobel & J. Kalman (eds.), *New literacies and teacher learning* (pp. 195–218). New York: Peter Lang.

Billen, M. (2015). *#Learningtoteach: Using Instagram to elicit pre-service teacher reflection.* PhD dissertation.

Borko, H. (2004). Professional development and teacher learning: Mapping the terrain. *Educational Researcher*, 33(3), 3–15.

boyd, d. (2008). A response to Christine Hine. In A. N. Markham & N. K. Baym (Eds.), *Internet Inquiry: Conversations about method* (pp. 26–32). Thousand Oaks, CA: Sage.

boyd, d., S. Golder, & G. Lotan. (2010). Tweet, tweet, retweet: Conversational aspects of retweeting on Twitter. Paper presented at the Hawaii International Conference on Systems Science, 43, IEEE, Kauai, HI.

Bruns, A. and Stieglitz, S. (2014). Metrics for understanding communication on Twitter. In K. Weller, A. Bruns, J. Burgess, M. Mahrt, & C. Puschmann, *Twitter and society* (pp. 69–82). New York: Peter Lang.

Britt, V. (2015). "Beyond the four walls of my building": A case study of #Edchat. PhD dissertation.

Burrell, J. (2009). The field site as a network: A strategy for locating ethnographic research. *Field Methods*, 21(2), 181–199.

Carpenter, J. (2015). Pre-service teachers' microblogging: Professional development via Twitter. *Contemporary Issues in Technology and Teacher Education,* 15(2), 209–234.

Carpenter, J., & Krutka, D. (2015). Engagement through microblogging: Educator professional development via Twitter. *Professional Development in Education,* 41(4), 707–728.

Chapman, D., & Ortlieb, E. (2015). Pin it! Maximizing the benefits of video usage in a pre-service teacher classroom using Pinterest. In E. Ortlieb, M. McVee, & L. Shanahan (Eds.), *Video reflection in literacy teacher education and development: Lessons from research and practice* (pp. 257–277). London: Emerald.

Cho, V., Ro, J. & Littenberg-Tobias, J. (2013). What Twitter will and will not do: Theorising about teachers' online professional communities. *LEARNing Landscapes,* 6(2), 45–62.

Coburn, C. (2001). Collective sense-making about reading: How teachers mediate reading policy in their professional communities. *Educational Evaluation and Policy Analysis,* 23(2), 145–170.

Cochran-Smith, M., & Zeichner, K. (Eds.) (2010). *Studying teacher education: The report of the AERA Panel on Research and Teacher Education.* Washington, DC: Routledge.

Cohen, D., & Hill, H. (2001). *Learning policy: When state education reform works.* New Haven, CT: Yale University Press.

Coiro, J., Knobel, M., Lankshear, C., & Leu, D. J. (Editors). (2008). *Handbook of research in new literacies.* Mahwah, NJ: Lawrence Erlbaum Associates.

Constas, M. (1992). Qualitative analysis as a public event: The documentation of category development procedures. *American Educational Research Journal,* 29(2), 253–266.

Creswell, J. (2015). *A concise introduction to mixed methods research.* Thousand Oaks, CA: Sage.

Curwood, J. S. (2013). Applying the design framework to technology professional development. *Journal of Digital Learning in Teacher Education,* 29(3), 90–97.

Curwood, J. (2011). Teachers as learners: What makes technology-focused professional development effective? *English in Australia,* 46(3), 68–75.

Curwood, J. (2014a). Between continuity and change: Identities and narratives within teacher professional development. *Teaching Education,* 25(2), 156–183.

Curwood, J. (2014b). English teachers' cultural models about technology: A microethnographic perspective on professional development. *Journal of Literacy Research*, 46(1), 9–38.

Darling-Hammond, L., & Sykes, G. (1999). *Teaching as the learning profession: Handbook of policy and practice.* San Francisco, CA: Jossey-Bass.

Davies, J. (2012). Facework on Facebook as a new literacy practice. *Computers & Education,* 59(1), 19–29.

Denzin, N., & Lincoln, Y. (2000). *Handbook of qualitative research.* Beverly Hills, CA: Sage.

Desimone, L. (2009). Improving impact studies of teachers' professional development: Toward better conceptualizations and measures. *Educational Researcher,* 38(3), 181–199.

Desimone, L., Smith, T., and Phillips, K. (2013). Linking student achievement growth to professional development participation and changes in instruction: A longitudinal study of elementary students and teachers in Title I schools. *Teachers College Record,* 115(5), 1–46.

DuFour, R. (2004). What is a professional learning community? *Educational Leadership,* 6(8), 6–11.

Esterman, M. (2013). A historic moment for TeachMeets. *Teaching History,* 47(2), 51–52.

Garet, M., Porter, A., Desimone, L., Birman, B., & Yoon, K. (2001). What makes professional development effective? Analysis of a national sample of teachers. *American Educational Research Journal,* 38(3), 915–945.

Gee, J. & Green, J. (1998). Discourse analysis, learning and social practice: A methodological study. *Review of Research in Education,* 23, 119–169.

Gerber, H., Abrams, S., Curwood, J., & Magnifico, A. (2017). *Conducting qualitative research of learning in online spaces.* Thousand Oaks, CA: Sage.

Greenhow, C., & Gleason, B. (2012). Twitteracy: Tweeting as a new literacy practice. *The Educational Forum,* 76(4), 464–478.

Hammerness, K., Darling-Hammond, L., Bransford, J., Berliner, D., Cochran-Smith, M., McDonald, M., & Zeichner, K. (2005). How teachers learn and develop. In L. Darling-Hammond & J. Bransford (Eds.), *Preparing teachers for a changing world: What teachers should learn and be able to do* (pp. 58–389). San Francisco, CA: Wiley & Sons.

Hine, C. (2008). How can qualitative Internet researchers define the boundaries of their projects? In A. Markham & N. Baym (Eds.), *Internet inquiry: Conversations about method* (pp. 1–20). Thousand Oaks, CA: Sage.

Hutchinson, J. (2015). The impact of social TV and audience participation on national cultural policy: Co-creating television comedy with #7DaysLater. *Communication, Politics and Culture,* 47(3), 18–30.

Khan, S. (2012). Getting started with Twitter: A "why and how" for teachers. *English Australia Journal,* 28(1), 55–60.

Lammers, J., Curwood, J., & Magnifico, A. (2012). Toward an affinity space methodology: Considerations for literacy research. *English Teaching: Practice and Critique,* 11(2), 44–58.

Little, J. (2012). Professional community and professional development in the learning-centered school. In M. Kooy & K. van Veen (eds), *Teacher learning that matters: International perspectives* (pp. 22–46). New York, NY: Routledge.

Little, J. (2002). Locating learning in teachers' communities of practice: Opening up problems of analysis in records of everyday work. *Teaching and Teacher Education,* 18(8), 917–946.

Lu, Y. & Curwood, J. S. (2015). Update your status: Exploring pre-service teacher identities in an online discussion group. *Asia-Pacific Journal of Teacher Education,* 43(5), 438–449.

Markham, A. (2003, October). Images of Internet: Tool, place, way of being. Paper presented at the Fourth Annual Conference of the Association of Internet Researchers. Toronto, Canada.

Marshall, C., & Rossman, G. (2006). *Designing qualitative research.* Thousand Oaks, CA: Sage.

Marwick, A., & boyd, d. (2011). I tweet honestly, I tweet passionately: Twitter users, context collapse, and the imagined audience. *New Media and Society,* 13(1), 114–33.

Mason, J. (2002). *Qualitative researching.* Thousand Oaks, CA: Sage.

Merriam, S. (2009). *Qualitative research: A guide to design and implementation.* San Francisco, CA: Jossey-Bass.

Miles, M., Huberman, A., & Saldaña, J. (2014). *Qualitative data analysis: A methods sourcebook.* Thousand Oaks, CA: Sage.

Opfer, V. & Pedder, D. (2011). The lost promise of teacher professional development in England. *European Journal of Teacher Education,* 34(1), 3–24.

Penuel, W., Fishman, B., Yamaguchi, R., & Gallagher, L. (2007). What makes professional development effective? Strategies that foster curriculum implementation. *American Educational Research Journal,* 44(4), 921–958.

Putnam, R., & Borko, H. (2000). What do new views of knowledge and thinking have to say about research on teacher learning? *Educational Researcher,* 29(1), 4–15.

Saldaña, J. (2012). *The coding manual for qualitative researchers. 2nd ed.* Thousand Oaks, CA: Sage.

Visser, R. Evering, L., & Barrett, D. (2014). #TwitterforTeachers: The implications of Twitter as a self-directed professional development tool for K–12 teachers. *Journal of Research on Technology in Education,* 46(4), 396–413.

Walshe, J. & Hirsch, D. (1998). *Staying Ahead: In-service Training and Teacher Professional Development.* Paris: OECD.

Webster-Wright, A. (2009). Reframing professional development through understanding authentic professional learning. *Review of Educational Research,* 79(2), 702–739.

Wilson, S., & Berne, J. (1999). Teacher learning and the acquisition of professional knowledge: An examination of research on contemporary professional development. *Review of Research in Education,* 24(1), 173–209.

CHAPTER SIX

The messiness of actor-network theory in an online gaming ethnography

The inside story of *Leet Noobs*

MARK CHEN

INTRODUCTION

This chapter describes processes through which, as a newbie to academic research, I sought to make sense of a massive amount of data. Indeed, according to conventional wisdom about the proper conduct of research, I had actually gone about things backward so far as theory-guided research is concerned (although I was in line with grounded theory). I had hundreds of hours of raw data, collected before knowing what I would do with it, and was in need of a theory. I needed help to understand what was going on and also some process for writing the data up that made sense to other scholars (a doctoral committee) who were unfamiliar with my setting. These matters seem especially relevant as I now advise new doctoral students about how to conduct and write their own research.

This chapter draws on my doctoral dissertation, subsequently published as a book, *Leet Noobs: The Life and Death of an Expert Player Group in* World of Warcraft (Chen, 2012). It is an ethnographic look at a group of players of the massively multiplayer online game (MMOG) *World of Warcraft* (WoW), and describes the learning trajectory entailed as the group's members negotiated how to communicate effectively, work together, and measure performance during large-group events known as "raids." Most of this study is written up using an actor-network theory lens (ANT; Latour, 2005), which involves considering the activity system as an assemblage or network of various entities working together to make the setting stable. The whole job took seven years to complete, from data collection to publication as a book. In fact, the writing evolved over time, informed by different theoretical tools as I encountered them and deemed them useful for understanding it all. The research began when I was fresh to graduate school, after many years away from academic study. My data were initially collected for a qualitative methods course as part of a year-long study in 2005/2006. The formal paper produced for that course became my first academic journal article, "Communication, Coordination, and Camaraderie in *World of Warcraft*" (Chen, 2009a).

Viewing academia generally as a place of inequity I tried to be as transparent as possible with my early academic work, and I posted all my course papers online for anyone to read, including "Communication, Coordination, and Camaraderie in *World of Warcraft*" (http://markdangerchen.net/papers/coordination-cooperation-and-camaraderie-in-world-of-warcraft). I wanted to document the iterative process of producing academic work, in case others found it helpful in allaying feelings of inadequacy often experienced by new scholars (including me, really—I mean, come on, who hasn't had the imposter syndrome in graduate school?). Hence, the online paper is an early version of the published article, where I'm working through ideas and evidently wrestling with how to do qualitative research rigorously. It hopefully reflects that I'm trying to be mindful and reflective while attempting to still do right by a community I cared deeply about. I was also struggling with an influx of new ideas, while also responding to problems I had found in relation to game theory and social dilemmas—including some of my earlier work attempting to design game theory informed experiments (Chen, 2005)—and seeking to reconcile it with what I saw happening in my everyday gaming life. Accordingly, some of what I was writing about in that early paper is pretty far removed from what I would later concentrate on. But in the interests of making academic production transparent, it's still online for anyone to see.

When it was time to choose a dissertation topic, I was all set to do a research study comparing guild life with work life, having access to some guild mates who all worked together in the same office (guilds are generally tight-knit groups of gamers who've aligned themselves together and have pledged allegiance to a common organization). Unfortunately, during the summer, while I was finalizing topics, some of those coworkers had a serious falling out. During a meeting with my advisor, it became apparent that I still had a substantial amount of unexamined data from my earlier coursework study. The "Communication, Coordination, and Camaraderie in *World of Warcraft*" paper had drawn on maybe a tenth of the data I had collected, and it had documented only the communication practices of the raid group. I began looking at other ways to analyze my data corpus. Meanwhile, I now had a couple more years of graduate schooling under my belt and had learned much more about research.

I could see how new-to-me concepts could apply very well to the data I had in hand. It made sense to write about gaming as a cultural phenomenon, where success meant participating legitimately (Gee, 2003) and accruing cultural capital (Malaby, 2009), and to document change-in-practice as a learning narrative with this player group I had spent a year with. I also could see how Science and Technology Studies-informed lenses could help me describe raiding practice effectively and convincingly, especially since a major part of the story of raiding involved how the group interacted with user-created modifications to the game in order to succeed. ANT, distributed cognition (Hutchins, 1995), and the "mangle of practice" (Pickering, 1993) accounts seemed more appropriate than other possibilities as a way to write about the convoluted intricacies of raiding in WoW.

Each chapter in my dissertation was written as a stand-alone paper, and to me it's clear how my thinking evolved over the course of their development. Ironically… or actually, probably completely typical of academic publishing, my "Communication, Coordination, and Camaraderie in *World of Warcraft*" paper (chapter 2 of the dissertation/book), which in part addressed problems I had with traditional social dilemma scholarship, was published the same year as my social and cultural capital paper (chapter 1), even though I hadn't really thought about social dilemmas and game theory for three years by the time those two were published. The final two chapters (4 and 5) of the dissertation (and then book) were new material, but I actually think they represent my most sophisticated analyses. Chapter 3 uses ANT to trace the adoption of a nonhuman add-on to WoW's interface to share in the responsibility of raiding. The last chapter took me the longest to write since I had to think about *how* to think about it, as it was a delicate topic: the group I studied and previously claimed was stable due to everyone being friends flame-warred itself out of existence.

This current write-up will attempt to describe the research methods I used to create *Leet Noobs*, starting with that early work and then tracing its evolution to published papers, to dissertation, and finally to book. Each version is better than the previous, better informed with more nuanced analysis. The whole process was "messy" as hell (Law, 2004).

PURPOSE OF STUDY AND HOW IT AFFECTED DATA COLLECTION

The initial questions I had for my research on WoW were: "What kind of communication was happening in the game in and around raids?" and "What kind of learning narrative could be seen in this communication?" The research had started out as an assignment in a course that had a grounded theory approach and, accordingly, the questions were intentionally broad and open. This prompted a straightforward procedure of recording as much of the communication that was happening as possible and hoping there would be something interesting to say about emergent patterns in the data.

This was not a simple task! I ended up recording about 600 hours of text chat data and 80 hours of video data of the group's endeavors. I *wanted* to video record everything that was happening in game while I participated with the group. Ideally, I would also have asked some key informants to record their points of view in the game, but, logistically, that seemed like an enormous favor to ask. It was difficult for me to allocate storage space for my personal recording (this was 2005, after all), and I couldn't conceive of realistically asking participants to devote gigabytes of space toward my project. I ended up having to settle with video recording only a portion of the sessions, focusing on new encounters the group faced and leaving out routine activities. Each session I recorded filled up a sizable amount of my available disk space until I had a chance to process and compress the videos for final archiving. I burned DVDs of the videos after each compression batch so that I'd have enough storage space for the next few sessions' videos. Even so, I had to settle for lower video quality than was ideal to make everything manageable. Now, more than ten years later, if I were to do it all over again, I'd relish the fact that I could save high-definition videos with very good quality compression due to both advances in storage capacity-to-cost ratios and higher fidelity compression algorithms.[1]

While compromising on the video data, I was still able to record all the in-game text chat the group used to coordinate our action. I felt this was a fair compromise since it was our main form of communication. In fact, thinking about what data to record forced some initial analysis. The raid group under study used several text chat channels to communicate (and most members also opted to unsubscribe from irrelevant default channels such as a trading channel). There were whole group channels, each with a different purpose, ranging from general chat to task-specific chat. There were also subgroup channels: one for each role specialization within the team, where members would coordinate internally or confer privately before sharing ideas with the whole group (see Table 6.1). This meant that, at some point, the group decided it needed multiple channels to play effectively, and this happened almost immediately in the life of the raid group, such that it seemed to be an assumed obvious step.

For my dissertation, text chat was displayed in full glorious color (more color images can be found at http://markdangerchen.net/2015/10/29/leet-noobs-color-images; I set this archive up to enable book readers to better see the images as I had wanted to include them in the book, but couldn't). For everything else, I had to reformat the text without color, which, unfortunately, makes it harder to scan over large bodies of text quickly to get a sense of chat patterns that were based on channel usage.

Table 6.1. Text Chat Channels the Raid Group Used to Communicate (In the game, these channels were rendered in color—as indicated in square brackets below—on a dark background).

say	only displayed talk from other players if they were near enough [white]
yell	displayed talk that is broadcast to a large region [yellow]
emote	displayed text for in-game character animations [brown]
whisper	displayed personal chat between two players [pink]
[Party]	for up to five players who had teamed up to complete quests or tasks [blue]
[Guild]	to send messages to guild members no matter where they were in-game [light green]
[Officer]	for the officers of a guild [dark green]
[Raid]	for up to 40 players, consisting of eight parties of five players each [orange]
[healsting]	for the healer classes to talk about who to heal [tan]
[madtankin]	for the warriors to talk about who would play certain roles [tan]
[splittranq]	for the hunters during a specific fight in MC [tan]
[madsheep]	for the mages to coordinate who would cast polymorph spells in certain encounters, turning enemies to sheep [tan]
[soulburn]	for the warlocks to talk about who to support and which monsters to banish [tan]
[madrogues]	for the rogues to talk about general rogue strategy like when to use poisons on our weapons [tan]

While most of the specialized role channels were private to players whose characters matched those roles, I subscribed to all channels so I could record all the text chat. A third-party tool was used to dump the chat into text files that were regularly archived along with the aforementioned videos. While capturing the communication data I marked in a separate text file anything that seemed important at the moment it occurred: one such file for each session.

I also saved many threads from the group's online forum when it was about particular strategies for new or difficult encounters in the game. When I presented posts from a thread as evidence in my writing, I tried to preserve their formatting, including grammatical errors and misspellings (see Figure 6.1).

Warren <The 7/10 Split> (2:12 p.m.)
ok Heres the deal. I am posting this for all to see. I dot care how pissed Max will be at me, I dont care if he kicks me out of the guild. This is retarded. Its a game. I am done with you drama queens

Fig. 6.1. An example of a forum post, as treated in my book. In my dissertation, this was in full color to match the online forum's color scheme.

Finally, I saved very many screenshots to later analyze and use to illustrate significant ideas and moments. Screenshots and video that an online researcher takes during data collection are hugely important in documenting what goes on in an online game. They provide context for the communication being studied. More than that, however, they also situate the researcher's point of view, making it easy to visualize the researcher's limitations; one player's perspective can hardly count as omniscient over the whole system. Being able to see what players see is also highly relevant for one of the main points of *Leet Noobs*: namely, that players' expertise depends on being able to use third-party visual modifications to the game. Successful play presupposes successfully distributing cognition and delegating responsibilities in the network among all its actors, including nonhuman ones. Permission to include a screenshot of these third-party adds-on could not be obtained from Blizzard Entertainment for either this book or *Leet Noobs* (a partial screenshot appears in Figure 6.4 later in this chapter). This presents an interesting conundrum for new literacies researchers wanting to make data obtained from commercial digital spaces transparent to readers.

ANALYSES AND ALIGNMENT TO THEORY

Once I began collecting data, I simultaneously started trying to analyze it. I went through certain fights and encounters multiple times on the way to finally arriving at the account presented in the dissertation and the book. With each successive pass, I had a clearer understanding of what went on, often coupled with a more sophisticated way of writing about it.

At first, when writing "Communication, Coordination, and Camaraderie in *World of Warcraft*," I was interested in describing the communication practices of the group. In that first pass I had a relatively straightforward task of unpacking game-specific jargon into something I could present to others outside of the domain. After seeing what the data contained, I was subsequently able to go through it again (Pass 2) and start categorizing particular exchanges, as well as code specific utterances within those exchanges. Visualizing the coding schemes also let me see patterns in the data that I could examine in more detail. Once these patterns emerged, I then realized I needed a way to explain the patterns satisfactorily. For that, I had to do yet another pass (Pass 3) through the data using a Science and Technology Studies-informed lens on the actor-networks in play.

Meanwhile, on top of the chat data I was collecting on raiding, I was also engaging in more general participant-observation of WoW, and I felt knowledgeable enough to write ethnographic narratives of daily life in the game (on my particular server, situated in an inclusive guild in the underdog faction). I was able to portray WoW as a cultural space where interactions and relationships with other players mattered just as much, if not more, than player-game interactions and relationships.

While this was happening, I basically ignored the last few months of data I had collected since I didn't really know how to think about it or write it up. I was fully occupied with describing typical sessions, painting a general picture of how things worked and then a detailed picture of how raids worked. I only started thinking about the breakup of the raid group several years after having already analyzed the earlier data and describing the story of the group's learning trajectory and expertise development. Fortunately, the ANT lens I used to talk about raiding was also useful in understanding the dissolution of the group. I could write it in ANT terms (disruption, failure of translation and enrollment, instability, etc.). All of this would ultimately support an early point I had identified during my first analytic pass: namely, the importance of trust in order for a group to be stable and perform well cannot be overemphasized.

Pass 1

I've heard the phrase "massaging the data" from a handful of researchers over the years. Initially, I was puzzled by this, but now I nod instead because I think about how I had to format my WoW data so that I could analyze it. The chat data were dumped to text files, each line with a date/time stamp, the channel the utterance occurred on, and the content of the message. For most of the massaging, I used a text editor that supported regular expression (https://en.wikipedia.org/wiki/Regular_expression) functions for search and replace. In my initial pass, I ended up deleting most of the data before analyzing, since the majority of the chat data actually consisted of system or add-on messages normally hidden from the player. I also used search/replace for the aliases on each player's username to change it to a pseudonym. The example below includes numerous lines in the "druidlovin" channel, but these are auto-generated messages from the KLHTM third-party add-on (the nonhuman actor analyzed in *Leet Noobs*) that my group of players was using to help us manage raid battles. In game, this channel is hidden, so that I'm not inundated with messages.

3/5 17:21:06.625 Waynard has gone offline.
3/5 17:21:09.265 [2. druidlovin] Thoguht: KLHTM threat 0
3/5 17:21:14.421 [2. druidlovin] Thoguht: KLHTM threat 0
3/5 17:21:19.296 [2. druidlovin] Thoguht: KLHTM threat 0
3/5 17:21:24.421 [2. druidlovin] Thoguht: KLHTM threat 0
3/5 17:21:29.546 [2. druidlovin] Thoguht: KLHTM threat 0
3/5 17:21:34.453 [2. druidlovin] Thoguht: KLHTM threat 0
3/5 17:21:39.265 [2. druidlovin] Thoguht: KLHTM threat 0
3/5 17:21:44.296 [2. druidlovin] Thoguht: KLHTM threat 0

3/5 17:21:49.453 [2. druidlovin] Thoguht: KLHTM threat 0
3/5 17:21:54.453 [2. druidlovin] Thoguht: KLHTM threat 0
3/5 17:21:59.437 [2. druidlovin] Thoguht: KLHTM threat 0
3/5 17:22:04.453 [2. druidlovin] Thoguht: KLHTM threat 0
3/5 17:22:09.453 [2. druidlovin] Thoguht: KLHTM threat 0
3/5 17:22:14.437 [2. druidlovin] Thoguht: KLHTM threat 0
3/5 17:22:19.625 [2. druidlovin] Thoguht: KLHTM threat 0
3/5 17:22:24.546 [2. druidlovin] Thoguht: KLHTM threat 0
3/5 17:22:29.562 [2. druidlovin] Thoguht: KLHTM threat 0
3/5 17:22:34.531 [2. druidlovin] Thoguht: KLHTM threat 0
3/5 17:22:39.593 [2. druidlovin] Thoguht: KLHTM threat 0
3/5 17:22:44.640 [2. druidlovin] Thoguht: KLHTM threat 0
3/5 17:22:49.671 [2. druidlovin] Thoguht: KLHTM threat 0
3/5 17:22:54.718 [2. druidlovin] Thoguht: KLHTM threat 0
3/5 17:22:59.625 [2. druidlovin] Thoguht: KLHTM threat 0
3/5 17:23:04.609 [2. druidlovin] Thoguht: KLHTM threat 0
3/5 17:23:09.531 [2. druidlovin] Thoguht: KLHTM threat 0
3/5 17:23:14.734 [2. druidlovin] Thoguht: KLHTM threat 0
3/5 17:23:19.687 [2. druidlovin] Thoguht: KLHTM threat 0
3/5 17:23:24.781 [2. druidlovin] Thoguht: KLHTM threat 0
3/5 17:23:29.609 [2. druidlovin] Thoguht: KLHTM threat 0
3/5 17:23:34.562 [2. druidlovin] Thoguht: KLHTM threat 0
3/5 17:23:39.765 [2. druidlovin] Thoguht: KLHTM threat 0
3/5 17:23:44.796 [2. druidlovin] Thoguht: KLHTM threat 0
3/5 17:23:49.765 [2. druidlovin] Thoguht: KLHTM threat 0
3/5 17:23:53.750 To Maxwell: Hi!
3/5 17:23:54.703 [2. druidlovin] Thoguht: KLHTM threat 0
3/5 17:23:58.218 Maxwell has invited you to join a group.
3/5 17:23:59.796 [2. druidlovin] Thoguht: KLHTM threat 0
3/5 17:24:00.156 Looting changed to group loot.
3/5 17:24:00.156 Loot threshold set to Uncommon
3/5 17:24:00.375 Maxwell whispers: heya =)
3/5 17:24:03.687 You have joined a raid group
3/5 17:24:04.546 Looting changed to master looter.
3/5 17:24:04.546 Maxwell is now the loot master.
3/5 17:24:04.734 [Raid] Lester: Howdy!
3/5 17:24:04.812 [2. druidlovin] Thoguht: KLHTM threat 0
3/5 17:24:07.046 [2. druidlovin] Pliance: KLHTM threat 0
3/5 17:24:09.859 [2. druidlovin] Thoguht: KLHTM threat 0
3/5 17:24:10.234 [Raid] Maxwell: hello!

Thus, after deleting the KLHTM lines, all the above becomes something much more readable:

3/5 17:21:06.625 Waynard has gone offline.
3/5 17:23:53.750 To Maxwell: Hi!

3/5 17:23:58.218 Maxwell has invited you to join a group.
3/5 17:24:00.375 Maxwell whispers: heya =)
3/5 17:24:03.687 You have joined a raid group
3/5 17:24:04.546 Looting changed to master looter.
3/5 17:24:04.546 Maxwell is now the loot master.
3/5 17:24:04.734 [Raid] Lester: Howdy!
3/5 17:24:10.234 [Raid] Maxwell: hello!

Furthermore, in game, the text is color-coded, depending on which channel an utterance occurred. Owing to my web design background, I decided that the easiest way to start seeing patterns and analyze the text was to create HTML files of the transcripts so that I could use the same color-coding scheme. I added HTML tags around each line, giving each channel its own "id" attribute marked in color. I also made each line a new row in a table and added an extra column to the table that I then populated with my personal translations of the chat (see Figure 6.2).

19:30:00.953 : [2. madrogues] Rebecca: good... poison up... assist wei	-'good' refers to the fact that no Rogues said they have not done this fight. Even so, Rebecca clarifies our role—use poisons on our weapons and focus-fire on Wei's target.
19:30:02.484 : [5. madtankin] William: where is wallace tonight?	-madtankin channel for the Warriors. wallace is a character who usually comes to our raids.
19:30:07.703 : [Raid] Maxwell: Henry peels to Marcie	-role assignment
19:30:10.468 : [3. healsting] Drusella: *runs around like crazy people*	-Druids are getting a little silly now...
19:30:12.656 : [3. healsting] Sven: We could... DPS shaman, Holy Nova priests?	-more suggestions on turning certain healers into damage dealers instead
19:30:15.312 : [5. madtankin] Wallace: I didn't make it in time. Rawr!	-Wallace is still subscribed to the madtankin channel even though he is not part of the raid. These custom chat channels exist independently from any other channels in the game.
19:30:17.453 : To Lori: May I have a healthstone pretty please?	-Healthstones made by different Warlocks sometimes have different amounts of healing they can do (depending on how a player has 'specced' the character) which means they can be stored in one's inventory at the same time. In this case, I know Larry and Lori create different types of healthstones, so I've requested one from each.
19:30:17.687 : [Raid] Maxwell: Horace peels to Mary	-role assignment
19:30:19.640 : [4. soulburn] Lori: Les-for this fight you will be ssing Derek.	-what to do with that one soulstone that Lester has available

Fig. 6.2. Example chat log with annotations (right-hand column) that I later added to help make sense of the data.

After converting the chat in this fashion for a few sessions, I started to get a good idea of what typical chat during WoW raiding looked like. I could begin to generate a coding scheme, categorizing utterances into things like "strategy," "greetings," "question," or "off-topic." It also gave me confidence to start making certain claims about WoW game play, leading to my "Communication, Coordination, and Camaraderie in *World of Warcraft*" paper: specifically, that the quality of chat going on during a session could be used as an indicator of how well the group was performing. More joking around meant the group had routinized certain parts of raiding and was having a good night. Tension in the chat clearly pointed to friction within the group, and it was certainly evident during nights of low performance and frustration.

I focused on two nights in particular for the "Communication, Coordination, and Camaraderie in *World of Warcraft*" paper, but it was just the start. I knew I wanted to keep analyzing my data to find other patterns. This initial analysis and treatment of the data, however, was not a quick process. In principle I could just methodically go through all my data this way. For sanity's sake, however, I realized I needed a way to focus on only part of my data corpus. I went back to my initial questions about communication in WoW and felt that I was adequately answering them with the "Communication, Coordination, and Camaraderie in *World of Warcraft*" write-up. I became dissatisfied with these snapshots of WoW raiding, however, as I felt like they didn't give a longitudinal view of the practice players developed around the game. I wanted to document *how* the group's practice became routine—how it changed from its first month to its last few months. I began to define learning as adaptation or change over time, which meant I needed to compare chat and practice over time while the group was performing the same task during each compared session.

Pass 2

Narrowing my focus to specific boss fights—namely ones that were new—helped me identify a slice of the data to look at ("boss" monsters are bigger and tougher than others, requiring careful coordination and teamwork to defeat). Luckily, I had an inclination earlier on that the big-event fights and how a group learned to deal with them were the most interesting parts of raiding. In addition to the text dump, I had also video-recorded many of these sessions and, therefore, was able to interleave their transcription with the relevant portions of text data.

For this second pass, I opted to use Microsoft Excel instead of converting each session's logs into an HTML file. Using a text editor again, I added tabs to delimit different parts of each line so that I could then import them to Excel, creating separate columns for date, time, time-by-minute, channel, actor, and utterance. For the channel and actor columns, I extracted this data from the utterance part of the line if it occurred in "say," "whisper," or was an "emote." Thus:

2/24 21:52:38.484 [Raid] Maxwell: Rags hits like a truck
2/24 21:53:05.046 [2. madrogues] Rand: yeah, I stayed in there on the last knockback because I didn't think any warriors where in melee range
2/24 21:53:18.187 Lex creates: Major Healthstone.

became this:

2006/02/24 21:52:38.484 21:52 [Raid] Maxwell Rags hits like a truck
2006/02/24 21:53:05.046 21:53 [2. madrogues] Rand yeah, I stayed in there on the last knockback because I didn't think any warriors where in melee range
2006/02/24 21:53:18.187 21:53 [Emote] Lex Lex creates: Major Healthstone.

Once these Excel files were created, I added another column to put in codes and categorize or tag data, based on content. I then exported the data to a custom Flash app that creates charts to visualize each session (see Figure 6.3), counting number of utterances per minute. The entire process is documented in "Visualization of Expert Chat Development in a *World of Warcraft* Player Group" (Chen, 2009c). This analysis let me start identifying general trends in the data. Overall, for example, the group shifted talk to more informal off-topic banter as the months passed. I could also identify a disproportionately small share of the talk by women, lower than would be expected given their share of the group composition.

Selected play sessions were also written up as narrative events, using Rogoff et al.'s (2002) *functional pattern analysis*. These include sufficient detail to generate patterns of practice across the set of narratives (examples of these narrative accounts can be found at: http://markdangerchen.net/leet-noobs/leet-noobs-unpublished-appendix-functional-pattern-analysis). Hence, two methods of writing up or visualizing the data were used in my attempt to find patterns and to be able to present a general view of what raiding was like and how it changed over time for this group.

Pass 3

From the charts, it seemed clear that general patterns emerged around when and what we talked about during a boss fight. Interestingly, many of the text chat lines emanated from a third-party modification the group used to help manage boss fights (the darker parts of some of the bars in the top chart in Figure 6.3). This add-on, CT Raid, kept track of events and announced them to the group during a fight. Most of these messages appeared to come from the raid leader, but they were actually automatically generated by the add-on. This is similar to the crazy amount of lines of text generated by KLHTM (seen in Pass 1 above), except in CT

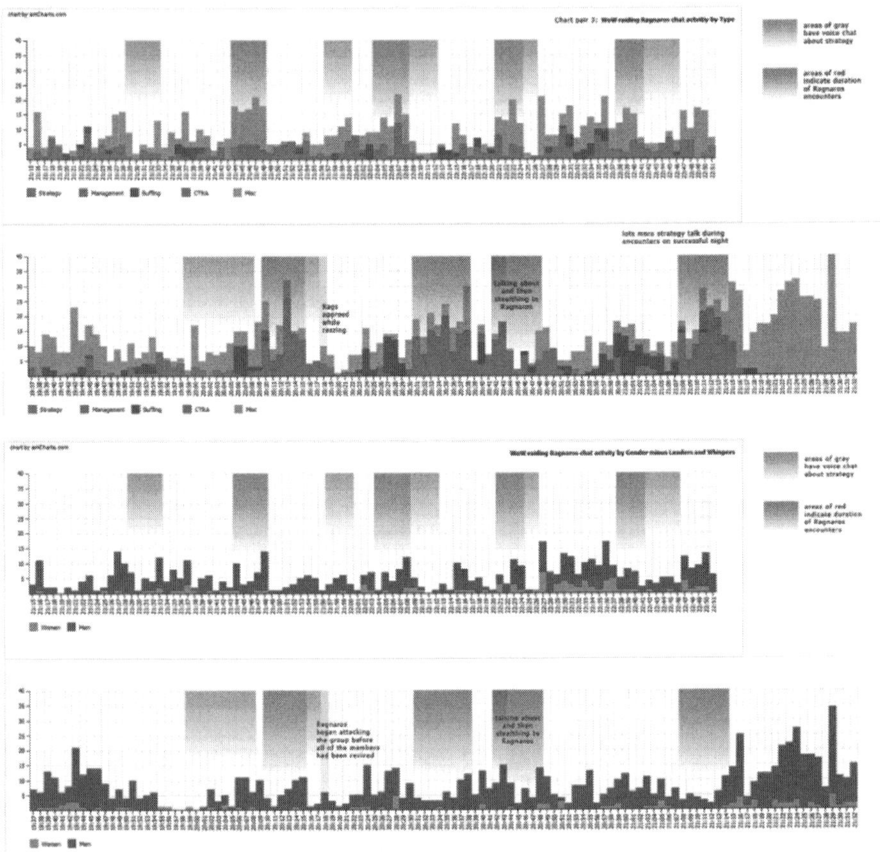

Fig. 6.3. Example charts of utterances per minute, comparing two different sessions in *World of Warcraft*. The first shows the proportion of talk that was about strategy, and the second by gender. The latter clearly shows a male dominance (approximately 90% of the talk), which is interesting given that about a quarter of the group was women.

Raid's case, they were used to convey in-the-moment information rather than to work invisibly in the background crunching numbers for us. I decided I couldn't count these add-on messages as having originated from the raid leader, since he would react to them just as the rest of the group would react. The system (we had arranged) was telling all of us, including the raid leader, what to do. This was strikingly different from how I had been thinking about group activity, assuming all actions and intent in the hands of the players. Instead, I needed some new way to think about how to analyze this technical, nonhuman participant in the raid events.

Serendipitously, around the time I was finishing up my visualization paper (Chen, 2009c), I was taking a concurrent course on situated technology use led by Reed Stevens. This course included readings from Science and Technology Studies about sociomaterial practice (e.g., Orlikowski, 2007) and, specifically, a conceptual theory about how to look at and analyze an activity system that treated human and nonhuman participants equally. This was Actor-Network Theory, or ANT (cf. Latour, 2005). Indeed, ANT seemed to offer an ideal way to understand the raid events in WoW since so much of the group's activity was dependent on these third-party tools, which not only acted among the group but also forced its members to react and act differently. The nonhuman actors were full participants and were agentive in their own right (for more on this, see Chen, 2012).

Fig. 6.4. A section of my user interface during a raid battle, showing various add-ons in use. The KLH Threat Meter can be seen on the left side, displaying the top ten current threat levels of various members of the raid group. Warren and Wendy, at the top, are the main tanks for the group. Roger, Thoguht, Mandy, and Hall are all damage dealers (DPSers). Their threat level is nowhere near the tanks', thus they can up their damage output without fear of drawing aggro. All of these terms are explained in Chen (2012). Image cropped from *World of Warcraft*® provided courtesy of Blizzard Entertainment, Inc.

Using ANT to reexamine raiding in WoW led to the deepest analysis chapter for *Leet Noobs*, one in which I trace the history of the aforementioned KLHTM add-on as it became part of the group. This adoption was set against the backdrop of overall WoW raiding practice and its sea change during early 2006. Among the players, KLHTM was also known as KTM (and this is how I refer to it in *Leet Noobs* and how the rest of this chapter will refer to it), standing for KLH Threat

Meter. KTM is the first add-on that displayed a threat meter for the players to view as they are engaged in fights (see Figure 6.4). It was developed and made available by others while the raid group existed, and was slowly adopted into the group's practice over several sessions and with different subsets of group members from week to week until, finally, the group had formally enrolled KTM into its activity. Once fully enrolled, its use was instrumental in helping the group to diagnose the Ragnaros boss battle successfully, leading to the group finally taking the Fire Lord down.

This tracing took time, and, once I had decided this is what I needed to do, it became clear that I had an incomplete picture of its history in my data corpus. This is because all my data had been recorded from my point of view. I had not asked others to record their chat or activity, so it was impossible to name exactly who started using KTM when. I could only see evidence for when I used it and when the players I was working with were also using it; but they might have picked it up with other groups of players. Accordingly, the chapter that deals with this aspect of the research conveys a sense that I try to deduce KTM's use by narrowing down events and dates that were notable to the group and then just documenting the add-on's use in those events. To help get it all straight in my thinking, and to help readers also understand KTM's history as situated within the history of the group, I again used tables and charts as visual scaffolds (see Table 6.2).

Creating these tables meant going back to each session's logs and paying new attention to the use of KTM. This was reasonably straightforward, except that readers will recall that in Pass 1 I deleted all those lines! This is an example of where it pays to keep back-ups and never to modify source files. Even with back-ups available, I nonetheless needed around 3 days of desperate searching to find my archived DVDs.

Using KTM allowed the rogues in the raid group to diagnose an issue we were having with the fight against Ragnaros. By Week 24, the raid group had fully enrolled KTM into its network, and in Week 27 the rogues could see that a theory we had about the fight with Rags was mistaken. We had assumed certain rogues were being killed because we were doing too much "spike" damage to the monster, thereby drawing its attention away from the warriors who were supposed to be taking the brunt of the damage from Ragnaros. Yet KTM showed us that this wasn't happening at all. In fact, the rogues were nowhere close to the threat level needed to grab and hold aggro. Confronted with this evidence, the rogues had to come up with other possible explanations, leading them to reason that the main problem during the fight was to do with where characters were positioned in the game during the fight's multiple stages.

An aside is in order here about this conceptual change: Evidence for it existed in our group's change in practice and only a little bit of talk during one of the nights, where it isn't clear that all of the rogues understood what was being discussed. In other words, the kind of learning happening in the game may have

Table 6.2. Partial History of Raiding with Regular Raid Group and Separate Guild Group.

Wk	Date	Zone	Boss Wall	Notes
18	2/22/2006	MC		
	2/24/2006	MC	Rags	first serious attempt at killing Rags
	2/25/2006	AQ20		first time in Ruins of Ahn'Qiraj with raid group, first mention of KTM
	2/26/2006	Ony		first use of KTM in Onyxia by Rand and Thoguht
19	3/1/2006	MC		
	3/3/2006	MC		first use of KTM in MC, only Thoguht
	3/5/2006	Ony		stopped using KTM
20	3/6/2006	ZG		first time in Zul'Gurub with the Booty Bay Anglers; didn't use KTM
	3/8/2006	MC		first use of KTM in MC by Rebecca, Rand, Thoguht, and Pliance
	3/10/2006	MC		
	3/12/2006	Ony		
21	3/15/2006	MC		
	3/17/2006	MC		
	3/19/2006	Ony		
22	3/20/2006	ZG		Anglers ZG with no KTM
	3/22/2006	MC		
	3/24/2006	MC		
	3/26/2006	Ony		
23	3/27/2006	ZG		Anglers ZG with no KTM
	3/29/2006	MC		
	3/31/2006	MC	Rags	Ragnaros fight wouldn't reset properly
	4/2/2006	Ony		now tanks, raid leaders, and some others using KTM regularly
24	4/3/2006	ZG		Anglers ZG with no KTM
	4/5/2006	MC		
	4/7/2006	MC	Rags	KTM part of standard practice now
	4/9/2006	Ony		
25	4/10/2006	ZG		Anglers ZG with no KTM
	4/12/2006	MC		
	4/14/2006	MC	Rags	Ragnaros fight buggy again
	4/16/2006	Ony		
26	4/17/2006	ZG	Panther	first use of KTM in ZG with Anglers
	4/19/2006	MC		
	4/21/2006	MC		
	4/23/2006	Ony		

(*Continued*)

Table 6.2. (*Continued*)

Wk	Date	Zone	Boss Wall	Notes
27	4/24/2006	ZG	Raptor	
	4/26/2006	MC		
	4/28/2006	MC	Rags	diagnose rogues' aggro problem with KTM
	4/30/2006	Ony		
28	5/1/2006	ZG	Panther	Panther down!
	5/3/2006	MC		
	5/5/2006	MC		Wendy leaves raid
	5/7/2006	Ony		
29	5/8/2006	ZG		
	5/10/2006	MC		
	5/12/2006	MC	Rags	no data, but first Ragnaros kill
	5/14/2006	Ony		
30	5/15/2006	ZG		
	5/17/2006	MC		
	5/19/2006	MC	Rags	Ragnaros killed on 3rd attempt
	5/21/2006	Ony		

Note: The "Boss Wall" column details which boss we were attempting to kill that night. If none is listed, the raid was not attempting a new boss and ended after routine fights. The "Notes" column displays significant moments when a boss was killed for the first time and/or when the groups started using KTM. Raiding activity ramped up over thirty weeks, starting from two nights a week and ending at four nights a week by the time the regular group completed Molten Core. (To save space, this table displays Weeks 18+.)

been only tacit and expressed through behavior change. This might call into question why education favors explicit knowledge. Alternatively, if we agree the gold standard on whether someone has learned something is whether they can talk about it, can I honestly consider the players in my group to be "experts?" I still wonder about this. Ultimately, however, it is clear the raid group succeeded in the in-game tasks, and it was due to this new collective understanding of how the game worked.

Either way, we now knew that the fight with Ragnaros was more than just numbers. This shifted our focus to the 3D space of the world and to being aware of our positions during the fight. As I uncovered this through the chat log data, I realized that a better accounting of nonverbal action needed to happen. I needed to examine the video data in a much more systematic way than I had previously managed. Eventually, describing the activity through video interaction analysis methods (Goodwin, 1994; Jordan & Henderson, 1995; Stevens & Hall, 1998) gave me a way to express how rhythmic the raiding experience can be.

General *World of Warcraft* Life

Throughout the duration of making these three passes through the raiding data I was still participating more widely in WoW gaming and culture. I had a lot of nonraid data that could serve as examples of typical life in the game. I knew there were certain things I wanted to highlight, and I spent quite a bit of time finding examples of all these moments. It pays dividends if, during data collection, one makes field notes during or immediately after each session. This helps when you have to search for specific examples; with good data collection practices, finding specific examples is as easy as searching through one's field notes.

Within this general participation in WoW, I found that playing the game really felt like two separate activities: the general day-to-day questing and leveling up in the game (i.e., stage one) versus the end-game raiding (i.e., stage two). This was described by some of the players I was participating with, but it was also a lived experience of mine—as I hit the level cap and searched for almost half a year for a raid group to join as a regular member.

Thinking about and describing the game in terms of two stages, and seeing how gaining access to the second end-game stage was not a given for all players, led directly to thinking about structures of expertise in the game; and to Chapter 1 in my dissertation and book: "Social Dimensions of Expertise in *World of Warcraft*" (Chen, 2009b; see also a visual representation of these stages at: http://markdangerchen.net/pubs/chen-poster-leet-noobs-portrait-final.pdf). Thomas Malaby's *Making Virtual Worlds* (2009) had made clear to me the concepts of social and cultural capital, and how accruing these forms of capital were necessary for access to expert play (i.e., stage two). To my mind, this exploded and undermined many conventional definitions of expertise, establishing it as being more of a social phenomenon that emerges through relationships with others in the community than solely as an individual cognitive phenomenon (cf., Collins & Evans, 2007). In the case of WoW, becoming expert presupposed enculturation into a particular set of practices that was continually redefined as players' understanding of the game changed. Describing the game as taking part in two stages also led me to the title "Leet Noobs," since players who were expert or elite (AKA "leet") during stage one needed to relearn how to play in stage two, making them novices or newbies (AKA "noobs") again.

The Last Chapter

I mentioned earlier that all of the analytic passes and writing about life in WoW kept me busy enough that I continued to put off looking at the last few weeks of data on the raid group I was studying. This is because the group fell apart, and it was not an amicable breakup. I was befuddled, to be sure, since I did not know how to reconcile this occurrence with my earliest work in "Communication, Coordination, and Camaraderie in *World of Warcraft*," which practically lauds the group for its stability and argues that it was due to extremely strong bonds born out of friendship and trust.

The conclusions in the "Communication, Coordination, and Camaraderie in *World of Warcraft*" chapter were revised for the dissertation and book, which explains differences that exist in their published iterations. I maintained that trust was necessary for the group to be successful and that evidence of trust could be found in how the group members communicated during raid events and in the online forums between sessions. Furthermore, levity during raiding was evidence of trust during an event.

I still believe this to be true, but the original "Communication, Coordination, and Camaraderie in *World of Warcraft*" paper attributes trust to the social bonds that existed between group members. In the ANT chapter of my dissertation and book, it became more and more apparent that the group was using this new technology—this new nonhuman actor that was fully participating in our activity—as a surveillance tool, and trust through friendship was being replaced by trust through numbers and performance. Just as the group offloaded the task of remembering and keeping track of certain numbers for them, the group offloaded the task of trust appraisal to KTM.

I was able to make these claims by analyzing the discourse of the group, especially in its external web forums. Namely, it was a lot of gathering data and looking for evidence of relationships between events and talk and how certain ideas propagated through the network. It was messy and uncertain, and I am continually reminded of what Latour says is a successful social sciences write-up: one that presents a convincing story (2005). Taken at face value, this sounds pretty cynical and dastardly. The main thing to remember here is that most of the convincing has to happen internally with the researcher/writer (and it's pretty unethical to write up a qualitative account if you don't yourself believe in what you're saying).

One thing that strikes me as notable is that I only looked at two discussion forums: the main one used by the raid group and the one used by my guild. The raid group comprised members from multiple allied guilds, including the one I jointly ran with some friends. When the raid imploded, my guild talked about this implosion at length, speculating on the nature of friendship, progression, and what it meant to play WoW. I assume this sort of discussion occurred in the forums for the *other* guilds that were affected by the raid group meltdown, too, but I was not privy to that information. My tracing of events and how ideas propagated through our network, it could be argued, was incomplete. Yet, as with any research, out of practical necessity, there comes a time when one has to decide where to stop, where to set boundaries on what to analyze or include.

I felt that I had enough data to tell a compelling story that accounted for what happened.

Another note is that the methods used to save forum data seemed unsatisfactory. After searching around for a time for an app or a tech solution to download forum data, I ended up settling on manually saving specific pages of content. Part of this was motivated by the thought that the content should not be divorced from its original presentation. Some of the tech solutions I found would strip the formatting and theme surrounding the forum posts. I could have used an app that downloaded everything in a forum, but I reasoned that I would then still have to manually read everything and mark specific threads that were relevant for later analysis. If I was going to do that, why not just do it with the source material instead of a duplicate copy? Making the duplicate copy would actually add time and require more storage space on my hard drive.

REPORTING

I am fully aware that my dissertation research is not how most people do this work. I did not have a methods chapter. I did not have a literature review chapter. These things were integrated into each of my chapters as needed for that chapter's argument. It made the most sense to do it this way because my dissertation was an edited collection of papers that I had been publishing or was working on as I grappled with different themes I saw in my WoW data. Part of it was that I didn't know any better. I didn't know that a dissertation normally has a lit review and a methods chapter and only one conclusion chapter. Truth to tell, we can blame Constance Steinkuehler for this, since I admired her work deeply and saw how her dissertation was a collection of papers on literacy practices around the MMOG *Lineage*. I thought that's how dissertations were written! To this day, I still find it odd to hear people carve out chapters from their dissertations for publication. I don't think I could have done it that way. I needed journal and conference deadlines to stay productive. Did I mention my dissertation was on *World of Warcraft*, sometimes referred to as *World of Warcrack*?

As mentioned earlier, a compromise I made by submitting work to journals was that they often did not print in full color. I found the color extremely useful for analysis and display of data. When I was preparing the dissertation manuscript, I took advantage of not having the same limitations. The color reproduction makes clearer which chat channels were being used and how interleaved all the chat was for a player. It took a bit of getting used to as a player who would often have to deal with several channels at once, sometimes scrolling through the chat window blazingly fast. This color fidelity benefit also extended to the numerous screenshots I included in the dissertation, which, in addition to including far fewer owing to potential rights issues, were printed in black and white for the book.

FINAL THOUGHTS

This chapter is messy, but I hope it is clear that it's partly because it's an attempt to describe messy research. I don't know what kind of advice I can give to new scholars attempting to do similar research other than say that I suspect a lot of the details of research and how intricate and convoluted and full of "aha!" moments it can be has to be experienced to be understood. As I was going through graduate school, there was not a single academic term where I did not see new connections to new-to-me theories or methods to use to analyze the massive amount of data that I had collected.

I owe my success to strong collaborations and academic deadlines. Whenever possible, I chose to cowrite or copresent work. Almost always this activity led to a deeper understanding of my topic, even though it often did not lead to new publications. Part of me feels like we have ethical obligations to collaborate. If I know someone out there is struggling with the same themes I am, why would I not try to work with them so that we collectively can understand what the hell is going on?

More data are always better data. One researcher working alone does not have enough data or insight into the object of study. While I had massive amounts of WoW data, almost as an accident due to a course assignment where I overcollected, I still feel like it wasn't enough. I often found I wanted more from more varied sources or from other players' points of view. Additionally, I was constrained by my own schedule. I could not capture *everything* since I had other obligations as well. This means I missed the very first session when my raid group killed Ragnaros!

I cannot think of doing this research and not having it be deeply personal. Finding ANT to explain how nonhuman actors participated with(in) the raid group was transformative. I think of the world through this ontological posthuman lens now. Nor can I think of the interpretation and reporting of the research as not being heavily influenced by who I am. And truth to tell, I was learning the game at the same time I was becoming a games scholar. My misconception about how threat worked in the game was one I shared with my participants. I learned with them. I learned through writing about me and them, about us.

This process took time. From start to finish, it represents roughly seven years of my life. It required time to reflect, to think through concepts and problems, and it took time to write. I also realize that I was extremely fortunate to have funding through the LIFE Center at the University of Washington, which supported the last couple of years of my graduate studies so I could finish writing. I cannot imagine doing similar work without that financial support.

NOTE

1. Who knows if I'd actually be satisfied at the hardware, though. Many high-end computers are already rendering games at 4K quality, and tech continues to struggle to keep up. In fact, for my undergraduate thesis, I struggled with the exact same problem, having completed the first 3D rendering art degree at Reed College, which required hundreds of dollars of hard drive investments (something like $500 for 350 MB!).

REFERENCES

Chen, M. (2005). Addressing social dilemmas and fostering cooperation through computer games. Digital Games Research Association (DiGRA), Vancouver, Canada.

Chen, M. (2009a). Communication, coordination, and camaraderie in *World of Warcraft*. *Games and Culture,* 4, 47–73. Available from: http://dx.doi.org/10.1177/1555412008325478

Chen, M. (2009b). Social dimensions of expertise in *World of Warcraft* players. *Transformative Works and Cultures, 2*. Available from: http://dx.doi.org/10.3983/twc.2009.0072

Chen, M. (2009c). Visualization of expert chat development in a *World of Warcraft* player group. *E-Learning,* 6(1), 54–70. Available from: http://dx.doi.org/10.2304/elea.2009.6.1.54

Chen, M. (2012). *Leet noobs: The life and death of an expert player group in* World of Warcraft. New York: Peter Lang.

Collins, H., & Evans, R. (2007). *Rethinking expertise.* Chicago: University of Chicago Press.

Gee, J. (2003). *What video games have to teach us about learning and literacy.* New York: Palgrave Macmillan.

Goodwin, C. (1994). Professional vision. *American Anthropologist,* 96(3), 606–633.

Hutchins, E. (1995). *Cognition in the wild.* Cambridge, MA: The MIT Press.

Jordan, B., & Henderson, A. (1995). Interaction analysis: Foundations and practice. *The Journal of the Learning Sciences,* 4(1), 39–103. Available from: http://www.jstor.org/stable/1466849

Latour, B. (2005). *Reassembling the social: An introduction to actor-network theory.* New York: Oxford University Press.

Law, J. (2004). *After method: Mess in social science research.* New York: Routledge.

Malaby, T. (2009). *Making virtual worlds: Linden Lab and Second Life.* Ithaca, NY: Cornell University Press.

Orlikowski, W. (2007). Sociomaterial practices: Exploring technology at work. *Organization Studies,* 28(9), 1435–1448.

Pickering, A. (1993). The mangle of practice: Agency and emergence in the sociology of science. *American Journal of Sociology,* 99(3), 559–589.

Rogoff, B., Topping, K., Baker-Sennett, J., & Lacasa, P. (2002). Mutual contributions of individuals, partners, and institutions: Planning to remember in Girl Scout cookie sales. *Social Development,* 11(1), 266–289.

Stevens, R., & Hall, R. (1998). Disciplined perception: Learning to see in technoscience. In M. Lampert & M. L. Blunk (Eds.), *Talking mathematics in school: Studies of teaching and learning* (pp. 107–149). Cambridge, UK: Cambridge University Press.

CHAPTER SEVEN

Classroom digital literacies as interactional accomplishments

IBRAR BHATT

When you wish to discover the new unexpected actors that have more recently popped up and which are not yet bona fide members of "society," you have to travel somewhere else and with very different kinds of gear.

—Latour (2005, p. 22)

INTRODUCTION

Modern classrooms are sites where new technological dynamics are rapidly displacing classic pedagogies. With new literacies emerging from old, and information, knowledge, and meaning-making themselves being redefined for what they contribute to the efficacy of learning and teaching, the nature of what we investigate as researchers is as important, and uncertain, as the methods of investigation themselves. Take, for example, the study discussed in this chapter: the established and commonplace activity of writing a course assignment. Every day, and in classrooms everywhere, assignment tasks of many kinds are given to students by their teachers. These can be anything from dissertations and short essays, to digital and paper-based portfolios, and so on. These tasks can, on the one hand, be procedurally framed to acknowledge elements of new digital literacies; yet they also can remain grounded in an educational system that valorizes more traditional kinds of literacies. Added to this mix is the range of new textual practices with digital media that proliferate in students' lives more generally (e.g., Ito, 2010). What therefore emerges in the writing of a course assignment is far from a predictable set of practices. Within this problematic, this chapter provides an account of the research methods adopted to investigate the digital literacies of students' own assignment tasks while situated within a classroom setting. Building on the ethnographic tradition of the New Literacy Studies (outlined below), the focus here is on the practicalities of data collection and, specifically, what was added by the incorporation of a detailed videography of the writing process.

Through investigating the literacies that were drawn into cases of assignment writing, this research study uncovers practices of digital literacy which otherwise would go unnoticed using traditional methods of ethnography dominating many current literacy inquiries. These include such techniques as field notes and observation accounts supported by still images. A step-by-step account of the data collection procedure is outlined in detail below, and illuminates the study of digital and new literacies in a manner that is currently lacking in literacy research. Importantly, the methods detailed below are meant to build on, rather than replace, more traditional and analogue interpretative methods. I argue that new classroom ecologies, as arenas where knowledge is transfused and produced, are contexts within which new and digital literacies proliferate. It follows, therefore, as Bruno Latour (2005) contends in the quote at the head of this chapter, that to research them properly we should employ "very different kinds of gear." Proficiency with digital research tools is vital to this undertaking as but one aspect of the overall research process.

The chapter begins by discussing the context of the research, its theoretical influences, and how these influenced decisions regarding study design and directed data analysis. This is followed by a more extensive and step-by-step account of the videographic methodology adopted as part of a wider phased ethnographic approach to the research as a whole. The chapter ends by highlighting the need for such methods to augment the methodological repertoire of literacy research studies, thereby updating and refreshing the study of literacy in digital environments.

RESEARCH CONTEXT

Assessed assignment tasks are key moments in the lives of students as they navigate their way through a formal course, and for teachers and managers who also have a stake in an assignment's successful completion. In this respect, the practices through which assignments are characterized and accomplished are bound up with different texts and a multitude of discourses such as economic imperatives, managerial efficiency, and quality assurance procedures (Tummons, 2010). These discourses and texts or "actors" can influence a particular and dominant conception of what an educational assignment task is, how it should be completed, and the valorized literacies that it is designed to assess. But this does not always play out as intended in the workings of classroom life. Writing an assignment is therefore a *practical controversy* for producers and "overseers" alike, and what is required is a deep exploration of the constituent practices which give an assignment its character and enable successful achievement for student, teacher, line manager, head of department, parents, and all actors directly or indirectly involved in completing the written task.

With this in mind, the study of assignment writing detailed in this chapter, based on the work of Ibrar Bhatt (2014), posed a number of questions, including: *What digital literacy practices of learners are emerging as they work on writing assignments in a classroom setting? How do these literacies relate to the learners' everyday literacies and habits? Are there any discrepancies between the way learners carry out their work and the requirements and expectations of their course and, more broadly, the college?*

The focus of any research inquiry becomes even more controversial and textually rich as more complex actors become involved in the practices of assignment design, completion, and assessment. This is because academic content is but one aspect of assignment completion; situational practices are shaped by wider enterprises such as policy goals, which, in turn, shape a certain order in the day-to-day practices of a classroom (Hamilton, 2009). It is within this framing that a focus on the literacies of assignment writing within the learning process, and their role within the regulatory frameworks of assessment and quality in education, is a fruitful basis of inquiry in the sociocultural study of new literacies. One of the primary reasons for this is that among the complex actors at play during assignment writing are those that emerge through the noncurricular, or "vernacular" literacies of learners and the role these practices can play in an educational process (Ivanič et al., 2009). These aspects form a key part of the rationale for this study's methods, as outlined in the coming sections.

THEORETICAL BACKGROUND

Any exploration of how an entity is made in the world—such as the writing of an assignment—needs to be an investigation of the practices and sociomaterial relations (the entanglements of people and things) that constitute it, and give the entity its features and characteristics (Fenwick, Edwards, & Sawchuk, 2011). Understanding how practices of digital literacy can emerge from worlds far removed from the classroom and be mobilized to create something new, is to focus on the *ecology* of literacy practices (Barton, 2007) and their *performativity* (Law, 2012; Mol, 2002). That is, how a student's digital literacy practices, and the enactment of these practices, perform the "new" world of any assignment as a product of writing. The locus of this investigation therefore lies at the intersection of two empirical and conceptual traditions: those fields are New Literacy Studies and sociomaterial theory.

What follows is a brief discussion of these theoretical traditions and how, through them, I have developed and applied methodologies used in videography and workplace studies to research digital literacies. Given the emphasis here on the methods of the research and data management, the below discussion provides only a foundational basis to the methodological decisions as part of a broader commitment to ethnographic studies of literacy.

(a) The New Literacy Studies

In any foundational discussion of literacy research, it is important to highlight the work of Silvia Scribner and Michael Cole (1981), whose research on the Vai in Liberia aimed to uncover the roles of formal learning versus cultural knowledge acquisition in relation to cognitive ability. Scribner and Cole came to the conclusion that literacy is associated with, and realized through, "social practices." Among other important findings, this seminal work reported that formal schooling leads to rather specific abilities that are valued and rewarded in institutional contexts but which, in fact, constitute only one form of literacy among other possible "literacies" that people in a given society may be socialized into. Following this vein of thought and later works (cited below) brought a paradigm shift in the literacy studies field from a singularly conceived and autonomous notion of *Literacy*, to a broader view of multiple and interrelated literate activities, or *literacies* (plural).

Subsequent investigations into the social construction of literacies (e.g., Street, 1984; Barton & Hamilton, 2012; Baynham, 1995) drew attention to the social practices at play, including power relations and sociocultural histories embedded within literacy activities. The autonomous and singular model of literacy as a "uniform set of technical skills" (Street, 2001, p. 2) to be applied in the same way everywhere was subsumed by a new, multiple, and ideological view (ibid.). As a result of this conceptual view of literacies as primarily social, New Literacy Studies perspectives came to take *context* as their starting point, and main focus of enquiry. The "new" here refers to this branch of research and theory as a new way to study literacies at the time of its emergence in the 1980s. It is, of course, now no longer new but has retained this name (see Gee, 2008).

Arising from this ideological shift in the notion of literacy came a new framework of ethnographic study which made a distinction between "literacy events" and "literacy practices" (Barton & Hamilton, 2000). "Events" refer to observable and empirical moments that are integral to literacy activities. The configuration of "practices" is what makes up the sociocultural construct of a typical literacy event. What becomes central, then, in the exploration and analysis of literacy events is the "configuration of action, talk and text" (Prinsloo & Baynham, 2008, p. 8) and the network of actors (social, material, political, etc.) implicated in ensuing practices.

The New Literacy Studies, through its decidedly ethnographic approach, argues that literacies are a matter of social, institutional, and historical practices within particular contexts. Added to this, with the new and multitudinous ways of meaning-making by means of digital media, a related field of study has emerged that focuses its attention on the study of "new literacies" (see Coiro et al., 2008; Lankshear & Knobel, 2011). Like the "New Literacy Studies," the study of new literacies applies ethnographic approaches to studying and conceptualizing literacy, and seeks to go beyond the competencies of the individual in understanding the new, emergent literacies of digital media environments and their cultural logics. This orientation focuses on the myriad ways of making meaning in digital environments, how these shape and give rise to new ways of being and knowing, and new kinds of social relations and communities, and so on (for more on this, see the section on *Digital and new literacies*).

This aspect is salient, especially when it comes to the literacies drawn into assignment work and other assessed tasks in education. Were it that the evaluation of literacy were singular, then "new literacies" might have remained solely a theoretical matter of social science inquiry, leaving out the complexities of wider student experience and learning environments. But the assessment of literacy is not a singular matter of pass/fail or literate/illiterate any more than literacy is a matter of text void of meaning. And assignment tasks, as outlined earlier, are bound up within different discourses and interests (economic, managerial, etc.). It is not only learners who are concerned with their results. Understanding the literacies of assignment tasks against the new literacies of a dynamic and multifaceted learning environment (with its new digital actors) becomes essential. The problem is that the interrelationships are complex and the literacy practices are difficult to detect with traditional research methods alone. This requires a need to engage and critique research methods when investigating new literacies, and a commitment to identifying "new unexpected actors" (Latour, 2005, p. 22) that have emerged through pervasive Web connectivity and a new, widespread digital sociality.

In short, digital literacy activities which emerge through prolific Internet use and other digital media tools in the classroom bring new research challenges and subsequently necessitate relevant research techniques to overcome them (de Roock, Bhatt, & Adams, 2015). This is largely due to the unique character of digital literacies and the kinds of practices that go into student work, practices which Chris Bigum and colleagues (2014) dub the "secret learner business"; that is, the practices beneath what is commonly made visible in a learning situation. They argue that an exploration of secret learner business can expose "the fuzzy, pragmatic and messy business" of all the practices leading up to a moment of learning (Bigum et al., 2014, p. 1).

There are parallels here with work in the field of Science, Technology, and Society. For example, studies on the doing of science and the processes of knowledge construction (e.g., Latour & Woolgar, 1986; Latour, 1987) show how much of the messy business and non-coherence of the workings of a laboratory are excluded from the final stages of "fact production" and glossed over in scientists' final reports. Similarly, accounting for new and unexpected actors that now emerge in practices of student assignment writing requires us to expand both the theoretical tools of the New Literacy Studies, and the ways in which literacy ethnographies are done. In the sections below, I outline my approach to digital literacies and sociomaterial theory, drawing on work done in the field of Science, Technology, and Society.

(b) Digital and new literacies

Following the shift from *Literacy* to *literacies*, outlined above, accounts of "digital literacy" are also many and comprise different conceptualizations of what digital literacy means and what it portends in educational contexts. Colin Lankshear and Michele Knobel (2008), in their formulation of a sociocultural understanding of literacy, draw attention to the pluralized form of "digital literacies" and use it to relate to myriad meaning-making practices evoked across different settings, communities, and identities in digital environments. Digital literacy practices can therefore relate to multiple aspects of learners' lives (friendship groups, collegial networks, family, etc.) and can take many forms (blogs, social media posts, tweets, gaming activities, etc.). This multitude of practices have at their core a set of "enculturations" (Lankshear & Knobel, 2008, p. 7), exploration of which is the genesis of a sociocultural approach to digital literacy.

The conception of digital literacy as a singular skill set denies not only its influences, but also its impact. Since all text-mediated interaction cannot be reduced simply to transmitting and receiving information (Knobel & Lankshear, 2006, p. 15), a conception of digital literacies that is useful within and beyond the classroom must not ignore surrounding social practice, materiality, and how these impact meaning-making. The enculturations are a story that needs to be told, especially when we look at them in the context of students' assignment writing. The convergence and multiplicity of competencies in being digitally "literate" become not so easy to define, especially in light of college policy discourses which often describe a need to "upskill" and "train" staff and students in developing an autonomous form of digital literacy.

In any study of student assignment writing, meaning-making is also significant. Students' digital literacy practices, which when taken together formulate a finished piece of work, can encompass a plethora of social practices. These include processing and drawing on multiple textual sources, navigating links, evaluating content suitability, and mobilizing actors (friends, teachers, texts, algorithms, etc.) for aid. These practices are part and parcel of meaning-making and often are enacted beyond the sight of teachers and researchers, and typically emerge via a variety of static and portable devices being used in a typical classroom setting: desktop computers, laptops, tablets, smartphones, etc. As many of these digital literacy practices occur below the radar of traditional ethnographic observation and recording, a researcher's province of interest and analytic lens must expand to include wider contexts and interactions than is typically the case in classroom ethnographies. This, in turn, stimulates new avenues of research inquiry, and highlights the need for new methodological approaches to exploring precisely how digital literacies saturate new and developing classroom ecologies.

(c) A sociomaterial understanding

The "social" is not a monolithic construct (Latour, 2005); the material world and humans meet in every interaction (Orlikowski, 2007). This means that any entity, and any practice, is built upon an entanglement of people and things. The current digital age has only served to make these entanglements even more complex, nuanced, and, according to some, more embodied than previously was the case (Hayles, 2012). A sociomaterial perspective on practice, therefore, is one in which the human is not the sole agent of anything "social." This speaks directly to classroom environments where a student is not the sole generator of a completed assignment, nor is a researcher the sole creator of anything scholarly. Rather there are networks of actors, epistemic and pedagogical underpinnings, and negotiations with the physical world, which are also at play in any act of knowledge creation. In this way, and drawing from the field of Science, Technology, and Society, my perspective on digital literacy is deeply informed by sociomaterial approaches to literacy (Bhatt & de Roock, 2013; Gourlay & Oliver, 2013). This then leads me to understand the term "social" as also incorporating material artifacts (such as laptops, desks, paper) as actors in how literacy practices are done, rather than these things being merely mediating tools.

There are a number of ways that sociomaterial theory provides a useful basis from which to approach the study of digital literacies. Here I highlight one particular affordance of this theory: that of *performativity*. From this orientation, an investigation of a student sitting at their classroom desk writing an assignment begins with the view that entities such as *the teacher*, *the student*, *the class*, *the assignment*, etc. are all *performed* through an assemblage of practices which make them who or what they are. It thus begs to be asked of the product that emerges from those practices: "How does it come to be as it is?" and "Could it be done differently?"

Thus, in my own examination of written assignment work, what eventually came to be known and recognized by all those involved as an "assignment" was assembled by a choreography of practices and performances of these practices. These practices, as my research revealed, originated from different worlds (friendship groups, family chats, work-based reports, etc.), yet they were mobilized into the assignment-writing event in the classroom and collectively assembled the somewhat precarious entity of the "assignment."

Practices appear to hold the assignment together, but a close examination of them shows that they do so only through *precarious interactions* with each other. For example, in a typical and very brief moment in one of the cases of assignment writing in this study, a student discusses the contents of her assignment with the teacher, her friend sitting next to her, and another friend on Facebook via her own device (which contravenes college policies on classroom ICT use). While doing this she also scrolls through reports from her previous employer's website, and dips into a previous assignment on a related topic, among other things. The relations between these actors is not stable in this brief period; they rely on various elements working together collectively to hold the moment together, such as personal devices used beneath the table to avoid being noticed by the teacher, friends who are online and available, chat applications and Internet connections effectively working, etc. The composite result of all of these practices is content for a student's assignment in that particular moment.

To understand assignment writing, therefore, I needed to empirically examine the practices that students engaged in to produce them, and the ways in which these practices were organized and systematized as part of writing strategies, along with focusing on how they gain their meaning and function as dynamic elements of something else, hence their precarity (Law, 2012).

Importantly, some sociomaterial assemblages gain their stability from a perpetual performance of sets of practices. In a typical classroom scenario we need to look at how and why this is the case, and what holds an assemblage of practices together. For example, in the case of quality inspection reports, reactive directives are often issued to improve provision and make better use of digital media for learning. This also holds for things like learning technology "good practice" guides and digital literacy frameworks, which tend to idealize certain quintessential attributes of what good digital literacy and effective teaching ought to look like. These kinds of initiatives collectively attempt to exert a structuring agency upon what occurs in the day-to-day workings of classrooms. But the impositions of procedural practices do not always interact well with the emergent practices of a connected classroom, and we should ask: how and why do they get circumvented and opposed by students in the doing of their work? In this respect, echoing John Law (2012), ethnographers should "look for the gaps, the aporias and the tensions between the practices and their realities" (Law, 2012, p. 171).

Understanding any actor, therefore, requires following its influences and examining its relational work with other actors. Similarly, understanding digital literacies requires viewing the entirety of an interactional context—human and nonhuman, online and offline. Thus, not knowing what interactions I might capture, I nonetheless needed methods that would allow me to perform *in situ* monitoring of students' activities around their assignment writing. These methods needed to be broad enough in view to enable me to identify as many relevant actors as possible and to capture all technologies and interactions employed or performed by students, including those actors and practices commensurate with, and also subversive toward, the teacher's supervisory and evaluative role.

(d) Videographic methodologies

This study captured the entire procedure of students' on-screen composition as a digital recording (screencast), alongside an embedded video recording of their movements and vocalizations around the writing of their course assignments. The video-based data collection method deployed in this study of digital literacies has its roots in the fields of ethnomethodology and workplace studies (e.g., Luff, Hindmarsh, & Heath, 2000), with some influences drawn from multimodal analysis (e.g., Bezemer & Mavers, 2011). The methodology adopted therefore aims to prioritize "the situated and interactional accomplishments of practical action" (Heath, Hindmarsh, & Luff 2010, p. 1). "Practical action" within the context of this assignment-writing study refers to the practices of digital literacy occurring as the students complete their assignment tasks in classrooms. Their "interactional accomplishments" are uncovered through parsing out the choreography of actors—social and material—which give specific literacy practices their qualities. This methodology thereby complements and builds on attempts to bring together ethnography and multimodality (e.g., Dicks, et al., 2011), connective ethnographies (e.g., Fields & Kafai, 2009), and new methods of literacy research (e.g., Albers, Holbrook, & Flint, 2014).

When it comes to capturing practices of digital literacy, in order to problematize how technologies mediate meanings and social lives, traditional methods can fall short (Snee et al., 2015). And when it comes to the writing of course assignments and completion of classroom tasks, some practices, such as the conflation of practices evident in the example discussed in the previous section, are virtually invisible, inaccessible, or unanalyzable using traditional and analogue research methods. But new digital research and data collection methods also pose new practical and theoretical challenges, some of which I address in the following sections.

DATA COLLECTION AND ANALYSIS

(a) General approach

The kind of data collection and analysis that emerges from an ethnographic commitment to the New Literacy Studies and the sensibilities demanded by a sociomaterial approach led me to take account of learners' digital practices across time and place and in online/offline spaces during their assignment writing. In short, a composite picture of learners' writing was required to capture the moment-by-moment digital literacies that were being drawn into class work and identify which actors were mobilized to make these happen. I have addressed some of the theoretical underpinnings of this methodology and what it affords literacy research in more detail in other work (e.g., Bhatt & de Roock, 2013; Bhatt, de Roock, & Adams, 2015). What follows here is a discussion that is oriented more toward the practicality of how data were collected in a number of ethnographic case studies in my investigation of student assignment writing, and how these data were managed and analyzed in light of the aims of the study.

Data for the study were collected in three overall phases, phase two of which is outlined in detail for this chapter (as a series of steps described below). The data collection discussion that is presented below is commingled with analysis in order to give insights into how my data analysis outcomes were interpreted at every stage in the methodological process, and how I was able to draw out conclusions to do with capturing the nuances of digital literacy practices. But first it is necessary to see how this fits within a broader ethnographic methodological framework.

(b) Overall procedure

The study was carried out within the context of U.K. Further Education colleges,[1] where a mixture of academic, vocational, and school-level education takes place. The data were collected from three such research sites, each of which eventually led to a case study of assignment writing in progress for a particular college course. Key considerations in the selection of the college courses for this study were that they have embedded vocational elements (related to job training, such as childcare or teacher education), and that there were significant differences in the course-related activities of the learners across the sites, including in terms of assignment formats and processes. This variation and distinctiveness of the three sites was ascertained during an initial institutional observation phase. The vocational element was important in order to gain insight into the kinds of digital literacy practices influenced by, and drawn from, work spheres of participants' lives, and how particular work practices may influence the outcome of an assignment. Importantly, these practices can emerge from, interact, or compete with other practices during assignment writing (to be recorded later in the research process during phase 2 of the study).

Each site was investigated in three phases, the first of which involved weekly visits across a period of three to five months. Phase 1 involved ethnographic observations of institutional culture and classroom activities. From this phase of data collection, I selected a learner in each of the three sites whose assignment writing I planned to record and trace during class time, as part of phase 2 of the data collection process. This entailed using the videographic recording technique discussed earlier in this chapter and outlined in more detail in the step-by-step procedure below. In the methodology outlined below, I have drawn examples from two of the three case studies from the original study. Participants for these two cases were Sara and Paulo (pseudonyms are used for all participants and the colleges in this study). At the time of undertaking the research, Sara was in her early 20s and studying Childcare at a pre-University level (i.e., UK QCF level 3),[2] and Paulo was in his late teens and enrolled in an English for Speakers of Other Languages (ESOL) and Information, Communication, and Technology course at level 1.

After the video recordings of assignment writing events as part of phase 2 were completed, I interviewed each student about their digital literacies across home, work, and college lives. This represented phase 3 of the data collection process for this study. In keeping with a participatory ethnographic research approach (cf. Emmel, 2008), this part of my study design was enhanced by incorporating a Venn diagram task and a postassignment interview as data collection methods. The Venn diagram task aimed at having participants identify and map practices of digital literacy and tools for personal, classroom, and work use, and the "boundary crossings" (Ivanič & Satchwell, 2007) among them. In the three student interviews I conducted, discussion centered around where and how, within the video recording of their assignment work, practices "flowed" across different spheres of life activity (work, home, etc.) and how practices initiated in one sphere of life became mobilized by them as resources within their classroom-based assignment writing.

In addition to field notes made during initial observations, photographs taken of the college environment, and transcribed discussions with the three student participants, video data became central to the "thick description" (Geertz, 1973) required by the classroom literacy practices emerging in the research. Indeed, each data mode and each step of data collection illuminated the other. For example, by means of the video recordings, I was able to draw attention to the moment-by-moment literacy practices of assignment work, and uncover how these practices emerged from established networks of actors during assignment work (*learners doing what they should be*) and sometimes how other practices broke down networks of institutional culture (*learners not doing what they should be*).

(c) Videography

Step 1: Data set up

This first step in collecting videographic data had a multimodal nature and was a methodological choice well justified by current researchers in the New Literacy Studies tradition. According to Bella Dicks et al. (2011), for example, a multimodal approach can constitute anything from research using video recorders, observation of bodily movements, or analysis of material objects and environments. Thus, data collection instruments—screen capture software, cameras—were set up in the manner shown in Figure 7.1. The teacher is visible in this screen shot,[3] and the larger image in Figure 7.1 shows Sara's screen. This is dubbed a "screen-in-screen" image (see below). All three of them (i.e., Sara, her classmate, and her teacher) are interacting with each other during the writing of the assignment, and all of their vocalizations are recorded alongside the iterative process of on-screen composition.

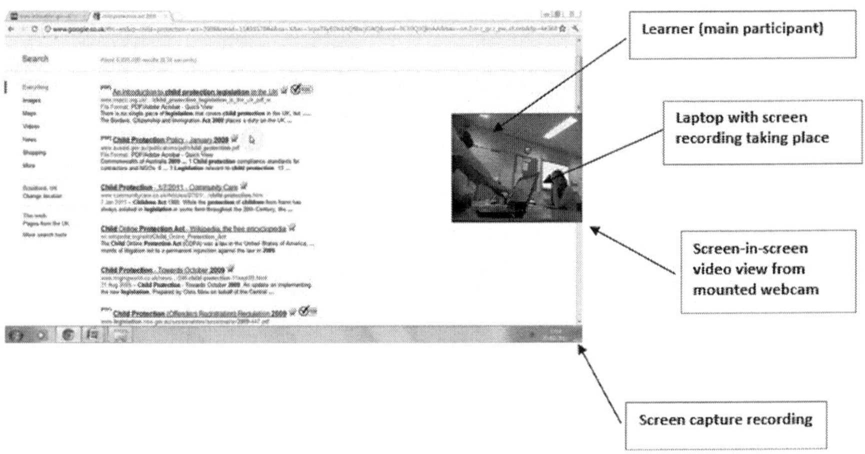

Fig. 7.1. Data capture setup used a screen recording with embedded video recording and audio of surrounding vocalizations.

The webcam used was not the built-in webcam of Sara's classroom laptop. Rather, through attaching a better quality webcam to the side of her I was able to achieve an angled view and more coverage of her movements. This webcam also had a more sensitive and omni-directional microphone, and effectively captured the interactions between Sara, Lauren, and the teacher. I was able to observe this lesson in person and note how the whiteboard instructions, texts from previous lessons, and departmental documents (on digital media policies and quality) all played an important role in the practices of Sara's assignment and within this particular lesson.

Step 2: Screen-in-screen recording

The software chosen for this multidimensional type of recording was Blueberry Flashback recorder. This software captures the entire process of on-screen composition with an embedded webcam recording of the learners' movements together with an audio recording of verbalizations around the tasks at the time of writing. This data collection setup resulted in an ongoing screen recording with an embedded video recording integrated as a "screen-in-screen" format, as shown in Figure 7.1. Once recorded, the films were converted from Blueberry Flashback's standard file format to mpeg.

The recording provided a rich, multimodal rendition and *in situ* monitoring of the assignment writing event during classroom time, on- and off-screen, and simultaneously captured Sara and Lauren's interactions with each other (including discussions and gestures) and real-time interactions with the computer (typing, copy-pasting, browsing, etc.). I collected three videos to view, one for each case being explored, and meticulously transcribed segments as part of the analysis. This is outlined in the next steps below.

Step 3: Analytic video logging

The data recordings were rendered into accessible video logs (see Table 7.1 for an extract) chronicling, at short intervals, learners' activities and interactions during in-class assignment writing. Following this work salient moments during the recordings which related directly to, and addressed, the research questions were then selected and considered for further analysis. This made the data more accessible and allowed for ease of categorization and breakdown of participants' interactions and practices in a manner that allowed me to address the research questions methodically.

Selection of what to include in the analytic video logs was based on a range of concerns influenced by the research questions, observational notes, collected documentation from the sites (obtained in phase 1 of data collection), and other relevant and supporting data. Close attention was paid to the practices and salient moments during in-class assignment writing. The most important feature of the analytic video logs entails providing a detailed account of "what happened." At this stage, the event was broken down into segments, which were decided by salient moments during assignment writing. Moments in the recordings which revealed such things as information-hunting and copy-paste practices, social media interactions, circumventions and violations of college policy on digital media use, instances when things did not go to plan, and other mundane aspects of interaction were all represented as "segments" and part of this breakdown in the logs.

With video data, it is important to avoid the risk of oversaturation brought about by a potentially overwhelming amount of data. There is, after all, a lot to note in even a few minutes of video data. Consistent with Christian Heath, Jon Hindmarsh, and Paul Luff's work (2010), I decided to divide the video logs into segments within identified events as described above. These were of varying

Table 7.1. Extract from the video log for Paulo's assignment.

Time and segment	Researcher notes	Description
00:00–00:42	Waiting for the programme to upload. The lesson was delayed at the start as T couldn't find the key to the room. It was held by an ICT technician.	Paulo sits in front of the computer, takes a brief look of his notes on this assignment. Looks at the screen and at the notes one after the other. Pauses between glances, up and down.
00:42–01:52	Paulo is still mulling what is required of him. Seems a little confused, possibly due to the multiple forms of input.	He opens Microsoft Word. Responds to T's instructions to him specifically regarding "the different sections of the report" which is a task drawn from the results of a survey. He asks her to clarify something for him. T then turns to address the entire class to offer the same clarification and instructions.
01:53–03:50	Use of the Moodle VLE is insisted on by T. This is based on a college managerial directive.	Starts typing "My Report" while T addresses the class, then stops and listens again to T. He opens a new tab (Google) and searches for "Northdale College—Virtual Learning Environment." He logs in to his account and then clicks on "My Course: 15–18's ESOL research" option.
04:14–05:02	He reaches the VLE interface to get his work. But now needs help.	Clicks on "Participants" under the "My Course: 15–18's ESOL research" option and then he seems unsure for a while about what to do next, until he decides to go back to "15–18's ESOL research."
05:12–06:18	Other actors are on stand-by to be called in, and they are: an ICT technician enters the room and helps Paulo get to the right part of the VLE for his work.	Asks for help from T. She asks him if he's in the wrong course and approaches him to help but he's in the right one. He goes on the left top of the page and clicks on the "Course Overview: 16–18 ESOL Bridging Course." One of ICT support staff, who was already in the room, comes over to help. He sees the "Topic Outline" of the course.

Time and segment	Researcher notes	Description
06:19–07:16	Things are not cohering: VLE restrictions (enrolment key and password problems), an absent student's lack of preassignment work makes him ill prepared.	Paulo goes to the Enrolment options. According to the support staff member an "enrolment key" for the course is required to get in to the relevant pages of the VLE which he needs access to. T is a little frustrated because of this delay and confusion. In the meantime, a student has to leave the class in order to find the person who can provide him with his password. While waiting for that T tells the rest to work on their reports. Paulo goes back to Microsoft Word and starts typing again "in my report." Looks at the paper with his notes for a second that he now places in front of his keyboard, and goes on typing. T gently chastises a student who has no survey results to work from because he was absent yesterday.
07:16–08:00	The enrolment key is another type of key, which allows access to another kind of space. A network of actors holds the formal teaching procedure together.	The ICT technician, who had left the classroom, now has to come back in. Paulo is mid-sentence, but manages to enroll himself into the VLE to get the resources he needs. He and T both look frustrated.

Key: T = the teacher, VLE = Virtual Learning Environment.

lengths, which made for easy repeated viewing. Where necessary, I was able to decide which of these segments demanded further analytic scrutiny (as detailed in the next step). What becomes apparent in using this approach is that while the unit of analysis is the unfolding "literacy event," when we "follow the actors" (cf. Latour, 2005) we see that each literacy event is instantiated by practices which point to other events beyond the "here and now."

Step 4: Narrative vignettes

Textual data from the video logs, field notes, and other sources were then integrated and rendered into the form of narrative vignettes to "tell a story" of how the assignments were written. Points highlighted as noteworthy were drawn together with the data from prior steps (as outlined above). Vignettes transform the data to gloss over some of the messiness and fuzziness, or the "secret business" (cf. Bigum et al., 2014), that is associated with the processes of data collection and research presentation. My story-like reconstruction of the events at this step allowed the data to be transformed into a manageable and easily accessible form for reading and further analysis, and enabled me to examine and reflect on the writing and digital practices of the learners as they unfolded.

In the above video log, Paulo gets started with his assignment. How Paulo then goes on to cope with the multitude of instructions given by his teacher about his assignment emerges throughout his writing, and is evidenced in the following vignette extract, which also provides an example of how the data are transformed in this particular step:

> Ten minutes of the class have now elapsed. Paulo switches windows from Moodle to Microsoft Word; the latter contains his report, and he alternately types and looks at his notes. He has to go back and forth across different web pages and his Word file which has received little attention thus far since he has spent the last few minutes merely getting organized and figuring out what to do. When he does get into the flow of writing, he is interrupted: he is asked to return to the web page of resources in the virtual learning environment. He scrolls down and clicks on "Homework Social Networking Report" to download the file (i.e., right click "Show in Folder") and then drags the file onto his desktop. He opens the file, then goes back to his report and continues typing. The teacher directs everyone to look at the extra information on the board, which lays out the paragraphs for the report. This is worded as follows:
>
> **Paragraph 1: Introduction, what I will write about**
> **Paragraph 2: The pros and cons, comparing 4 networking sites**
> **Paragraph 3: Class survey on social networking results**
> **Paragraph 4: How I use social networking**
> **Paragraph 5: Conclusion**
>
> Paulo then focuses on the look of the page, tweaking its layout (margins, font etc.) as he types. This lasts into the twelfth minute. While writing his report, he looks at his notes, pauses momentarily, and then writes about how Facebook, Twitter, and YouTube are currently the most popular social networks. He does this continuously.
>
> Meanwhile, the teacher is heard in the background giving instructions, reminding students of what is required. Paulo is looking at his notes the whole time while typing. Spell checker interrupts often, he acquiesces, but one of these corrections leads to another mistake, albeit not a spelling related one. (for more details, see Bhatt, 2014)

In the above vignette, Paulo faces another interruption: a reminder to write the assignment a certain way, in a certain format, and with certain protocols in mind. These interruptions, as detailed below, represent a crucial aspect in the practices of his assignment writing: lots of small tasks nested within a greater task. These smaller tasks occur throughout his assignment writing and require a certain level of capability: scanning an online bookmark list for links to readings, addressing the language and grammar elements explicit in the rubric, the skills of navigating around the virtual learning environment, interpreting different types of assignment instructions, etc. Some of these "tasks within tasks" are less explicit, and part of what we could describe as belonging to the "dramaturgy of formal learning," that is, an assemblage of practices held together through their regularity. The work for these other, nested, tasks is instantiated by different digital literacy practices. Importantly, college documentation collected as part of phase 1 of this study reveal that the teacher's insistence on such things as using the Moodle learning environment for this task stems from institutional digital learning policy directives, which set the learning standards for and expectations regarding classroom technology use. These exert a structuring agency within the classroom, leading to the dramaturgy of formal learning and an imaginary of how this assignment, and other classroom activities, *should* be completed. Throughout the entire assignment writing process, and culminating in its final submission, we see Paulo either choosing to comply with these directives or circumvent them. Sometimes they are shaped by something "not going to plan" which necessitates the intervention of other actors (e.g., the ICT technician) to hold things in place or to move things along.

Whatever the case, the juggling of these and other elements while getting the assignment completed means that Paulo's digital literacies are contested—they certainly are not monolithic or even college-centric—and emerge through the network of different actors at play in the assignment. His multitasking was remarkable, even though he felt as though he was floundering at the start.

Step 5: Digital transcription

Screen capture video proved to be the most revealing in terms of tracing the choreography of practices drawn into the assignment writing process. But, in some cases, scrutinizing these practices alongside the video logs required a further layer of analytic work. This additional work necessitated the use of a computer-assisted qualitative data analysis software program known as ELAN to manipulate the recordings (e.g., slowing down, transcribing). Computer-assisted qualitative data analysis has very much become standard practice in many forms of qualitative analysis, especially those involving video data. Its use in my own study emerged from a need to explore certain segments of the analytic video logs in much more detail, and to slow them down for a more granular analysis. In previous work, I have described this kind of analysis as "diving deep" into practices of digital literacy (Bhatt et al., 2015). By diving deep, literacy researchers can expose the complex interplay of practices, including web-mediated intertextual work (Barthes & Heath, 1977), occurring as students work on their assignments.

An example of a salient moment in the recordings is an interaction when Sara is discussing her work with her peers and the teacher, and searching online for information. In the particular segment produced below (see Figure 7.2), I sought to better understand, and to slow down, the multitude of interactions at play in the performance of her digital literacy practices, and to understand how these related to her assignment goals. We see in Figure 7.2 that Sara is interacting with Lauren and the teacher, as well as with the Google search algorithm, an actor that is far removed from the classroom but core to Sara's assignment writing strategies. In this interaction, Sara is misguided by a Google search result but is redirected by her teacher who tells her that her results are irrelevant for the task. How Sara dealt with this disjunction is interesting in terms of exploring her digital literacy workarounds and the moment itself warranted further scrutiny. By slowing this clip down and then transcribing the interaction to highlight pauses, I was able to consider Google's algorithmic-based interventions as akin to a "turn" in interaction around the text (see Bhatt & de Roock, 2013). Google's auto-complete action interrupts mid-word keying and, as they would with a human interactant, Sara and her teacher pause to consider its displayed responses. What is important here is that, as an actor that is apparently far removed from the classroom interaction (i.e., based largely on servers in California), the search engine is far from neutral in its suggestions and results (Baker & Potts, 2013).

When such moments arise in recorded literacy events, the qualitative data analysis program, ELAN, facilitates the organization, transcription, and analysis of multimodal data from multiple sources in a manageable interface. It uniquely allows for the syncing of video files with a horizontally depicted transcription in tiers, giving methodological flexibility alongside the video data (Halverson, Bass, & Woods, 2012). Figure 7.2 is an example screen shot depicting the representational system created through this software.

Sara's movements, her talk around the task, her interactions with others in the classroom and with digital interfaces are significant. The practices she engages in are not always evident in the final written assignment submission, but, as we see, they are essential to the final assignment and meaningful in its formulation. Using CAQDAS tools such as ELAN to manage key segments in the recording allowed for deeper insights into the character of Sara's interactions. Such tools afford manipulability (slowing down, segmentation, etc.) and multimodal transcription (Bezemer & Mavers, 2011) to account for the complex interplay of the practices we see Sara engaging in. The representational system of ELAN allowed me to integrate the practices with other activities occurring simultaneously, yet also to parse them out for analytic attention, all within the context of assignment work being done.

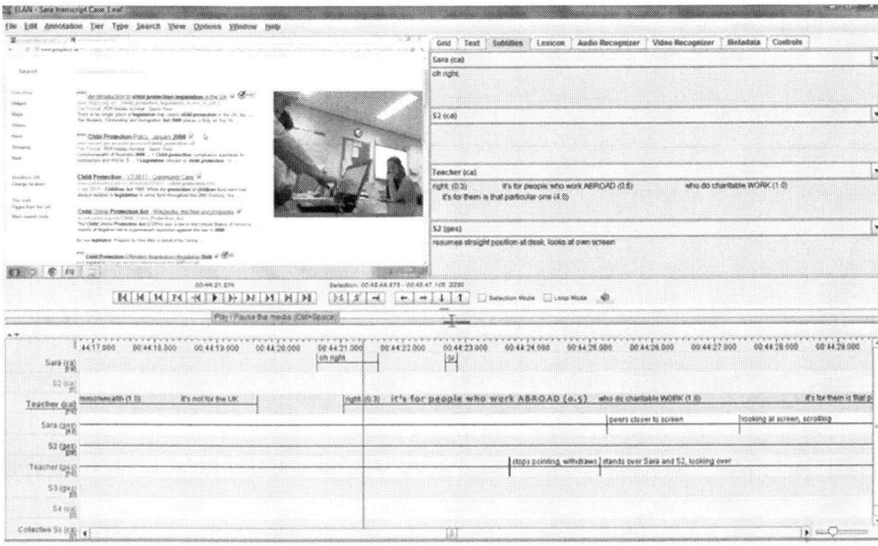

Fig. 7.2. A transcript screenshot of using ELAN from the study.

These tools allowed for the further exploration of practices. Some of those which emerged were in contrast to the dominant institutional conception of what an "assignment" actually is and how it should be written by the students. This relates fundamentally to the valorized schooled literacies that college assignments are designed to assess and which are implemented by force of documents such as institutional "acceptable use" policies, mandatory courseware management systems like Moodle, digital learning guides, and the culture of classroom procedure.

What therefore begins as a general "forest-wise" (Erickson, 2006) account of what happened, aided by earlier layers of data management (e.g., video logging), then brought me to a "tree-wise" (ibid.) understanding of salient moments. Through careful and repeated viewing of the screen-in-screen recordings and video logging, and drawing on the call to "follow actors" (Latour, 2005), I observed that learners readily drew from other texts to complete their work, used algorithmically mediated practices (e.g., via search engines), and used noninstitutional technologies to perform social acts which in some cases supported their assignment writing (for more on this, see Bhatt, 2014). Tree-wise understandings in data analysis refer to paying analytic attention to the choreography of practices and their precise roles in the greater event being observed and recorded. This is not just about identifying practices such as text *re-mixing*, *curating*, Google searching, etc., but also about understanding where they came from and their role in meaning-making as part of the final products of writing. Tree-wise and forest-wise analyses sensitize researchers to the rich details of visually recorded data alongside the broader patterns within which those very details fit.

CONCLUSIONS

Although grounded in the ethnographic tradition of the New Literacy Studies, by exposing the complex digital literacy practices at play in the work of assignment writing, my research highlights the need for literacy researchers to adapt their methods to new learning environments and new forms of digital sociality. David Barton's (2007) description of the ecological nature of literacy as being embedded in human activity, social life and thought, and its position in history draws attention to the sociocultural environment in which literacy events occur. This study, in recognizing the complex environments of new literacies in classrooms, makes the case that literacy research methodologies must adjust to changing environments in order to be insightful and contribute meaningfully to a developing discussion on digital literacy theory and digital learning policies.

Through my method's attention to synchronizing a video view with screen capture, in order to capture interactions unfolding as learners wrote their assignments, I came to see how digital literacy practices are practically achieved and span multiple digital platforms, programs, devices, time/space parameters, and what would ordinarily be dubbed "formal" and "informal" domains. Yet these same practices were vital to successful completion of the assignment tasks. Key among the things this dynamic approach uncovered was the role of search engine algorithms in digital literacy practices, something underexplored in literacy research. I was also able to see how some digital literacy practices are privileged over others, and how these tensions are handled in specific moments within a literacy event. Disjunctures such as these have a lot to do with the control and agency of college procedures and protocols associated with teaching quality and what is deemed "good practice."

While acknowledging the interconnectedness of in-class and outside-class literacy practices in student writing is not new in literacy research (e.g., Maybin, 2007), precisely capturing the complex nature of student practices with technologies in the moment-by-moment unfolding of classroom tasks has rarely been achieved. The methods presented here therefore supplement and extend the existing methodological repertoire of literacy research inquiries, refreshing the study of literacy, and thereby allow for new kinds of data to be collected or generated and new kinds of research questions to be asked.

NOTES

1. Further Education is a sector within the United Kingdom and Ireland, which refers to postcompulsory education and training. Further Education colleges can deliver vocational training, university-level degrees, and second-chance school education. It is similar to "continuing education" in the United States.

2. For a breakdown of the levels of the UK's Qualifications & Credit framework (QCF) for the participants' levels see http://www.accreditedqualifications.org.uk/qualifications-and-credit-framework-qcf.html
3. Consent to publish pictures was obtained at the time of the research.

REFERENCES

Albers, P., Holbrook, T., & Flint, A. (2014). *New methods of literacy research*. Abingdon, UK: Taylor & Francis.

Baker, P., & Potts, A. (2013). "Why do white people have thin lips?" Google and the perpetuation of stereotypes via auto-complete search forms. *Critical Discourse Studies*, 10(2), 187–204.

Barthes, R., & Heath, S. (1977). *Image-music-text*. London: Fontana.

Barton, D. (2007). *Literacy: An introduction to the ecology of written language*. Oxford, UK: Blackwell.

Barton, D., & Hamilton, M. (2000). Literacy practices. In D. Barton, M. Hamilton, & R. Ivanič, (Eds.), *Situated literacies: Reading and writing in context* (pp. 7–15). London: Routledge.

Barton, D., & Hamilton, M. (2012). *Local literacies: Reading and writing in one community* (revised ed). London: Routledge.

Baynham, M. (1995). *Literacy practices: Investigating literacy in social contexts*. London: Longman.

Bezemer, J., & Mavers, D. (2011). Multimodal transcription as academic practice: A social semiotic perspective. *International Journal of Social Research Methodology*, 14(3), 191–206.

Bhatt, I. (2014). A Sociomaterial Account of Assignment Writing in Further Education Classrooms (PhD diss.), School of Education, University of Leeds.

Bhatt, I., & de Roock, R. (2013). Capturing the sociomateriality of digital literacy events. *Research in Learning Technology*, 21(4). Available from: http://dx.doi.org/10.3402/rlt.v21.21281

Bhatt, I., de Roock, R., & Adams, J. (2015). Diving deep into digital literacy: Emerging methods for research. *Language and Education*, 29(6), 477–492.

Bigum, C., Rowan, L., Wright, S., Hamilton, M., & Haxell, A. (2014). *Looking for black cats and lessons from Charlie: Exploring the potential of public click pedagogy (February 2014 version of Working paper)*. Updated 9th April 2014. Available from: http://chrisbigum.com/downloads/PCP-NLC.pdf

Coiro, J., Knobel, M., Lankshear, C., & Leu, D. J. (2008). *Handbook of research on new literacies*. New York: Taylor & Francis.

de Roock, R., Bhatt, I., & Adams, J. (2015). Video analysis in digital literacy studies: Exploring innovative methods. In H. Snee, C. Hine, Y. Morley, S. Roberts, & H. Watson (Eds.), *Digital methods for social sciences: An interdisciplinary guide to research innovation* (pp. 105–121). Hampshire, UK: Palgrave Macmillan.

Dicks, B., Flewitt, R., Lancaster, L., & Pahl, K. (2011). Multimodality and ethnography: Working at the intersection. *Qualitative Research*, 11(3), 227–237.

Emmel, N. (2008). *Participatory mapping: An innovative sociological method. Real life methods*. ESRC, National Centre for Social Research. Available from: http://eprints.ncrm.ac.uk/540

Erickson, F. (2006). Definition and analysis of data from videotape: Some research procedures and their rationales. In J. Green, G. Camilli, & P. Elmore (Eds.), *Handbook of complementary methods in education research* (pp. 177–205). Mahwah, NJ: American Educational Research Association.

Fenwick, T. J., Edwards, R., & Sawchuk, P. (2011). *Emerging approaches to educational research: Tracing the sociomaterial*. London: Routledge.

Fields, D., & Kafai, Y. (2009). A connective ethnography of peer knowledge sharing and diffusion in a tween virtual world. *International Journal of Computer-Supported Collaborative Learning*, 4(1), 47–68.

Gee, J. (2008). *Social linguistics and literacies: Ideology in discourses*. London: Routledge.

Geertz, C. (1973). *The interpretation of cultures: Selected essays*. New York: Basic Books.

Gourlay, L., & Oliver, M. (2013). Beyond "the social": Digital literacies as sociomaterial practice. In R. Goodfellow & M. Lea (Eds.), *Literacy in the digital university: Critical perspectives on learning, scholarship & technology* (pp. 79–94). London: Routledge.

Halverson, E., Bass, M., & Woods, D. (2012). The process of creation: A novel methodology for analyzing multimodal data. *The Qualitative Report*, 17(21), 1–27.

Hamilton, M. (2009). Putting words in their mouths: The alignment of identities with system goals through the use of individual learning plans. *British Educational Research Journal*, 35(2), 221–242.

Hayles, K. (2012). *How we think: Digital media and contemporary technogenesis*. Chicago, IL: University of Chicago Press.

Heath, C., Hindmarsh, J., & Luff, P. (2010). *Video in qualitative research: Analyzing social interaction in everyday life*. Thousand Oaks, CA: Sage.

Ito, M., et al. (2010). *Hanging out, messing around, and geeking out: Kids living and learning with new media*. Cambridge, MA: MIT Press.

Ivanič, R., Edwards, R., Barton, D., Martin-Jones, M., Fowler, Z., Hughes, B., Mannion, G., Miller, K., Satchwell, C., & Smith, J. (2009). *Improving learning in college: Rethinking literacies across the curriculum*. London: Routledge.

Ivanič, R., & Satchwell, C. (2007). Boundary crossing: Networking and transforming literacies in research processes and college courses. *Journal of Applied Linguistics*, 4(1). DOI: 10.1558/japl.v4i1.101.

Knobel, M., & Lankshear, C. (2006). Digital literacy and digital literacies: Policy, pedagogy and research considerations for education. *Nordic Journal of Digital Literacy*, 1(1), 12–24.

Lankshear, C., & Knobel, M. (2008). Introduction. In C. Lankshear & M. Knobel (Eds.), *Digital literacies: Concepts, policies and practices* (pp. 1–16). New York: Peter Lang.

Lankshear, C. & Knobel, M. (2011). *New literacies: Everyday practices and social learning*. New York: McGraw-Hill.

Latour, B. (1987). *Science in action: How to follow scientists and engineers through society*. Milton Keynes, UK: Open University Press.

Latour, B. (2005). *Reassembling the social: An introduction to actor-network-theory*. Oxford, UK: Oxford University Press.

Latour, B., & Woolgar, S. (1986). *Laboratory life: The construction of scientific facts*. Princeton, NJ: Princeton University Press.

Law, J. (2012). Collateral realities. In F. Rubio & P. Baert (Eds.), *The politics of knowledge* (pp. 156–178). London: Routledge.

Luff, P., Hindmarsh, J., & Heath, C. (2000). *Workplace studies: Recovering work practice and informing system design*. Cambridge, MA: Cambridge University Press.

Maybin, J. (2007). Literacy under and over the desk: Oppositions and heterogeneity. *Language and Education*, 21(6), 515–530.

Mol, A. (2002). *The body multiple: Ontology in medical practice*. Durham, NC: Duke University Press.

Orlikowski, W. (2007). Sociomaterial practices: Exploring technology at work. *Organization Studies*, 28(9), 1435–1448.

Prinsloo, M., & Baynham, M. (2008). Introduction: Renewing literacy studies. In M. Prinsloo & M. Baynham (Eds.), *Literacies, global and local* (pp. 1–16). Philadelphia, PA: John Benjamins.

Scribner, S., & Cole, M. (1981). *The psychology of literacy*. Cambridge, MA: Harvard University Press.

Snee, H., Hine, C., Morley, Y., Roberts, S., & Watson, H. (2015). *Digital methods for social science*. Hampshire, UK: Palgrave MacMillan.

Street, B. (1984). *Literacy in theory and practice*. Cambridge, UK: Cambridge University Press.

Street, B. (2001). *Literacy and development: Ethnographic perspectives*. London: Routledge.

Tummons, J. (2010). Institutional ethnography and actor–network theory: A framework for researching the assessment of trainee teachers. *Ethnography and Education*, 5(3), 345–357.

CHAPTER EIGHT

Discourse analytic approaches to understanding new literacies in online fan fiction writing communities

REBECCA W. BLACK

ISSUES AND QUESTIONS ADDRESSED

When I began this research project in 2002, fewer than 600 million people were online globally—a number which comes into sharper focus when compared to the 1.09 billion daily *Facebook* users in 2016 (Facebook, 2016, n.p.). At the time, the notion of online communities as an object of academic inquiry was still relatively novel, especially in the domain of education and literacy studies. However, as a former English language instructor, I was intrigued to find online communities devoted to writing and reading, especially when some of these spaces were populated with young people from a variety of cultural and linguistic backgrounds who were interacting primarily in English. This sort of voluntary engagement with and around written texts was in direct contrast to the sort of resistance to writing that I often encountered as a teacher in school classrooms.

The primary context for the study discussed in this chapter, Fanfiction.net, was, and probably still is, the largest and one of the best-known online *fan fiction* archives. Fan fiction is writing in which fans reimagine existing media storyworlds, such as movies, books, television series, and video games, in order to explore alternate plotlines, settings, and possibilities for character interactions. For example, a fan might explore a romantic relationship between Harry Potter and Hermione Granger or develop a prequel that explores Harry Potter's childhood. In 2006, Fanfiction.net housed over a million fan texts, published in at least 13 languages, and attracted authors from all over the globe. On the site, fans composed and publicly posted stories based on their favorite media canons, and readers had the option of publicly posting reviews or feedback on the texts. Thus, Fanfiction.net provided a context where young people could write, read, and interact around story worlds that were of great interest to them.

THEORETICAL GROUNDING: NEW LITERACY STUDIES AND STUDIES OF NEW LITERACIES

At the time, I was steeped in readings focused on the New Literacy Studies (e.g., Bazerman, 1989; Cazden, 1988; Cook-Gumperz, 1986; Gee, 1987; Graff, 1979; Heath, 1983; Scollon & Scollon, 1981; Scribner & Cole, 1981; Street, 1984, 1997; Wertsch, 1985) and new and digital literacies (e.g., Coiro et al., 2008; Gee, 2004, 2007; Kist, 2004; Kress, 2003; Knobel & Lankshear, 2007; Lankshear, 1997; Lankshear & Knobel, 2003, 2006; New London Group, 1996). Proponents of the New Literacy Studies presented a challenge to prevailing views of literacy as a purely cognitive process located within individual minds. Instead, they viewed literacy as a sociocultural practice through which individuals participate in social events. Scholars within the New *Literacies* Studies built, in many ways, on the work of the New Literacy Studies and adhered to the notion of literacy as social practice; however, their focus was on new digital forms of literacy that were becoming increasingly relevant and prevalent with growing access to computers. I was drawn to the New Literacy Studies notion of literacy as a social practice because it resonated with what I witnessed in my classroom as students struggled to acquire aspects of the English language that went beyond what was explicit in the linguistic code. And the new literacies studies conception of literacy also resonated with what I was seeing online as young people used a range of digital texts to forge social connections and develop a sense of community with their peers. Second language acquisition and literacy researchers were just beginning to explore in earnest the possibilities that technology-mediated communication might offer for language and literacy development, and for English language learners' (ELLs) identities (see Lam, 2000). I viewed my study as a potential contribution to this emerging literature on young people's many uses of digital texts.

I designed the project to be a virtual ethnography (Hine, 2000) of the entire Fanfiction.net site. However, in early analyses of different media-based subsections of the site (i.e., Harry Potter, *Star Wars*, *Lineage*), I realized that there seemed to be many more self-identified ELLs composing in the anime and manga-based subsections. So, while I still used ethnographic methods to gain a holistic picture of Fanfiction.net, I shifted my focus to an exploratory case study (Yin, 2003) of ELL writer and reader interactions around *Card Captor Sakura*, a popular anime-based subsection. Drawing from my experiences with ELL students' resistance to writing in classroom settings, combined with my initial observations of high levels of textual engagement within Fanfiction.net, I developed the following overarching research questions for the study: In what ways does participating in online fan fiction spaces provide ELLs with access to literacy learning and literate practices in areas where many school-based approaches have not succeeded? How might the digital mode of communication scaffold or promote affiliation with composing and interacting in English?

COLLECTING DATA IN ONLINE ENVIRONMENTS

In order to gain a robust understanding of what was actually happening on the site, I spent three years as a participant observer on Fanfiction.net. This included approximately ten to twenty hours per week of writing and publicly posting my own fan fiction stories, providing feedback for other writers' texts, and interacting with a diverse group of fans both on Fanfiction.net and in the broader fan fiction community. In addition, I sought to identify focal participants for my study. The following paragraph is a neat description of what ended up being a messy process of identifying and recruiting participants.

> By examining the linguistic features of posted fan fiction texts and information presented on the authors' accompanying personal pages that included biographical information, I was able to identify six potential adolescent ELL participants. The study also involved a purposive nonprobability form of snowball sampling in that the links from one member's personal page acted as a referral to another member's personal page and texts (Miles & Huberman, 1994). Additionally, conceptually-driven sequential sampling (Miles & Huberman, 1994) was used to identify participants who engaged in notably different forms of participation—for example, some members were very active in writing on the site, while others were more active in reading, socializing, and posting reviews of others' texts. (Black, 2009, p. 403)

The process of recruiting participants was messy for two main reasons. First, due to the relative novelty of this sort of online research, the Institutional Review Board at my university struggled with how to reconcile protections developed for material contexts with studies designed for digital spaces. In particular, they were concerned with the recruitment process and how I would obtain parental consent. Ultimately, we settled on a cumbersome process by which minors who were interested in joining the study visited, with a parent or guardian, a password-protected research website and entered their mailing address where I could send parental and participant consent forms that could then be mailed back to me. Because my participants were all over the world, and because I wished to minimize any inconvenience on their part, this process also entailed purchasing the appropriate return postage materials for each country and including them with the forms that were sent out—a task which sometimes proved to be an interesting logistical challenge for the local post office.

The second complicating factor, closely tied to the first, stems from the sometimes highly personal nature of fan fiction texts. Because many young people use their fan texts to explore emotionally charged topics from their own lives (e.g., sexuality, popularity, date rape, suicidal ideations), many of these teenaged authors were understandably reluctant to draw their parents' attention to these narratives by asking them to sign a human subjects consent form. Relatedly, even though fan authors used pseudonymous pen names, I was reluctant to include participants who posted certain kinds of sensitive materials, even if they consented to be in the study. As a particularly salient example, there was a young, Latino ELL who was interested in being a participant in the study. Many of his stories focused on a young, male protagonist who comes out as homosexual to his friends and family. Upon reading his biographical information and interactions with readers on the site, it became clear that these stories represented issues with sexuality and family dynamics that he was struggling with in his own life. And, even though he considered the risk of accidental disclosure to his parents to be low because they were not skilled Internet users, I thought it best not to include him in the study. These are examples of the sort of ethical challenges that new literacies researchers still face in an age of ever-more networked, shareable, and "googleable" text.

Once my focal participants were selected, I gathered data from multiple sources over a three-year period. The primary sources were fan fiction texts written by three focal participants, and reader reviews of these texts. Fanfiction.net provides an "Alert" option that sends an e-mail notification when specified members update their texts. Thus, I was able to download new and revised versions of participants' texts as they were posted to the site. I was also able to download readers' reviews of these newly updated texts. I also visited participants' personal pages on a biweekly basis to note and/or download any changes to their biographical information. I ended up with hundreds of chapters of focal participants' fan fiction texts and over 10,000 reader reviews of these texts. In terms of process, while I read over these data multiple times, I only conducted close analyses of approximately 50 chapters and accompanying author's notes (fan fiction on Fanfiction.net tends to be stories comprising single through to multiple chapters), and around 500 reader reviews. In retrospect, while the fine-grained, discourse analyses of these data were invaluable for understanding participants' experiences in this space, I wish I had also incorporated some sort of quantitative corpus analyses into the study to shed light on broader patterns of participation within Fanfiction.net.

Over the three-year study period, I conducted semi-structured interviews and had numerous informal e-mail and Instant Messenger exchanges with participants about their activities in the fan community, in school, and at home. At the time, videoconferencing tools such as Skype were not readily available, so the interviews were conducted via Instant Messenger and were approximately one hour long. Given the choice, I would probably have used a combination of video and written exchanges with participants as this would have provided further insight into both their spoken and written ways of using English. The participants were formally interviewed twice during the study, with the first interview taking place three to six months after initial contact, and the second interview taking place approximately one year after the first interview. The interview protocols focused on participants' experiences with and impressions of fan fiction writing. This included questions about how they became interested in fan fiction, what types of fan fiction writing they engaged in, their reasons for writing fan fiction, and the role that participation in the fan community plays in their lives. Interviews also covered biographical topics, such as language background, experience with English, and home and family life, and included questions about how participants perceived the relationship between their fan fiction writing and school-based literacy activities.

DISCOURSE ANALYTIC APPROACHES TO ANALYSIS

Although the study focused on ELLs' access to affiliation with English language literacy in a broad sense, in this section I will focus on data analysis aimed at answering a subquestion that emerged during the study: *What kinds of "work" are writers and reviewers doing with their texts in this space?* Understanding the sort of linguistic, social, and identity work being done via texts was an integral component of understanding why these ELLs felt an affiliation with writing in this space, and for understanding how such textual work differed from academic literacy activities in schools.

In online spaces, multimodal discourse plays an important role in the "work" of designing identities and in having others recognize such identities. James Paul Gee's (1999) notion of big-D/little-d discourse is both a theory and method of analysis that is well-suited for understanding the social work being done via language. In Gee's construct, little-d discourse refers to language in everyday use, while big-D discourse refers to the ways that various semiotic (i.e., multimodal), material (e.g., clothing, tools, technologies), and expressive (e.g., paralinguistic cues, genre conventions) resources work in tandem with everyday language to help individuals "pull off" certain socially situated identities. In order to deepen my understandings of the ways that language was being used as part of social practice, I also incorporated elements of systemic functional linguistics. In particular,

I relied on Michael Halliday and Ruqaiya Hasan's (1985/89) detailed interrogations of the *speech function* that each utterance serves (e.g., requesting information [question], providing information [statement], demanding action [order]).

The data were analyzed as part of a cyclical process that involved several iterations of different stages of analysis. The first stage involved repeated reading and broad, descriptive coding of patterns that I noticed in the Fanfiction.net site texts. The main patterns that I looked for were aligned with what J. Amos Hatch (2002) suggests: Similarity (things that happen the same way), Difference (they happen in predictably different ways), Frequency (they happen often or seldom), Sequence (they happen in a certain order), Correspondence (they happen in relation to other activities or events), and Causation (one appears to cause another) (p. 155). The next stage involved coding for recurrent themes in fan texts and reader reviews of texts, as well as noting structural and generic (having to do with genre) patterns and characteristics of each of these types of fan texts.

In the next stage, I identified texts that were illustrative of certain patterns and broke these texts down into lines or "idea units" where each line introduced a new idea (see Gee, 1986, 1999). For example, the following statement, "Important note: English is my second language and I only spoken it for 2.5 years" would be broken down into two lines. The first would be "Important note: English is my second language," because it introduces the idea that the writer is an ELL. The second would be "and I only spoken it for 2.5 years" because it introduces related but distinct information about how long the writer has been learning English. In the next stage, lines were grouped into topical segments, or "sets of lines about a single minimal topic, organized rhythmically and syntactically so as to hang together in a particularly tight way" (Gee, 1999, p. 94). As an example, the following lines would be grouped into a stanza because they are all focused on thanking readers for their patience waiting for her chapter updates and explaining why it has taken her so long to write them.

L6 A/N: Konnichiwa minna-san!!
L7 I'm back! ^^
L8 Okie, I am trying my best to finish up this story,
L9 but I also have to have time to study for my exams. ><;;;;

It is also worth noting that at the time, I was dissatisfied with the user interfaces of existing qualitative research software programs and felt disconnected from my data when using them. Thus, I did the majority of the early coding for this project in *Microsoft Word*. This was a laborious process in which I entered each line of text into a table and coded to the right (see Table 8.1). Over time, however, this became too unwieldy, and I began using qualitative coding software. Not surprisingly, the software made it much easier for me to code larger amounts of text, keep track

Table 8.1. Example of early coding in Microsoft Word.

Text	Genre, Discourse, Style	Function
A/N: Konnichiwa minna-san!!	G: Author's Note, Japanese D: Fan community (interactive), Multicultural S: Informal, Enthusiastic	Greeting audience Affiliating with Japanese origins of anime Expressing enthusiasm
I'm back! ^^	G: Asian emoji D: Youth, Online chat, Multicultural S: Informal	Acknowledging delay in updates Affiliating with Japanese origins of anime
Okie, I am trying my best to finish up this story,	G: D: Writer duty to readers S: Informal	Mitigating complaints
but I also have to have time to study for my exams. ><;;;;	G: D: Youth, Online chat, multicultural, responsible student S: Informal	Explaining delay Expressing regret for delay (through crying emoji)

of my analytic notes, and identify patterns across my data (i.e., fan texts, reader reviews, interviews, field notes, analytic notes).

In the final stage of analysis, I developed a detailed typology of different kinds of social functions and meanings of these texts. Genre, discourse, and style are three particular types of meaning that can be used to understand how a text relates to the microcosm of a social event as well as the macrocosm of the broader cultural, political, and historical contexts in which that event happens (Fairclough, 2003). *Genres* are codified ways of conveying meaning in social events. Features of genre include the thematic structure of a text, cohesion devices, word choice, metaphorical language, politeness conventions, and interactional patterns (Fairclough, 2003; Rogers, 2004). In my study, repeated patterns of structuring fan fiction texts and conveying messages to readers would be coded as examples of genre. *Discourses* refer to ways of representing self, others, and the world (Fairclough, 2003). Features of discourse include themes, voices and perspectives, and ideologies of a text (Rogers, 2004). The ways that writers represented themselves as language learners, adolescents, and fans, as well as their beliefs about writing (e.g., writing as recursive, writing as fun) would be coded as examples of discourse. *Style* refers to ways of using language to align oneself with particular discourses and/or genres through linguistic features such as modality, transitivity, active and passive voice, and word choice. Language choice, social registers, and emojis would be coded as examples of style. To illustrate what this sort of analysis looks like, in the following section, an adapted version of speech function, and genre, discourse, and style is used to explore the sort of social and identity work that Grace, a focal participant from my study, was doing on Fanfiction.net.

WORKED EXAMPLE

Grace was a particularly prolific and popular fan fiction writer from the Philippines who had written many anime-based stories on Fanfiction.net since 2001. Grace considered Kapampangan her home language, but she also started learning Filipino, a standardized version of Tagalog, at a very young age, as it was required for most grade school activities in the Philippines. English, an official language of the country, was taught in school starting at around age seven years, and Grace primarily used English to participate in classes, to communicate with people online, and to write her fan fiction stories. The excerpt below is from *Heart Song*, one of Grace's popular *Card Captor Sakura* fan fictions that was first published in May 2001. *Card Captor Sakura* is a manga and anime series that centers on the adventures of a young Japanese girl named Sakura Kinomoto or Cherry Blossom.

The following excerpt contains two generic patterns, *headers* and *author's notes*, that can be found repeatedly in fan texts. Over the course of my analysis, it became clear that these generic elements were being used by authors to enact important social and identity work. Headers are included at the start of a fan fiction to provide readers with information about the content of the narrative, and they typically contain information such as media canon, story genre, age-appropriateness rating, romantic pairings, and warnings about material that readers might find objectionable (e.g., explicit content, character death). Author's notes (A/Ns) are messages from the writer to the reader that generically can be distinguished from headers by location (i.e., they commonly appear at the start or finish and sometimes within a story narrative), and by content (i.e., they usually contain information about the writers' thoughts and ideas on various topics). However, as can be seen in the following excerpt, this is not always a clean delineation; Grace integrates typical elements of a header with typical elements of an author's note in stanzas 1–6.

Stanza 1:
L1: I LOVE YOU SO MUCH PHILIP
L2: God HAS GIVEN YOU! and I REJOICE NOW FOR GOD HAS LEADME TO YOU :D

In this first stanza, Grace begins with a form of dedication as she acknowledges her love for her romantic partner and thanks God for bringing him into her life. At the level of style, Grace is indexing the importance of broader religious Discourses in her life, as evidenced by her emphatic use of caps and her word choice (i.e., God, rejoice). In addition, Grace aligns herself with youthful, online communicative Discourse with her use of an emoji.

Stanza 2:
L3: Disclaimer: all CCS [*Card Captor Sakura*] characters belongs to CLAMP

The second stanza is a copyright disclaimer, a genre element that appears with high frequency in fan fiction headers and author's notes. At the level of discourse, these disclaimers index the broader sociocultural and financial contexts in which fan fictions are situated in terms of debates over fair use of media content by fans and the intellectual property rights of corporations and copyright holders (Tushnet, 1997). In terms of function, these disclaimers attempt to head off any legal action on the part of Clamp, the copyright holder for *Card Captor Sakura*. At the level of style, Grace appears to be emphasizing Clamp's claim to the copyright through her use of caps.

Stanza 3:
L4: and English is not my FIRST LANGUAGE

This third stanza is also a generic element that appeared with some frequency in some ELLs' notes to readers. This sort of self-identification as an ELL does the work of shaping how readers approach the text and mitigating potential critique of the author's English writing skills. In addition, the stylistic use of capital letters worked in tandem with the words to highlight the importance of these words and garner understanding from readers.

Stanza 4:
L5: Note: another S+S fanfic..
L6: by Grace
L7: Yeah.. the Fastest/quickest
L8: and yet Poor english Writer from the Philippines..
L9: Sighs.. I hope i can handle uh.. 3 new fanfics at the same time …-.-

Stanza 4 contains a mixture of typical generic elements of fan fiction headers and author's notes. In addition, these lines do a great deal of social and identity work. Generically, the first line exemplifies a common practice for headers of explicitly marking the romantic pairing of couples within a fan fiction. The S+S denotes a romantic relationship between the characters Sakura Kinomoto and Syaoran Li, with the letters representing the first names of each character. Functionally, this does the work of warning off readers who may object to this pairing and, by proxy, attempting to avoid conflict and negative reviews. This is an important rhetorical move in a fan community where members may have strong investments in how characters are represented. At the levels of discourse and style, the first line indexes into the broader Discourse of fan communities and marks Grace's membership in this community with her use of the appropriate method for denoting pairings, and through her abbreviation of "fan fiction" to "fanfic."

Lines 7–9 contain some common elements of many ELL author's notes, and some elements that can be viewed as unique to Grace. In lines 7–8, Grace is indexing part of the larger Discourse of participation in the online fan fiction community. Specifically, in order to successfully attract and maintain a readership, fan authors must continuously update or add new chapters to their stories. In terms of style, lines 7–9 use modality (Sighs.. I hope, uh), word choice (Poor), and emojis (-.-) to align herself with this Discourse by acknowledging this responsibility to her fan readers and expressing concern about whether she will be able to meet her obligations in this regard. In addition, these lines do the social and identity work of eliciting support from readers who are implicitly being asked to refute Grace's claims that she is a poor writer and assure her that she will be able to handle the three new stories that she is working on. It is worth noting that analysis of reviews revealed that readers do respond to the content of these author's notes by providing the support and encouragement that was implicitly requested.

Stanza 5:
L10: Onegai!!!
L11: R+R please..
L12: I hope you enjoy this fic as much as you enjoy the rest of my fanfics!

Stanza 6:
L12: I am still doing the Many worlds in 1 world story keke
L13: I want to make the chapter 4 funny but its hard Demoo..
L14: I'll post it tomorrow okay?
L15: in the meantime just check out my other fanfics

The fifth and sixth stanzas are similar in terms of the linguistic work that they do. Specifically, they index Grace's membership in the youthful online fan fiction community by using R+R, which is the abbreviation for "Read and Review," and terms such as "fic" and "keke" (for okay), while at the same time eliciting feedback and support from readers by asking them to provide reviews and read her other stories while they wait for an update for her *Many Worlds in One World* story. Stylistically, Grace's use of the Japanese terms "Onegai" for *please* and "Demo" for *but* also align her with the transnational nature of anime-based fan fiction communities.

Stanza 7:
L16: Heart Song …
L17: Chapter One: The famous Cherry
L18: Ccs Fanfic by Grace
L19: All rights reserved on CLAMP

Stanza 8:
"PLEASE WELCOME.. OUR VERY OWN!! … CHERRY BLOSSOM!!!!"
The crowds went wild, when the lights went out and then they heard a voice …
"Aitai na Aenai na … Setsunai na … Kono kimochi …"
Then one by one light went on.. and they saw a shower of Cherry Blossoms.. the audience gasp.. then they heard a voice again …
"Ienai no. … Iitai no … Chansu.. nogashite bakari"
Then a little spotlight focus on a girl.. going down, up from the sky.. wearing a pink dress with wings on the back, and a cherry blossoms at her hair.. she is sitting on a gold swing
"Datte. … Datte … tsubasa hiroge futari de … Sora wo marason Yume wo yunizon shitai"
"WE LOVE YOU CHERRY!!!!"
The singer smiles at them, then when her feet touches the stage, she smiles and continues to sing the slow melody.. without music … "Hora Catch You Catch You Catch Me Catch Me Matte …"

Stanzas 7 and 8 are the beginning of Grace's fan fiction text. Stanza 7 introduces generic information about the text, such as title, chapter, and author, and includes an additional copyright disclaimer. In terms of genre, the story is a fan fiction "crossover" or a text that mixes media genres. As evidenced by the story excerpt in stanza 8, *Heartsong* is a songfiction, which incorporates lyrics of a song into the story narrative. Her text combined lyrics from different songs ranging from the Romaji (Romanized Japanese) version of the *Card Captor Sakura* movie soundtrack, to ballads by Angela Bofill, a Latina rhythm-and-blues artist, and Barbra Streisand, a U.S. singer, with textual elements based on the anime series.

Use of the critical discourse analysis constructs of genre, discourse, and style also provided insight into fan fiction writing as both a social and academically oriented practice. When I first submitted my analysis for publication in a journal, a helpful reviewer pushed me to revisit my analysis and deepen my understanding of critical discourse analysis and the social functions of language by looking at the tensions and synergies between the three constructs. When I revisited the analysis,

I found that my focal participants shared textual patterns that, at the levels of genre, discourse, and style, indexed certain types of identities as authors, readers, and views of writing. To illustrate, Grace represented herself as an ELL and a "Poor english Writer" (sic). By representing herself as a poor writer, Grace implicitly positioned readers as experts who might notice and provide feedback on how to improve her texts. And, as mentioned earlier, these types of statements also served a mitigating function, warding off excessive critique of her English language skills. This view of online fan fiction writing as an interactive, social endeavor also was reflected in Grace's linguistic style, as she used caps, punctuation, word choice, and emojis to set an informal, personal tone for her textual interactions with readers. However, as discussed in Black (2009), at the level of discourse, these lines can be seen as representing a tension between two potentially conflicting notions of writing. One view, often prioritized in traditional classrooms, is that of writing being about form, conventions, and correctness. In contrast, the other view is that of writing as being about function, communication, and message.

> The misalignment or inconsistency between the ways of interacting (genres), representing (discourses), and being (style) (Rogers, 2004) across these participants' texts suggests that while they implicitly referenced an assumed, academically-oriented discourse related to conventions and correctness in writing, through their genres and styles of writing, they actually were presenting a challenge to this notion by asking readers to judge their texts based primarily on meaning. (Black, 2009, p. 414)

In this way, fans used language or Discourse to create social spaces in which they, as ELLs, could still take on the identity of popular and successful writers whose texts were valued for function (e.g., interesting storylines) rather than just form (e.g., grammaticality).

THE ROLE OF THEORY IN INTERPRETING FINDINGS

At the start of this project, my interpretation of the findings was influenced both by my experiences as a classroom teacher and by my reading of insightful scholarly work that focused on comparing learning and participation in fan spaces to the sort of activities that take place in traditional classrooms (Alvermann & Hagood, 2000; Alvermann, Moon, & Hagood, 1999; Chandler Olcott & Mahar, 2003). Thus, I initially interpreted my findings through the lens of Second Language Acquisition theory and focused on how fan fiction writing provided focal participants with resources for print-based literacy and access to a writing community where they could improve their English language skills. For example, Grace was able to rely on a ready-made cast of characters and preconstructed settings from the anime series as a support when developing her own narratives in English. Through her interactions on Fanfiction.net, Grace was also able to practice her conventional and pragmatic aspects of English, experiment with different genres of writing, and gain a great deal of discourse or communicative competence in an informal register through her written exchanges with other fans. Such activities also enabled Grace to develop an identity as an accomplished author of English language texts. While literacy and language development remained an important component of my study, as my literature base expanded, my interpretive lens expanded with it. I began to see online fan fiction through the lens of new literacies and cultural studies, and as a practice with value in and of itself, rather than something that had value only if it contributed to ELLs' mastery of school-based literacy.

Henry Jenkins' (1992) foundational work on participatory fan culture helped me to think about how they challenge the notion of fans as solely passive consumers as they actively "poach" from mass media as a resource for their own textual exchanges and identity construction in online spaces. My focal participants leveraged popular media to construct stories that served several social functions. For example, fan fictions provided ELLs with social connection to a community of peers who shared their interest in a particular fandom. In addition, fan fictions provided a safe way for participants to explore deeply personal issues by ventriloquating these issues through the media characters (e.g., having an anime character experience heartbreak, or bullying, or social isolation in school) and eliciting responses and possible solutions to such issues from the audience.

Work in media and cultural studies also helped me to think about how the use of multiple languages and semiotic resources in fan texts referenced a larger discourse—that of the cosmopolitan (Jenkins, 2006), transnational (this term eventually replaced "multicultural" in my coding) nature of contemporary media and popular culture. Within the anime fan community, being an ELL of Asian descent often served as an additive component of identity (Black, 2005, 2006; Lam, 2000, 2006). By using Asian emojis, Japanese words, and multiple languages in their texts, focal participants like Grace were able to leverage their transcultural identities and multilingual skills to gain status within the community. In addition, they were able to create texts that became part of a broader, transcultural *mediascape* (Appadurai, 1996) and were taken up and used by other fans in their own creative works and the larger popular cultural imaginary.

Theoretical perspectives on new and digital literacies also provided useful insights into what I was seeing in my data. For example, writing and reading within the fan fiction community seemed to be illustrative of the participatory, collaborative, and networked "ethos" characterizing many contemporary digital spaces (Lankshear & Knobel, 2006). Stories on Fanfiction.net were often products of various forms of collaboration. Some fans would compose the narrative together, other fans worked in tandem with beta-readers (fans who act as a personal reviewer/editor for a text) in the development of their story. Other fan fictions were posted and revised repeatedly in response to feedback from the audience. Learning how to leverage the networked capabilities of the online platform was another important component of participation. For example, the most successful fan authors were effective at making personal connections with the audience, either by linking to or reviewing readers' stories, or by mentioning readers in author's notes. Focal participants who employed these strategies had thousands of reader reviews, which allowed them greater access to feedback on their writing and served as outside affirmation of their identities as successful writers. The digital medium also provided a range of opportunities for participation in this space. For example, anime fans who did not write stories could instead develop websites, create fan art, or provide reviews as a way of engaging with the community.

EXPLAINING WHY ANYONE SHOULD CARE ABOUT THIS WORK

Navigating the "so what" component of a study that bridges both traditional and novel forms of literacy learning is often a challenge. I am reluctant to provide "instructions" on how to integrate fan fiction and popular culture-related activities into a classroom because each learning context is quite different, and teachers are the best judges of what will or will not inspire and support their students' learning. Moreover, popular cultural preferences are highly subjective, so a fandom that inspires one student will be anathema to another. I am, however, also reluctant to simply provide a descriptive account of a setting where important forms of learning and literacy development are happening. So, the "so what" of my articles tends to be an attempt to connect what we know about learning theory and social development to my findings in a way that is balanced between prescriptive and descriptive.

As one example, analysis of Grace's and other focal participants' texts suggests that digital media and online spaces can provide ELLs with new contexts for developing what Wan Shun Eva Lam (2000) calls a "qualitatively different relationship" (p. 468) with English literacy that comes from being able to effectively express themselves online. Rather than using text solely to emulate preexisting genres and participate in concretized social patterns, the youth discussed in this study creatively employed language and other representational resources to enact cosmopolitan identities, make trans-border social connections, collaborate with other youth, experiment with new genres and formats for composing, and challenge traditional author/reader and producer/consumer distinctions. In these spaces, ELL youth's linguistic and cultural resources were viewed as a benefit rather than a deficit, and they were able to use a variety of communicative modes (text, image, emojis, etc.) to express themselves. Attending to such extracurricular activities can provide a richer picture of youth's literate lives and also can offer insight into ways to leverage such spaces and forms of expression in the service of more formal literacy and language learning goals. In addition, understanding youth's online activities can also shed light on the ways that young people do and do *not* productively and critically engage with the linguistic, cultural, and ideological materials that they encounter in global online spaces. As youth increasingly turn toward such spaces as sites for communication, socialization, and self-representation, it is crucial that we, as researchers and educators, attend to the ways in which new media and information and communication technologies may be influencing modern configurations of imagination, creativity, and communication in order to best support, extend, or constructively offer critique on both the positive and questionable aspects of such configurations.

In addition, online fan fiction spaces help us to understand that substantive literacy instruction does not need to focus on learning as an elite and solitary enterprise centered on authorized interpretations of canonical texts (Newkirk, 2000). Instead, print literacy can be made "more attractive and possible by being imbedded in systems that are, at least initially, more attractive to the learner" (Newkirk, 2000, p. 297). Such systems might include social scaffolds such as collaborative writing through networks or multimodal writing through digital literacy and online authoring software. Or, such systems might include a range of student-selected pop culture and current event-related topics in which all students, including ELLs, have a frame of reference and/or a measure of expertise. Choosing such topics can provide a departure point for authentic communication as students use and develop literacy skills to discuss and debate topics and display various forms of expertise in areas that are meaningful and relevant to their identities and social worlds.

ACKNOWLEDGMENTS

Portions of this chapter were adapted from Black (2007) and Black (2009).

REFERENCES

Alvermann, D., & Hagood, M. (2000). Fandom and critical media literacy. *Journal of Adolescent & Adult Literacy*, 43, 436–446.

Alvermann, D., Moon, J., & Hagood, M. (1999). *Popular culture in the classroom: Teaching and researching media literacy*. Newark, DE: International Reading Association.

Appadurai, A. (1996). *Modernity at large: Cultural dimensions of globalization*. Minneapolis: University of Minnesota Press.

Bazerman, C. (1989). *Shaping written knowledge*. Madison: University of Wisconsin Press.

Black, R. (2005). Access and affiliation: The literacy and composition practices of English language learners in an online fanfiction community. *Journal of Adolescent & Adult Literacy*, 49(2), 118–128.

Black, R. (2006). Language, literacy, and culture in online fanfiction. *E-learning*, 3(2), 170–184.

Black, R. (2007). Digital design: English language learners and reader reviews in online fiction. In M. Knobel & C. Lankshear (Eds.), *A new literacies sampler* (pp. 115–136). New York: Peter Lang.

Black, R. (2009). Online fanfiction, global identities, and imagination. *Research in the Teaching of English*, 43 (4), 397–425.

Cazden, C. (1988). *Classroom discourse: The language of teaching and learning*. Portsmouth, NH: Heinemann.

Chandler-Olcott, K., & Mahar, D. (2003). Adolescents' anime-inspired "fanfictions": An exploration of multiliteracies. *Journal of Adolescent & Adult Literacy*, 46, 556–566.

Coiro, J., Knobel, M., Lankshear, C., & Leu, D. (Eds.) (2008). *Handbook of research on new literacies*. Philadelphia, PA: Lawrence Erlbaum.

Cook-Gumperz, J. (Ed.) (1986). *The social construction of literacy*. Cambridge, UK: Cambridge University Press.

Facebook (2016). *Investor Relations*. Available from http://investor.fb.com/releasedetail.cfm?ReleaseID=967167.

Fairclough, N. (2003). *Analysing discourse: Textual analysis for social research*. London: Routledge.

Gee, J. (1986). Units in the production of narrative discourse. *Discourse Processes*, 9, 391–422.

Gee, J. (1987). "What is literacy?" *Teaching and Learning*, 2(1), 3–11.

Gee, J. (1999). *An introduction to discourse analysis*. London: Routledge.

Gee, J. (2004). *Situated language and learning: A critique of traditional schooling*. London: Routledge.

Graff, H. (1979). *The literacy myth: Literacy and social structure in the nineteenth-century city*. New York: Academic Press.

Halliday, M., & Hasan, R. (1985/89). *Language, context and text: Aspects of language in a social semiotic perspective*. Deakin University Press/Oxford University Press: Geelong/Oxford.

Hatch, J. A. (2002). *Doing qualitative research in educational settings*. Albany, NY: State University of New York Press.

Heath, S. (1983). *Ways with words: Language, life, and work in communities and classrooms*. Cambridge, UK: Cambridge University Press.

Hine, C. (2000). *Virtual ethnography*. London: Sage.

Jenkins, H. (1992). *Textual poachers: Television, fans, and participatory culture*. New York: Routledge.

Jenkins, H. (2006). *Convergence culture: Where old and new media collide*. New York: New York University Press.

Knobel, M., & Lankshear, C. (Eds.) (2007). *A new literacies sampler*. New York: Peter Lang.

Kist, W. (2004). *New literacies in action: Teaching and learning in multiple media*. New York: Teachers College Press.

Kress, G. (2003). *Literacy in the new media age*. London: Routledge.

Lam, W. S. E. (2000). Literacy and the design of the self: A case study of a teenager writing on the Internet. *TESOL Quarterly*, 34, 457–482.

Lam, W. S. E. (2006). Re-envisioning language, literacy, and the immigrant subject in new mediascapes. *Pedagogies: An International Journal*, 1(3), 171–195.

Lankshear, C. (1997). *Changing literacies*. Berkshire, UK: Open University Press.

Lankshear, C., & Knobel, M. (2003). *New literacies: Changing knowledge and classroom learning*. Maidenhead, UK: Open University Press.

Lankshear, C., & Knobel, M. (2006). *New literacies: Changing practices and classroom learning. 2nd ed.* Maidenhead, UK: Open University Press.

New London Group. (1996). A pedagogy of multiliteracies: Designing social futures. *Harvard Educational Review*, 66, 60–92.

Newkirk, T. (2000). Misreading masculinity: Speculations on the great gender gap in writing. *Language Arts,* 77(4), 294–300.

Rogers, R. (Ed.). (2004). *An introduction to critical discourse analysis in education.* Mahwah: Lawrence Erlbaum.

Scollon, R., & S. Scollon. (1981). *Narrative, literacy, and face in interethnic communication.* Norwood, NJ: Ablex.

Scribner, S., & Cole, M. (1981). *The psychology of literacy.* Cambridge, MA: Harvard University Press.

Street, B. (1984). *Literacy in theory and practice.* Cambridge, UK: Cambridge University Press.

Street, B. (1997). The implications of the "New Literacy Studies" for literacy education. *English in Education,* 31(3), 45–59.

Tushnet, R. (1997). Legal fictions: Copyright, fan fiction and a new common law. *Loyola of Los Angeles Entertainment Law Review,* 17, 641–86.

Wertsch, J. (1985). *Vygotsky and the social formation of mind.* Cambridge, MA: Harvard University Press.

Yin, R. (2003). *Case study research: Design and methods.* Thousand Oaks, CA: Sage.

CHAPTER NINE

Games, films, AND media literacy

Frameworks for multimodal analysis

ANDREW BURN

In common sense terms, films, animation, and computer games each have a singular, unified identity. This is true in popular discourse—but it is also often the case in academic film studies or game studies. Thus, it is common practice to maintain an idea of "the language of film," as if it were a single mode. Similarly, we might talk over the last forty years or so of the developing "grammar" of computer games, especially pertinent for games scholars whose origins are in philology, linguistics, or natural language programming in computer science.

Multimodal analysis places the emphasis rather differently on the wide range of modes these forms combine through digital media synthesized on single platforms both at the points of composition (e.g., digital editing software) and distribution (e.g., digital film projectors or videogame consoles). The object of the exercise is to discover what each of the modes (language, visual design, music, and so on) brings to the table, while also working out how the combined whole makes something we recognize as a film, or a videogame. Having done this, the researcher faces the really important "so what" question: what meanings are produced by these cultural productions, for whom, and in whose interest? What are the implications of such analysis for contemporary models of media literacy?

The approach adopted in this chapter is to consider the related forms of film, computer game, and machinima as relatively settled cultural forms characterized by particular clusters of modes and media—dynamically multimodal, yet sufficiently stable for successive generations of designers and audiences to share some kinds of knowledge about "filming and editing" or "game engine."

The approach to multimodality here is rooted in social semiotics. It emphasizes how moving image media use semiotic processes (organized sign systems) across different modes and media in order to fulfill particular social functions: to represent the world, to construct relations between social groups, and to communicate particular interests, ideas, and emotions.

FILM: THE KINEIKONIC MODE

The kineikonic mode is a designation for the moving image as a multimodal form (Burn, 2014; Burn & Parker, 2003). Kineikonic is a portmanteau of the Greek words for move and image: *kinein* and *eikon*, respectively. While this theory draws on many of the classic conceptions of filming and editing as semiotic processes (e.g., Barthes, 1978; Bordwell & Thompson, 2001; Metz, 1974), it recasts them as orchestrating modes: as framing structures which construct spatial and temporal shapes around the sounds and images produced by other modes (embodied action, speech, music, architecture, and so on), conceived of here as contributory modes.

It also presents the opportunity for a range of different analytical strategies. Three of these will be briefly outlined below with references to further reading; the third of these will be developed more fully as an example.

ANALYTICAL APPROACH 1: SPATIAL AND TEMPORAL SYNTAGMS

One approach possible through multimodal analysis is to disaggregate the spatial and temporal syntagms (a syntagm is a combination of signs, usually employing structures which make sense through a shared understanding between producer and audience, such as the grammar of language). In effect, the "eikonic" element of the kineikonic mode is the visual image.

Step 1: The "eikonic syntagm"

The first step proposed here is to isolate a single frame from the film being analyzed. Here, the structures identified by Gunther Kress and Theo van Leeuwen in *Reading Images* (1996) in relation to visual images apply. So the frame can be analyzed as a still image, identifying structures such as:

- Represented participants or characters, and the relationship between them in terms of implied action (realized as vectors), gaze, proximity and orientation to each other and the spectator, attributes (costume, hair, adornment, instruments)

- Location
- Lighting
- Construction of foreground and background, center and margin
- Construction of left and right, top and bottom
- Camera angle (vertical and horizontal)

Example 1. The example here is taken from Laurence Olivier's 1948 film, *Hamlet.* The scene shows Ophelia in her chamber. The scene represents her confusion about Hamlet's behavior, and how he apparently was succumbing to madness in the aftermath of his father's murder. Figure 9.1 shows a single frame, with Ophelia in the foreground and Hamlet emerging from an archway behind her.

The frame presents a two-part action sequence, the relation between the two characters set up by the forward movement of Hamlet (denoted by the feet and arms vectors) and the backward glance of Ophelia toward him. Ophelia's location in the foreground establishes a proximity with the viewer, echoed in the voiceover we will hear in the kinetic syntagm, in which she narrates the scene. We could go

Fig. 9.1. A still from Olivier's *Hamlet* (1948).

on to analyze the lighting, scenery, costumes, hairstyles, and colors, and other features of the image. In general terms, the image presents uncertainty: the lighting is ambiguous, coming from the rear left and the foreground right; Ophelia's facial expression depicts apprehension in its slight frown (again complemented by the interrogative tonal contours of her voiceover).

Step 2: The "kinetic syntagm."

The second step proposed here is to analyze a segment of the temporal sequence containing the single frame analyzed in Step 1. Here, a critical division is made between the image track and the audio track. These contain a variety of distinct modes, which will be explored in more detail in Step 3. The analysis of the temporal sequence at this stage, however, might include:

- Action (the development of the action implied by the vectors in the still image)
- Music
- Speech
- Temporal sequence: the contraction of time (ellipsis), the expansion of time (stretch), the reordering of time (analepsis and prolepsis—flashback and flashforward)
- Camera movement (tracking, tilting, zooming)
- Editing (shot construction and transitions)

Example 2. Figure 9.2 shows a digital editing timeline containing this scene.

The time indicator is paused on a dissolve effect, indicating a transition in the visual sequence. The transition is from a close-up of Ophelia's face in the center of the shot to the image represented in Figure 9.1, denoting a gradual shift from Ophelia as the only character in the scene to the two-character structure observed in Figure 9.1. However, as we add other features from the different modes into the analysis, the meanings become more complex, even contradictory. The effect of the dissolve can be considered, for example. What is its function? Why can the camera (or zoom) simply not move back gradually? In either case, camera move or shot change, the film is performing something not possible for the theatre-goer. Figure 9.1 might very well be an analysis of a moment from a stage-play: the camera-frame is performing a similar function to the proscenium arch; the modes in play are all those that can be found in theatre. In the moving sequence, however, the mobile camera performs exactly those shifts in point-of-view that the theatre spectator in their fixed seat cannot. The move—especially the dissolve, which has no equivalent in theatre—draws attention to the cinematic nature of the

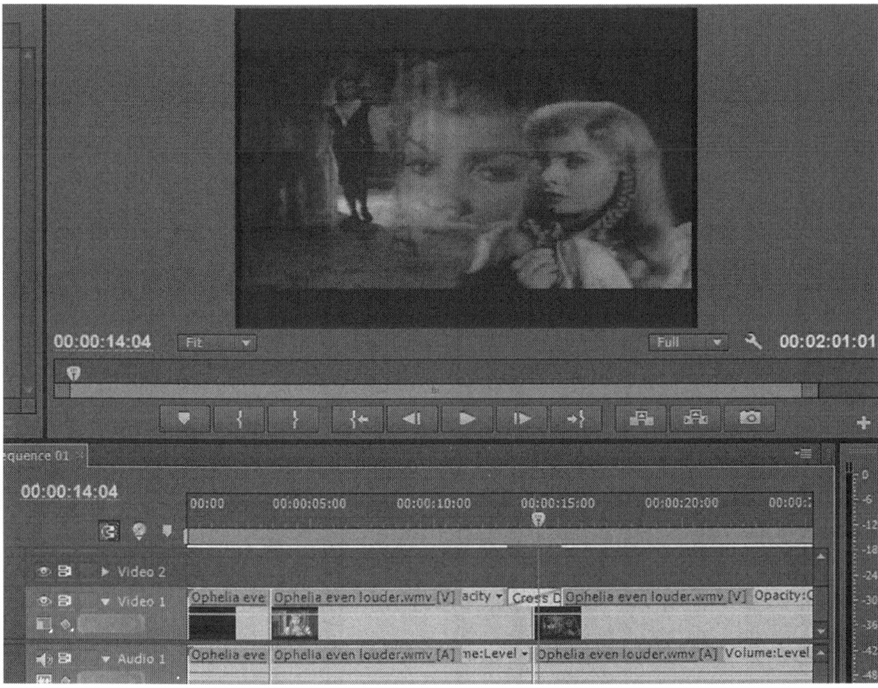

Fig. 9.2. Digital editing timeline.

sequence. We are reminded that this is a translation of William Shakespeare into the popular medium of film, a move that was controversial at the time of its production. Indeed, in the accompanying book (Cross, 1948), Olivier and his editor are adamant that their intention is to preserve the dramatic and poetic qualities of the play as they see them. Yet this scene is a good example of the new meanings conferred by the new medium. Indeed, the entire scene is transformed: it never takes place in the play at all, except as a narrated memory told by Ophelia to her father. Film allows the voiceover convention, the temporal framing of the scene so that we understand it is a flashback, and further laminations of image and sound, which, though not impossible in theatre, would be less likely.

ANALYTICAL APPROACH 2: THE METAMODAL KINEIKONIC

To look more closely at the interweaving of modes occurring here, this section presents a different analytical frame. *Metamodal* emphasizes the nesting of modes within modes in moving image texts. The prefix "meta-" is used to indicate "beyondness" and "adjacency"—cultural forms and modes within, beyond, and next to each other.

This model identifies *filming and editing* as orchestrating modes: the medium-specific meta-modes of the kineikonic. The process of filming and the process of editing effectively fall into two modes of design. *Filming* may resemble more the fluidity of speech; *editing* the fixity of writing. Filming produces spatial framing, angle, proximity, and camera movement and provisional duration, along with the orchestration of the "dramatic" modes: action, speech, set, and costume. Editing produces temporal framing, and the orchestration of other contributory modes, especially sound, music, and graphics.

In whichever way we approach the analysis of filming and editing, we must then consider the work of the contributory modes. This is not a new idea. For example, Roland Barthes, in his seminal work *Mythologies* (1957/1972), looks at a very specific aspect of Joseph Mankiewicz's 1953 film of Julius Caesar: the meaning of beads of sweat on the brow of Marlon Brando. This reminds us that the great signifying systems of language, painting, and music are not the only contributors to meaning: that a make-up artist dashing in to squeeze a drop of glycerin on Brando's forehead is part of the complex of contributory modes.

Each of the contributory modes breaks down into more specific signifying systems. Language breaks into speech and writing, and each into lexis and grammar; each of these categories further decomposes into specific resources, so that speech can be analyzed syntactically, lexically, metrically, phonologically, and in terms of features such as tone and tonicity (Halliday, 1985).

Dramatic action breaks down into gesture, itself further subdivisible into denotative, expressive, instrumental, symbolic, and other kinds of movement (cf. Kendon, 2004) such as facial expression, proxemics.

Music can be analyzed in terms of melody, tonality, harmony, rhythm, style, instrumentation, dynamics, and so on. As film theorists know, its function can be diegetic (music within the narrative) or non-diegetic (the more usual sonic coloring which we are encultured into accepting as part of an otherwise naturalistic mode of narrative). While it is often explained as an emotional accompaniment to film, it also has narrative properties, and, from a social semiotic point of view, carries particular social meanings (van Leeuwen, 1999).

A hierarchy can be constructed, then, from larger clusters of resources to minimal elements. The model shown in Figure 9.3 gives some idea of this, though it is indicative—many more semiotic resources are possible in individual moving image texts than can be represented here.

Step 1: Modal decomposition

One approach to the contributory modes, then, is decomposition: to break them down into progressively smaller resources, asking what the specialist role is of a

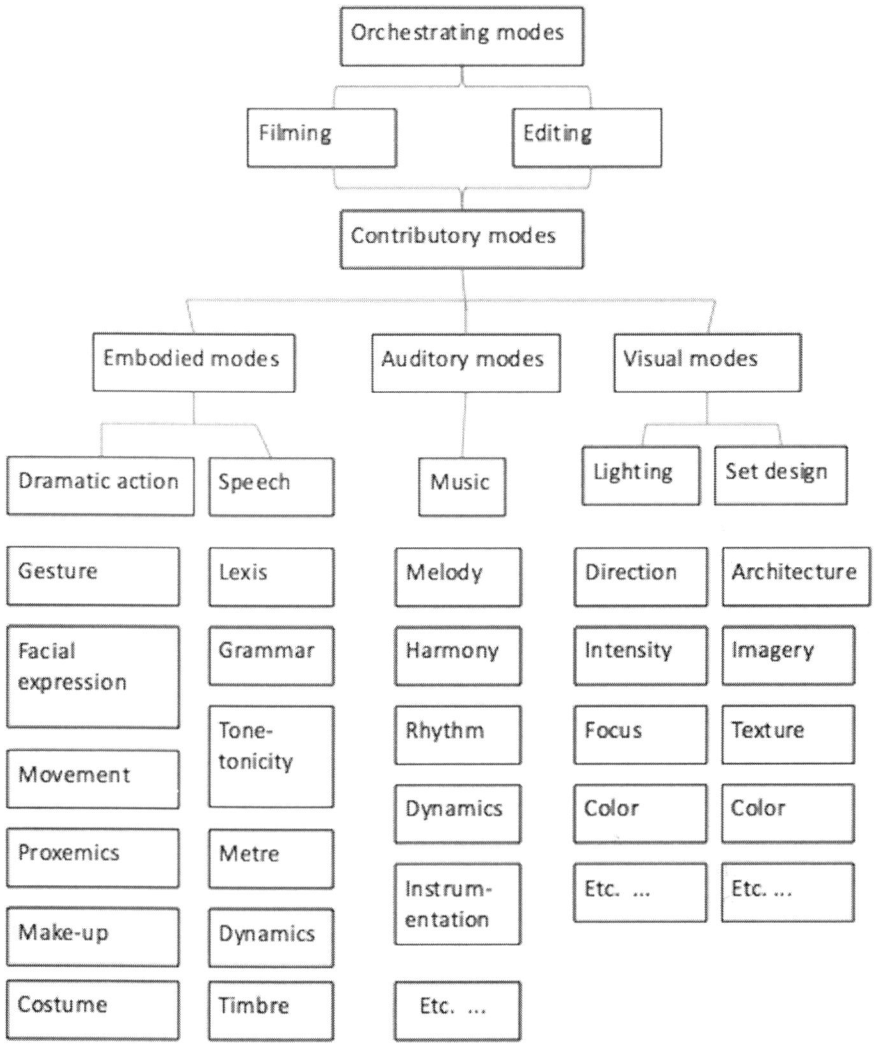

Fig. 9.3. Meta-modal structures.

particular resource. This may be because the researcher has a particular interest in the contribution of one or two modes: the music, or the language, for example.

Step 2: Intermodal functions

However, the distinctive insight offered by a multimodal approach is to see how the modes work together. Decomposition may be a valuable analytical route for some researchers; and all analysts need to decide at what level of granularity they want to work; but many researchers will want to look across and between modes, asking how they connect to make meanings, and what semiotic principles work across them. Some of the features of individual modes identified in Figure 9.3 are in fact applicable across many modes, as van Leeuwen's work on rhythm in music, speech, and editing amply demonstrates (van Leeuwen, 1985).

Example 3. Figure 9.4 shows a simple chart that transcribes the prominent modes in play in the *Hamlet* scene discussed earlier. The emphasis in this quite simple chart is on noting the modes and reading across them. No attempt is made to systematically represent space–time relations. The music column incorporates sections of William Walton's manuscript score for this scene.

Olivier was criticized for subordinating the high art of theatre to the popular form of cinema; but also for the opposite: producing cinema that was too "stagy." The effort to combine the forms can be seen in two decisions in this scene.

On the one hand, the scene is an example of Olivier's determination to fragment sequences of verse and drama as little as possible by cutting: it contains one of many very long shots in the film, which privilege dramatic continuity (in the same space and time) over cinematic continuity (constructed by editing shots to create the illusion of continuous space and time). Here, then, filming as an

SPEECH		MUSIC	ACTION	FILMING	EDITING
As I was sewing in my closet		Musical passage begins: D minor; low notes on 1st violin.	Sewing; raises head	Medium C/U; central framing	First shot of the sequence fades from black.
		1st violin passage continues.	Eyes move to L	Zoom to C/U	First shot
		1st violin passage continues.		Lighting dim to diffuse low-key	First shot
Lord *Hamlet* with his doublet all vnlac'd,		Insistent repeated phrases.	Head turn to L; Hamlet stands	Superimposed shot backlit; main shot still low-key-lit	Superimposition of long-shot of Hamlet; Fast dissolve to next shot
Pale as his shirt,		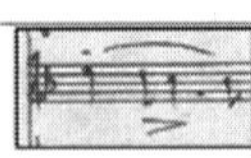 Falling phrase diminuendo	Hamlet walks forward	Wider two-shot (C/U and LS); key light raised; back and fill lights raised	Second shot continues ...

Fig. 9.4. Transcription of scene from *Hamlet* (1948).

orchestrating mode is used to promote the stage as the analogous orchestrating structure in theatre.

On the other hand, editing as orchestrating mode is used to provide a bracketing effect. Hamlet is introduced as a ghostly, superimposed figure (segment 4), suggesting both an otherworldly quality and that he is a product of her imagination or memory.

The introduction of the superimposed shot disrupts the apparent naturalism and theatrical continuity. Patrick Cook argues that this film, like the other three adaptations of Hamlet he considers, is firmly located in the mainstream "continuity" style of Western cinema, whose controlling aim is to efface the markers of fragmented space and time to produce the illusion of spatiotemporal continuity (Cook, 2012). The superimposition in this scene, however, disrupts this, briefly disorienting the viewer: is Hamlet in her mind, or in her chamber? And, in relation to constructions of cultural value in film aesthetics, is this a formulaic popular piece or an example of radical montage? The uncertainty not only testifies to the confusion felt at the time about how to view this piece of popular Shakespeare, but also indicates the fragility of such reductive cultural valuations.

Even this brief transcription draws attention to meanings beyond the scope of this chapter. For a fuller analysis of other modes and their interaction, including the language and verse of the dialogue, the music, and the embodied performance of the two actors, see Burn (2014).

MULTIMODALITY IN VIDEOGAMES

The cultural forms of theatre, cinema, and games are closely related. They all, for example, involve the depiction of imaginary worlds, narratives made up of dramatic action and role play, the combination of spatial and temporal structures of signification. They can be seen in terms of adaptation theory, which considers how narratives which might begin, for example, in literature, migrate across other media, and how they are transformed in the process.

In this case, the example used will be a sequence from a videogame adapted from Shakespeare's *Macbeth* by two 13-year-old girls. Before looking in detail at this sequence, it is worth briefly noting some of the possibilities for multimodal analysis of games.

ANALYTICAL APPROACH 1: PLAY, AVATARS, AND PERSON

In adventure games and role-playing games, the player typically adopts the character of the protagonist—the player-character, sometimes referred to as the avatar.

This is a good example of how the system of "person" which operates in the mode of language works differently in a computer game. The game presents itself in a kind of sustained second person, working through explicit or implicit offers and demands (you are in a gloomy dungeon; find the lost prisoner; will you take the left-hand corridor or the right-hand one?). The player is caught between a sense of first-person narrative (I *am* Harry Potter/James Bond/Gandalf), and can operate some functions in this mode; and a sense of third person, observing the avatar from outside the game, and not in control of some of its functions. For extended discussion of this in relation to Japanese role-playing games, see Diane Carr et al. (2006).

ANALYTICAL APPROACH 2: MODALITY IN GAMES

Like other moving image media, games often present a more or less naturalistic representation of a narrativized world, which may have cities, trees, lakes, people, and so on. Part of what makes it appealing is this naturalistic modality (Kress & van Leeuwen, 1996). Modality here (not to be confused with *multimodality*) means the claims made by the text to be true, authentic, valid, or credible, and how such claims are judged by the audience. The player may or may not find the streets, cars, water, and so on convincing—and as they explore the game, they will find other aspects of this naturalistic modality not available in films. They can, for example, experience the physics of this world—if they throw an object at a wall, it bounces off. However, modality in games is complex. The naturalistic representation of the city might suddenly be interrupted by a screen full of statistics—of health points, inventory possessions, levels, scores, and so on. This seems more like the kind of technological modality identified by Kress and van Leeuwen with maps, charts, and diagrams. But the player is of course not in the least disconcerted by this abrupt shift in modality. The interaction between this technological view of the game and the naturalistic view is learned within this genre, expected, and part of what makes the game authentic, believable, true to its genre. For an extended analysis of these kinds of modality in games, see Andrew Burn and David Parker (2003, Chapter 4).

ANALYTICAL APPROACH 3: COHERENCE AND COHESION IN VIDEOGAMES

These features of textual organization—how the text makes sense through the structures that "glue" it together—share some characteristics of coherence in language and other modes. The categories of cohesion identified by Michael Halliday and Ruqaiya Hasan (1976) are present, but require some adaptation. Their category of "reference," for example, operates across modes, as in any multimodal text. So a magic amulet might be represented by a phrase in a text box, by a character's speech, by an image, or by the 3D visual object itself; and the cohesion between these modes produces the aggregate meaning of the magic amulet. However, in the game, a further tie is present if the object is programmed to function in a particular way. If the player clicks on the amulet and it transports her to another place, then this additional cohesive tie, created through the procedural authoring of the game, provides an additional dimension, meaning, and function. For a detailed discussion of these forms of cohesion in videogame design, see Burn (2008).

ANALYTICAL APPROACH 4: CODE AS MODE

This approach looks at game design, rather than at the game as a played text. While many aspects of games can be analyzed in ways similar to those applied to film, looking at functions of the moving image, at systems of representation, and at structures such as point-of-view, the means by which the game is created requires another analytical move. Unlike literature, films, and theatre, videogames are computer programs, which work because they have been written as code. We need, as it were, to look under the bonnet of the car to see how this "engine" is put together (and the program running a game is referred to as a game engine). As Michael Mateas argues:

> Code is a kind of writing; just as literary scholars would not dream of reading translated glosses of work instead of reading the full work in its original language, so new media scholars must read code, not just at the simple level of primitive operations and control flow, but at the level of the procedural rhetoric, aesthetics and poetics encoded in a work. (Mateas, 2007, n.p.)

The programming of games occurs at different levels, however. At the root of any computer program is binary code, but this is not what programmers typically work in. They will use computer "languages" which make it easier and quicker to give the computer the necessary instructions. The more abstracted these languages become from the numerical base, the more "higher level" they are said to be. In the example below, the system for creating the rules which instruct the computer how to behave is not strictly a computer language at all, but a simple scripting system called a "rule editor." Children working with the game-authoring software construct three-part rules for every event in their game. A simple example might be "If the player | clicks the key | the door opens." These rules work like computer programming—they give the computer instructions. They also operate as procedural authoring: they devise a narrative sequence, which depends on the dynamic relationship between the human user and the program (Ferreira, 2015). The player may choose not to open the door, in which case the narrative will take a different turn. Or they may open the door, and the programmed sequence clicks into place.

The proposal here, then, is that "code"—whether it be binary code, a computer language, or a simple scripting tool like a rule editor—is a mode operating in videogames below the surface. It will have particular affordances, always related to the requirement that it resolve into numbers or on–off, true–false states. In the scripting tool used here, this is manifested in the conditionality of the rule—all rules are "if-clauses" in this particular case. The condition prescribed in the rule either will or will not be triggered. This translates into a very particular kind of narrative, characteristic of games: that is, the options available to the player.

Step 1: Identifying the code

The analyst applying this approach will need access to the design process. This may take different forms: observing the designers creating the game engine and its rules and algorithms; access to the design program itself; or the abstraction of the rules or a subset of them from the design process (as is the case in the example below). The analysis of advanced computer languages is beyond the scope of this chapter; rather, the example given will illustrate the broad principle of treating the code as a mode which orchestrates the other modes in play in the game (for a more detailed account of procedurality and multimodality, see Ferreira, 2015).

Step 2: Identifying the orchestrating functions of the code

The game engine orchestrates everything in the game, so some broad principles are necessary for the analyst's focus. Ultimately this will derive from the research question: the analyst may be interested in how much agency is afforded to the player; or in the behavior of the virtual world; or in the nature and meaning of combat sequences; or in the player's interactions with other players in avatar form, or with nonplayer characters, which are artificial intelligence entities functioning as characters in the narrative.

One focus might be derived from theories of play and game. One of the best-known and most frequently used models is the one elaborated by Roger Caillois in his book *Man, Play and Games* (2001/1958). Caillois presents six categories of play: Agon (competition); Alea (chance); Mimicry (role-play); Ilinx (vertigo); Ludus (rule-governed play); Paidia (loose, unstructured play).

So the analyst might be interested, for example, in the balance between Ludus and Paidia. Does the game tightly control the sequences of play—setting missions, for example, with clearly defined win–lose states? Or does it produce looser structures in which the player is free to wander, explore, socialize? So the analysis of the game engine would focus on how such states are prescribed. There might be a sequence of code, for example, which prescribes how much damage can be received by the player when attacked by an enemy within a mission, and what resources are made available for retaliation. Or there might be a sequence which prescribes how the game-world behaves in relation to how the player can move, what actions they can perform, what sensory experiences they can access, and so on.

Step 3: Relating the orchestrating and contributory modes

The analysis of the game engine can be related then to examples of play sequences. All media texts (indeed all forms of communication) present potential meanings, which wait to be actualized by a respondent's engagement. It is easy to forget this important point in the detailed business of textual analysis—but games remind us of it forcefully. A game engine is perhaps the most extreme version of a set of potential meanings, since the variations possible in play are limitless—not only in terms of interpretation, as is the case with literature or film, but in terms of the actual structure of the narrative sequence. Even where the narrative is tightly confined and prescriptive (often the case with games adapted from literature or film), the player may decide how long to take over certain events, where to look, how often to switch between play mode and statistics screen, and so on. So to explore the relation between the orchestrating mode of the code and the contributory modes of visual design, music, speech, virtual embodiment, and so on, a play sequence must be constructed and captured (e.g., by screen capture software) for analysis.

Example 1. This example is taken from a game made by two 13-year-old girls, in a project with Shakespeare's Globe to develop a game-authoring tool for Shakespeare plays based on the *Missionmaker* software. *Missionmaker* was developed by Immersive Education, and is now owned by MAGiCAL Projects at the University College London Institute of Education. The collaboration with Shakespeare's Globe, "Playing Shakespeare," was funded by the U.K.'s Arts and Humanities Research Council in 2012.

In the sequence discussed here, the player, as Macbeth, is able to kill King Duncan in his bedchamber. The task of the girls is to transform this event in the play into a game: to design a sequence in which the player has choices, multiple routes to follow, challenges to face, resources to meet them, and a win–lose state to complete the sequence. To do this, they create environments, characters, props, and so on, using prerendered assets available within the software. To some extent, we can use similar analytical methods to those outlined above for moving image texts. Games, at least graphical narrative games, share many properties with film: camera angle, framing, set, lighting, character behaviors and speech, and so on. There are differences, too, as noted in the brief suggestions made earlier in this section: the relation between the player and the characters is different, for example, so that the girls are really designing a kind of second-person offer and a first-person character. These are profound differences in the nature of games when compared to films.

Figure 9.5 shows the design screen of the two girls' *Macbeth* game. The large window shows the game world in design state, with the King Duncan character in the background. The transparent cylinder is a "trigger volume" invisible to the player—it is a programmed space, with a rule attached that specifies: "If the Player | enters the trigger volume | King Duncan wakes up."

The Rule Editor appears on the bottom left of the image. The rule active in the window specifies: "If Crown's state | becomes "owned by Player" | Player gets 600 Economy A points." The girls have programmed Economy A to be "Ambition," so that the player gains Ambition points, represented on a colored meter in the player interface, upon accomplishing particular tasks (an example of the "technological modality" described earlier).

The key characteristic of this procedural design is that it must produce conditionality—all programmed events depend on player interaction. This produces a particular kind of procedural narrative typical of videogames, and it can be analyzed in relation to the meanings of the game. In this case, for example, the player might choose to seize the crown after killing Duncan, eager to fulfill the ambition of the character, and hoping thereby to set in train a sequence of events leading to kingship—which could indeed be further programmed consequences in this case. Alternatively, the player might decide that they are overcome with remorse, and flee the scene, ignoring such rewards, and setting a different chain of events in motion.

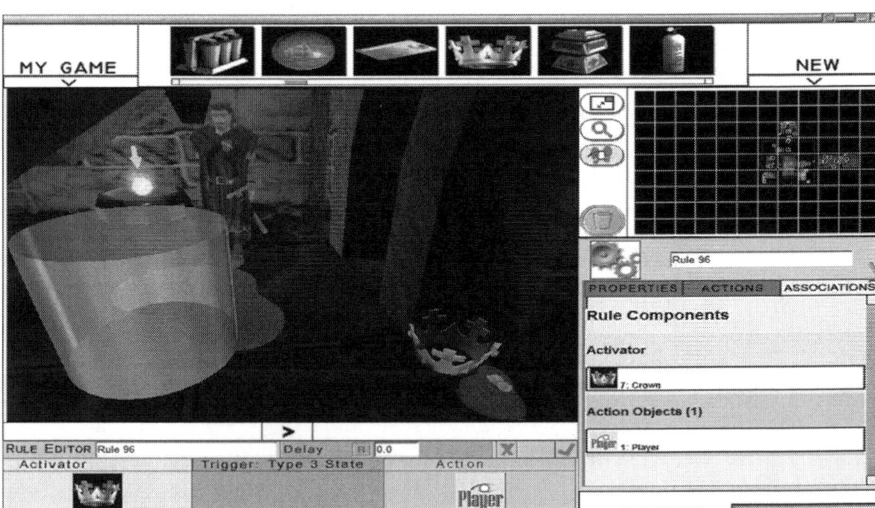

Fig. 9.5. The design interface of Missionmaker.

These articulations of rule-governed behaviors and multiple routes through a text are characteristic of procedural authoring. As a matter of interest, some argue that such procedurality is not unique to videogames, only that they produce the effect through the automated processes of the computers, thus allowing a quantitative leap in what is possible (Bogost, 2006; Ferreira, 2015). A closely related medium would be improvised theatre, in which actors might decide, from the resources available to them, to take one course of action or another (Boal, 1993).

The mode of code can be seen, as proposed in the case of filming and editing in the kineikonic mode, as the orchestrating mode of videogames. It creates the conditions which make the game possible; it determines how the game world and the characters within it can behave; it prescribes the options available to the player, extending or limiting their agency; it decides what sounds will play and under what conditions. It can be analyzed as a kind of language, especially since it is commonly expressed as a kind of language. However, as in the case of film, it needs to be articulated, in the analysis, with the other modes and clusters of modes nested within the game design. Just as in film texts, all the historic modes of theatre (action, speech, setting, music, light) are nested within the orchestrating structures of filming and editing, so, too, in games all the modes of drama and the moving image are nested within the procedural logic of the game engine.

One example of this is the way in which the two girls have inserted the witches from *Macbeth* into their game level. In their first design session, they showed a particular interest in the witches, seeing these as appealing fantasy figures who we might trace back to a rich vein of fantasy tales from fairytales and films that they had experienced. In Shakespeare's text, of course, the witches do not appear in the scene that the girls were assigned to adapt as a game level. Their solution is to bring the witches back into the murder scene, where they work as a reminder to the player of the witches' earlier prophecies and their consequences. These witches also provide the girls with satisfaction through their uncanny presence, which they represent by a combination of three character models from the software: an old woman's head, a female superhero's torso, and an alien creature's legs. The software allows the user to recombine the heads, legs, and torsos of the character models, as in the popular children's picture books where similar effects are produced by flipping the three sections of the pages. The girls also attach particular special effects to these models: to one, an animation of fire; to another an animation of rain. These elemental attributes, which are not part of the Shakespeare play, nevertheless lend an archaic, magical quality to the characters.

In addition, the girls' design for the witches incorporates their own voices, making the witches speak prophecies as the models lip-synch the girls' speech. This is the only place in the game where the girls use their own voices. Elsewhere, for Lady Macbeth and King Duncan, they use the prerecorded voices of professional actors. This choice suggests a particular motivation: to express empathy with the characters they are creating. Media literacy in this case is a multimodal combination of the virtual embodiment of the animated game characters with the actual voices of the girls as a dramatic performance, and the rules that the girls create to trigger the witches' speeches when a player walks into the invisible trigger volume. The media-literate practices consist of an association between the aspects of real and virtual embodiment (image and voice), and a subjective engagement with the fiction created by the teenage authors of the game and its players.

MACHINIMA

Machinima is a portmanteau word combining machine and cinema, implying animation and anime. It is defined by Matt Kelland et al. as "the art of making animated films within a realtime 3-D environment" (2005, p. 10). It can be thought of as animation made from the 3D environments and animated characters of computer games or virtual immersive worlds. The first machinima films were produced by players of the game *Quake* in the mid-1990s.

Analysis here must pay attention to the nature of the virtual world from which the machinima text was created: its construction, behaviors, affordances, and cultures. While in many ways machinima resembles any other film or animation, the elements within it are differently created.

The characters, for example, are digital characters made possible by the virtual world or software, and typically have a set of specific shapes that can then be customized by the player. In this sense, they are more like actors dressing up for a role, with costumes, wigs, ornamentation, make-up, and so on, than like animated characters which are drawn by the animator. Similarly, their movement is nothing like the frame-based motion created in traditional stop-frame animation. Instead, they will employ the animations provided by the software, allowing them to walk or run, dance or fight, fly or swim.

The metaphor adopted for this form of animation, then, is *lamination*. Lamination characterizes a particular thread in the history of the moving image, beginning with the superimposition of images through double exposure in photography, continuing through the forms of fantastic, magical animation exemplified by film-makers like Georges Méliès, and now evident in the practices of cinema effects, game design, and 3D animation.

Step 1: Identifying the laminates

The laminated layers are oriented to particular modes, so to identify them involves the kind of modal disaggregation employed in the first example in this chapter, most easily accomplished through a simple transcription table. This allows the analyst to select which modes and intermodal relations will best address the research questions.

The modes are layered over each other, as shown in Figure 9.6.

Fig. 9.6. Modal laminates.

So in any given sequence of the film, these laminates will appear. They are representational layers—layers of meaning—but also digital layers, which can be delaminated for editing (as appears in the example below), or for analysis.

Step 2: Drilling through the layers

Behind each layer, as it were, the production process exists in a further series of layers. To select character design as an example, the machinimator will need to begin by selecting a character template, then customize it with clothing, make-up, tattoos, spectacles, and so on; then make it speak, employ whatever animations for facial expressions and action are available, film it with the virtual camera available in the software, and finally edit it in much the same way as any other film. Figure 9.7 shows these production laminates. In selecting these and analyzing them in detail, the researcher may wish to explore the social motivations for the designs, and the meanings these contribute to the final animated film.

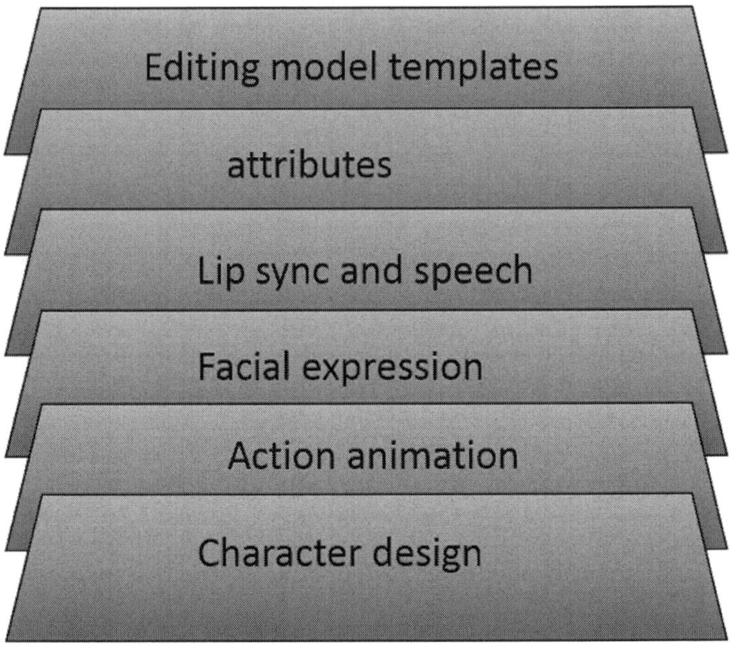

Fig. 9.7. Production laminate.

Example 1. This comes from an animated film made by a group of 11-year-old children, *The Moonstone*. (This 2012 project, "Montage, Mash-up, Machinima," was a collaboration with the British Film Institute and Moviestorm Ltd., and was funded by First Light.) This animated film presents the tale of a teenage girl, Lily, whose parents were lost in a plane crash. She sets out to find them with her grandmother and a strange Indian guide. He turns out to be a "good" werewolf, locked in combat with an evil werewolf. Lily helps him overcome his curse, beat the evil counterpart, and find her parents.

The children volunteered for four different design groups: set, character, voice acting, and music.

Finally, the class worked in pairs, each taking responsibility for a short section of the film. This involved drawing on the shared assets and using the 3D animation software, *Moviestorm*, to animate the characters through the action, attach dialogue, and construct shots and camera angles.

One instance from the making of *The Moonstone* film will serve as a detailed example of the nature of multimodal design in this project. It is a brief scene from the opening minute, in which the heroine, Lily, answers the door of her house to see a police officer who has the difficult task of breaking the news that her parents' plane has crashed. The visual scene is designed by two girls, working with three sets of resources: the set design of Lily's house and the street beyond it; the characters (Lily, her friend, and the policeman); and the prerecorded voice-acting of the children playing the parts of the three characters. Table 9.1 shows how the girls have constructed the sequence as four shots.

Table 9.1. Multimodal Analysis of Lily and the Policeman.

Shot	Framing and Camera	Action	Speech	Gesture	Face	Music
1	Mid two-shot (Lily and friend)from behind Lily	Lily goes to open door		Door opens	(Back of head)	Guitar and bass loop
2	Close-up two-shot (Lily and officer) from behind Lily	Lily opens door, revealing officer	Officer: "Is one of you Lily Woods?" Lily: "Yes, that's me"	Officer waves right arm	Officer's face neutral	Solo violin descending minor arpeggios
3	Extreme close-up (officer's face); camera pulls back to close-up (head and shoulders)	Officer gives the news	Officer: "Well, um, I've, I've come to tell you that [pause] the plane that your mum and dad were on has crashed, or has gone missing–"	Officer bows head and raises it again	Officer's eyebrows raise in the center, eyes widen	Violin continues …
4	Mid two-shot reaction (Lily and friend)	Lily weeps, comforted by friend	"– over the National forest".	Lily covers face; she and friend turn to each other	Lily's eyebrows raise; mouth turns down	Violin continues …

This transcription identifies the laminates and allows the first-stage analysis of the modes in operation to be conducted. The next stage of analysis drills down into three of these laminates: speech, facial expression (character design), and music.

Laminate 1: Speech. The voice of the policeman is acted by a boy, who described in an interview the specific function of the role, and explained the emotional nature of his part:

> *It's a bit upsetting to tell someone that their parents might be dead …*

And, drawing on his experience of an afterschool drama club, he describes the dramatic element in film:

> *Well in drama you have to use your face and your body, body language, and facial expressions: and in animated films you always also do that.*

His job is that of the traditional voiceover artist. From Disney through to Pixar, voiceover acting is recorded in advance, and the animation made to fit the voice, rather than the other way round. In multimodal terms, the modes of voice and body action, unified in "live" drama, are segregated, and put back together in postproduction. The voice retains its nature as dramatic performance, an embodied realization of character through intonation, dynamics of tempo and volume, and vocal timbre. By contrast, physical action, gesture, and facial expression are designed visually as a simulation of performance. Nevertheless, the boy is aware of the relationship between the modes: that fictional narratives in film involve the same kind of embodied expression as drama. From a multimodal point of view, then, media literacy cannot be separated from the expressive modes of dramatic action and vocal performance.

These insights have a particular significance in the pedagogy of media education and the development of media literacy. The fragmentation of the curriculum into subject domains cuts across the multimodal relationships of authentic cultural forms like film and games, and each domain tends to privilege its own modes. Media education (like film and media studies in Higher Education) may emphasize the orchestrating modes of filming and editing, and underemphasize important contributory modes such as dramatic action and voice. This constrained emphasis may occur in the day-to-day creative production work of teachers and children at least in part as a result of the conceptual frameworks they inherit from curriculum and examination designers. Nevertheless, it is not the case that specialist expertise should be abandoned. Film educators are necessarily expert in the art of filming and editing; music educators in melody and harmony; drama educators in embodied action and voice. It is a question of how each can become sufficiently aware of each other's domains, sufficiently collaborative at the right moment, and sufficiently creative in overcoming subject domain divisions.

Analysis of the boy's vocal performance shows that he delivers the lines with appropriate choice of intonation, volume, and pace. Although the lines are scripted, he introduces three hesitation indicators: "um," a repetition of "I've," and a pause (Table 9.1, Shot 3)—an improvised performance of the anxiety implied by the narrative.

Laminate 2: Character design. Another student has been responsible for building Lily and the police officer, using the layers of composition in *Moviestorm* to construct face shape, hair, eyes, eyebrows, nose, mouth, and clothing. The job of the girls here is to build the moving image sequence on the editing track of the software: organizing it into shots, reframing the image with a virtual camera to change point-of-view, shot distance, angle, camera movement, deciding how to represent actions and speech. In many ways, this orchestrating work of the mode of editing is similar to such work in conventional film. It involves, for example, learning the purpose and structure of shot-reverse-shot sequences to represent conversation (Burn, 2014).

However, the nature both of machinima and of this particular authoring tool, *Moviestorm*, produces some differences both from live action film and from conventional animation. The girls viewed the sequence in the rough edit of the whole film, and noticed that the policeman's expression did not convey the appropriate sentiment for his words. Aware of the mismatch between the modes, they amended the facial expression of the police officer, going into the relevant *Moviestorm* menus to find the slider tools to change the eyes, mouth, and eyebrows:

> when the policeman was telling Lily that her parents had gone missing then he was just like standing there with a really straight face and just saying sort of "I'm sorry your parents have gone missing" … and then we had to, we went on the mood bit [makes gesture of sliding from left to right] and then we, cos there's only like a few bits like sad, angry, and happy, romantic and stuff, went on the advanced one and we made him more sad and more sort of, with the wiggly faced one.

In terms of the kineikonic mode, this piece of compositional redrafting is distinctively digital. It would not be possible in live action film without reshooting part of the scene; nor in cel animation without redrawing the cels. Nor would it be possible in conventional machinima without reenacting the sequence with the virtual actors in the virtual world. However, the machinima here is really a blend of machinima and 3D animation, and has the options of 3D animation to rework the character on the fly, digging through the laminates to the layers that need adjusting. In semiotic terms, it consists of reworking the kineikonic syntagm (the plane of combination) through paradigmatic substitution (the plane of selection), making a closer intermodal match between the sorrowful intonation of the vocal track and the relevant parts of the facial expression. There is a selection of paradigmatic elements in play: replacing, in this child's words, "straight" with "sad," and working with a finer granularity of individual features. Such adjustments have similarities to the adjustment of lighting, audio volume, shot angle, and so on in the semiotics of film, in that they are distributed across a numerical scale. The film semiotician Christian Metz argued that such elements could not properly be considered part of the "grammar" of film, since they were continuous scales rather than discrete paradigmatic elements (Metz, 1974). However, we may dispute this because of the perceptions of the human signmakers, and the ways in which they realize degrees of the scale in language. This produces something more like paradigmatic choices: camera angles, though adjustable on a continuous scale, become low shot, high shot, bird's-eye shot, and so on. Lighting becomes high or low, hard or soft, top or below, key, fill, or back. Similarly, in these girls' choices, the slider scale filter for the policeman's eyebrows represents choices between neutral and sad.

Another point is worth mentioning. Since this is a digital medium, all choices at one level resolve into numerical ones. As Lev Manovich points out, this is one of the true distinguishing features of digital media (Manovich, 2001). However, once again, in terms of the interest of the signmaker (Kress & van Leeuwen, 1996), this numerical scale is transformed into paradigmatic choice. The child is interested in manipulating the representation of affect, and making a match between the modes of speech and virtual embodiment. In cultural terms, as noted above, we can see that the analogies are with similar activities in previously encountered virtual worlds which children have engaged with, such as *The Sims*, and, as Jackie Marsh observes, a range of other online virtual worlds including *Club Penguin*, *Neopets*, *Moshi Monsters*, and *Habbo Hotel* (Marsh, 2014).

In the context of the history of the moving image, these practices evolve from a different source than the emergence of film from stage drama, or the conception of film as a documentary record. Rather, the culture and practice of animation in early cinema derives from traditions of illusion, magic, "trick" photography such as double exposure, and their associated practices of overlay, lamination, filtering, and deceptive use of light.

In these children's machinima film, these practices are still apparent. The appeal of animation is its readiness to represent the "impossible image": fantasy elements of werewolf transformation, science fiction, time travel, and videogame play between virtual and "real" life.

Laminate 3: Music. The final layer to consider is the music layer. The music was composed by another group, using acoustic guitar, synthesized electric bass, and violin. The first sequence is a two-bar finger-picked ostinato, or repeated melodic pattern, with a bass line that suggests minor chords. The use of ostinato in film music can provide a dynamic, driving, insistent quality; or it can stabilize, even lead to monotony. Such ambiguity is well suited to this scene: the effect is of muted disquiet, appropriate for the dramatic mood of the piece, and anticipatory of the bad news to come (Figure 9.8).

The second sequence, which begins as the policeman starts speaking, is a soulful descending series of violin notes in a minor key. Minor keys traditionally signify sadness, while the melodic descent happens in steps: each bar descends, rises a little in the successive bar before descending further, and so on, so that an effect of a struggle against descent is conveyed. It has a baroque quality, accentuated by a trill on the penultimate note, a typical ornament of the baroque, suggestive

Fig. 9.8. The ostinato sequence accompanying Shot 1.

Fig. 9.9. The solo violin sequence accompanying shots 2–4.

of emotion (as in the music of Bach) (Figure 9.9). Here, the clear intention is to convey the tragic quality of the policeman's message.

The music is performing a range of functions in this sequence. The loop structure of the ostinato in the first section is reminiscent of videogames and the unpredictable duration of their game-play sequences. It also indicates the tension between the girls' (i.e., Lily and her friend) ordinary evening at home and the growing anxiety caused by the parents' lateness.

The abrupt shift into the tragic, legato (smoothly flowing) scales of the violin complements the policeman's message. The tonality of the violin, the downward trajectory of the arpeggios, and the minor key all work to emphasize the affective charge of the boy's performance, and the linguistic elements of the policeman's message.

This detailed analysis of the specific layers of vocal performance, visual design, and music composition reveals two orientations in terms of the semiotics of the moving image and its "technologies of inscription," or material media (Kress & van Leeuwen, 1996). One orientation is toward the traditional lamination processes of animation, as discussed in the earlier sections of this chapter: the bifurcation of vocal and bodily performance; the layering of visual imagery to produce the "impossible image"; and the additional layer of musical signification, common in moving image culture since its inception. The other orientation is toward the "language of new media": to the digital laminates of filters; the numerical scales of image adjustment and the new paradigmatic choices they produce; and to the playful compositional regimes of videogames and virtual worlds. We have also seen how this mix of practices requires the collaboration of educators with different specialisms across the arts: drama, literacy, music, media education, and ICT.

CONCLUSION: FROM TEXT TO CONTEXT

This chapter has focused on the textual analysis of three quite different moving image texts. While each requires some degree of specialized analytical approach, they share many features, and thus invite a number of common principles of analysis. Most obviously, these are the ways in which they integrate the visual modes orientated to spatial logics, and the auditory modes orientated to temporal logics. This chapter has proposed in addition a metamodal approach, in which dominant processes of framing in space and time, realized in film as filming and editing, and in games as code, can be analyzed in relation to the modes they orchestrate.

The models proposed here also attend to the nature of digital composition: to the realization of modes as elements of digital editing timelines; to the digital code underlying game sequences; to the digital laminates overlaid on each other to create the actions and expressivity of machinima and 3D animation more generally.

These aspects of media texts also imply, as the game and machinima examples showed, an expanded model of media literacy and by the same token media education. Media literacy is multimodal, and cannot be constrained to a narrow focus on the orchestrating modes of filming and editing, but must connect with the modes of dramatic performance and computer code.

There remains a cautionary note. The texts explored here, like all text, remain systems of potential meaning until someone actually views or plays them. At this point, the research methodology must find ways to analyze the meanings made in this negotiation between film and spectator, game and player. Similarly, however, the production process cannot be fully deduced from the textual elements themselves. In the examples provided above, the researcher has talked to the producers or read their accounts to seek explanations and evidence of the sign-maker's motivation in their discourse. Methodologically, this requires some form of multimodal discourse analysis beyond the scope of this chapter (e.g., Burn & Parker, 2003, Chapter 5). Researchers in this field are urged to ask always what is significant about the meanings produced by the analysis; how they are situated in their sociocultural context;

whose interests they serve. A simple but effective set of reminders, and a good way to end any chapter on multimodal methodologies, is the design analysis framework proposed by Mary Kalantzis and Bill Cope (2012, p. 200):

1. Reference: What do the meanings refer to?
2. Interaction: How do the meanings connect the people who are communicating?
3. Composition: How does the overall meaning hold together?
4. Context: Where are the meanings situated?
5. Purpose: Whose interests do these meanings serve?

REFERENCES

Barthes, R. (1957/1972). *Mythologies*, translated by Annette Lavers, New York: Hill and Wang.

Barthes, R. (1978). *Image-music-text* (trans. S. Heath). New York: Hill and Wang.

Boal, A. (1993). *Theatre of the oppressed*. New York: Theatre Communications Group.

Bogost, I. (2006). *Unit operations: An approach to videogame criticism*. Cambridge MA: MIT Press.

Bordwell, D., & Thompson, K. (2001). *Film art: An introduction* (6th ed.). New York: McGraw-Hill.

Burn, A. (2008). The case of *Rebellion*: researching multimodal texts. In J. Coiro, M. Knobel, C. Lankshear, & D. Leu (Eds.), *The handbook of research in new literacies* (pp. 149–177). New York: Laurence Erlbaum.

Burn, A. (2014). The kineikonic mode: Towards a multimodal approach to moving image media. In C. Jewitt (Ed.), *The Routledge handbook of multimodal analysis* (pp. 375–385). (2nd ed.) London: Routledge.

Burn, A., & Durran, J. (2013). Playing Shakespeare: Macbeth—narrative, drama, game. *Teaching English*, 1, 1–4.

Burn, A., & Parker, D. (2003). *Analysing media texts*. London: Continuum

Caillois, R. (2001/1958). *Man, play and games* (M. Barash, Trans.). Champaign: University of Illinois Press.

Carr, D., Buckingham, D., Burn, A., & Schott, G. (2006). *Computer games: Text, narrative, play*. Cambridge, UK: Polity.

Cook, P. (2011). *Cinematic Hamlet: The films of Olivier, Zeffirelli, Branagh and Almereyda*. Athens, OH: Ohio University Press.

Cross, B. (Ed.) (1948). *The film Hamlet*. London: Saturn Press.

Ferreira, D. (2015). The meaning potential of procedurality: Initial considerations on procedural semiotic resources. Working paper. DARE, UCL Institute of Education. Available from: http://www.7luas.com.br/all/research/articles/the-meaning-potential-of-procedurality/comment-page-1/

Halliday, M. (1985). *An introduction to functional grammar*. London: Arnold.

Halliday, M., & Hasan, R. (1976). *Cohesion in English*. London: Longman.

Kalantzis, M., & Cope, B. (2012). *Literacies*. New York: Cambridge University Press.

Kelland, M., Morris, M., & Lloyd, D. (2005). *Machinima*. London: Course Technology PTR.

Kendon, A. (2004). *Gesture: Visible action as utterance*. Cambridge, UK: Cambridge University Press.

Kress, K. & van Leeuwen, T. (1996) *Reading images: The grammar of visual design*. London: Routledge.

Manovich, L. (2001). *The language of new media*. Cambridge MA: MIT Press.

Marsh, J. (2014). The relationship between online and offline play: Friendship and exclusion. In A. Burn & C. Richards (Eds.), *Children's games in the new media age* (pp. 109–132). Farnham, UK: Ashgate.

Mateas, M. (2007). *Procedural literacy: Educating the new media practitioner*. Pittsburgh, PA: ETC Press, Carnegie Mellon University. Available from: http://press.etc.cmu.edu/node/205

Metz, C. (1974). *Film language*. Chicago IL: Chicago University Press

van Leeuwen, T. (1985). Rhythmic structure of the film text. In T. van Dijk (Ed.), *Discourse and communication* (pp. 216–232). Berlin: de Gruyter.

van Leeuwen, T. (1999). *Speech, music, sound*. London: Macmillan

CHAPTER TEN

Connecting content coding AND Discourse analysis TO investigate online affinity spaces

SEAN C. DUNCAN

In the study of games and learning, much time and effort have been devoted to understanding games *for* learning and games *as* learning. This reflects a way of thinking about games as tools to employ in crafting learning environments or as a basis for critical calls to change institutional education (Duncan, 2016). In both of these traditions, games have been seen as technological artifacts that can, through their effective design, "deliver something," such as content to learners, a means for assessing learning, scaffolding important practices, or even providing researchers with "data exhausts" (Steinkuehler & Squire, 2014) to fuel learning analytic/educational data mining systems. Games are, for many, technical systems first and foremost, with their roles as cultural touchstones and *media* often sidelined in favor of the goals of furthering educational design.

And yet, there has been a significant but understudied alternate tradition that focuses on games in the world, and understanding how learning may be embedded in the fan practices around games. James Paul Gee coined the term "affinity space" (Gee, 2004, 2005) to describe typically virtual, online spaces wherein *ad hoc* learning communities form around shared interests and passions (ranging from practices, such as knitting to digital games, such as *World of Warcraft*, to media fandom, such as *Star Trek*). In Gee's affinity space notion, at least in its earliest conceptions, "affinity spaces" were often synonymous with "online forum discussions" around games, televisual media, or other interest-driven topics. Focusing mostly on the forum discussions associated with commercial games, researchers have duly investigated the concept of affinity space in multiple forms, across many games (e.g.,

Civilization, *Dance Dance Revolution*, *World of Warcraft*; Hayes & Duncan, 2012), as well as around nongaming media (e.g., *NeoPets*, *The Hunger Games*; Lammers, Curwood, & Magnifico, 2012). Because the affinity space concept is fluid and has changed quite a bit in the past decade, it is still up for grabs as to which approaches might yield the most fruit in helping us to analyze learning within these spaces.

There have been discussions of methodological concerns in investigating learning within affinity spaces (see Lammers, Curwood, & Magnifico, 2012, for example), but, as yet, there has not been any significant step-by-step discussion of scholarly ways of characterizing, understanding, and tracking practices within affinity spaces. In this chapter, I will attempt to do just that, focusing on three cases—three connected studies of different sets of gaming affinity spaces—drawn from work I have either been involved in or directed over the past decade. I intend to build an argument not only for how affinity spaces can be studied, but to outline a specific mixed-methodology approach that can leverage the benefits of quantitative analyses as well as qualitative approaches. I begin with early content coding approaches to analyzing affinity spaces (based on the informal scientific reasoning emphasis presented in Steinkuehler & Duncan, 2008), then describe subsequent work that attempted to meaningfully tie content coding methods to Discourse analysis (Duncan, 2010a). Finally, I will discuss recent innovations and challenges in revising the method I've implemented in order to deal with structural and interactional changes that have accrued within online discussion spaces since these studies began.

INVESTIGATING INFORMAL SCIENTIFIC REASONING

The first case is one where we attempted to create a data coding scheme to describe and analyze "scientific" practices within online affinity spaces. The impetus for this work initially came from Constance Steinkuehler and Marjee Chmiel's (2006) pilot study of informal scientific reasoning within *World of Warcraft* forums, wherein they focused on discussion spaces in which players discussed strategies for improving their play. These early attempts at coding had several key goals. First, I argue, there was an implicit advocacy goal: Steinkuehler and Chmiel (2006) were avid gamers as well as researchers, and had witnessed firsthand what they had seen as complex reasoning practices in *World of Warcraft* forum spaces which they suspected were worthy of further investigation. They illustrated that there was significant potential for understanding gamer discourse through the lens of informal scientific reasoning, but exactly *how* one should study informal scientific reasoning in these spaces was still unclear.

With the goal of understanding the typicality of posited informal scientific thinking practices, Steinkuehler and I iterated multiple coding schemes in the development of the work that would become the informal scientific reasoning project reported in Steinkuehler and Sean Duncan (2008). Beginning with the "benchmarks" created by the American Association for the Advancement of Science (AAAS, 1993), we first struggled with the high degree of specificity of the benchmarks that were not relevant to understanding activities within the gaming context (e.g., "Fossils can be compared to one another and to living organisms according to their similarities and differences. Some organisms that lived long ago are similar to existing organisms, but some are quite different"). Quickly, we iterated our coding scheme to address hypothesized practices that captured elements of informal scientific practice as well, with the goal of this coding scheme to serve as an *interpretive tool* to aid in understanding the nascent "scientific" practices demonstrated within the game space. That is, the initial emphasis on the forms of science encoded in the AAAS standards that we initially planned to use to inform and guide our coding necessarily yielded to a broader conception of scientific thinking and practice, simply because *World of Warcraft* is, ultimately, a game and not an overtly scientific enterprise.

Initially, we wished to utilize Michelene Chi's (1997) guidelines for analyzing verbal data, but quickly moved toward the development of an *a priori* coding scheme that could capture "scientific thinking" independent of specific scientific context. Our coding scheme came together into "three major groups of codes: Scientific discursive practices (including social knowledge construction), systems- and model-based reasoning, and tacit epistemologies" (Steinkuehler & Duncan, 2008, p. 533). These focused, in turn, on the means by which participants within the space discussed *World of Warcraft* (e.g., building on each other's ideas or referencing external resources), the explicit or implicit manners in which affinity space discussants utilized systems- and model-based reasoning (e.g., understanding play-related feedback systems within the game or creating mathematical models), as well as the tacit epistemologies reflected through their speech (e.g., an "absolutist" perspective in which the poster expressed that there was one correct answer to a problem versus an "evaluative" one in which the poster appeared to wish to engage in discussion to evaluate knowledge; based on work by Deanna Kuhn, 1991).

These codes were painstakingly applied by four coders to nearly 2000 posts randomly selected from a data corpus of thousands of "Priest" class forum posts (downloaded manually, page by page, over a twelve-hour period). Without restating all the results from our 2008 paper, I'll note that the study yielded several interesting and important findings. First, the degree to which "social knowledge construction" was prevalent in this particular gaming affinity space (86% of all posts) was surprising to us at the time, given that "gamer discourse" was often portrayed in the media as superficial and as negatively correlated with intellectual work. Additionally, the high degree of "evaluative" tacit epistemology (65%

of posts) was strikingly higher than Kuhn's (1991) findings regarding informal argumentation (only 15% of which were evaluative). While the amount of mathematical reasoning and mathematical computation found in the data was startlingly small, when we scratched the surface of what these gamers were actually doing, it became clear that there nonetheless was a small but significant proportion of participants engaging in extremely complex mathematical model-building.

However, a central assumption of this work was not so much that these spaces *could be* interpreted using a framework of "informal scientific reasoning," but that this analysis would reveal something about how the discourse in and around games represented an informal scientific reasoning *practice* of some sort. As Steinkuehler and Duncan (2008, p. 531) asked, "if the inquiry activities used currently in education are unable to foster the right attitudes toward science, what can? Games, potentially." The appeal of this work was, ostensibly, to illustrate that the activities within affinity spaces could be seen as informal scientific thinking practices and so we hoped to encourage more widespread consideration of these games as sites for studying informal scientific thinking.

However, it was never particularly clear what the participants themselves thought of their gaming activity. Were they seeing their gaming practices as "science" or perhaps some other activity? Shortly after completing this initial study, I immersed myself further into these affinity spaces and began to listen more deeply to the tenor of gamer discussions. It became clear to me that many participants were most interested in discussing potential changes to the game's *design*. The discussions that they were engaged in were previously described as "scientific thinking," but perhaps a more careful assessment of the microstructure of their speech might help uncover how their intent—of honing and expanding the design of *World of Warcraft* itself—was worthy of further study, as a contrast to our study of informal scientific thinking.

Accordingly, for the next project, I began to iterate the next step in this method. This involved working toward developing a new set of content codes to attempt to capture *design talk* as it was evinced in multiple gaming affinity spaces and simultaneously trying to better capture participants' meaning of their own discursive practices. Beyond reapplying the method to a different set of concerns (design, rather than informal scientific reasoning), I was also explicitly concerned with refining the method by extending it into a case that provided the opportunity for interpretive, qualitative analysis. If the Steinkuehler and Duncan (2008) piece reflected a potential imposition of the researchers' goals (viewing the affinity space activity as "science") over the meaning made of the activity by the affinity space participants themselves, then the content coding approach could only tell us so much.

For the next project, I decided to focus on informal design practices and aimed to supplement content analysis with other methods—specifically, using it to create the groundwork for later, qualitative Discourse analysis (Gee, 2014), as a way to better understand the intent and goals of participants in these affinity spaces. In the next section, I will go into much more detail regarding how this investigation into informal design practices was considered—both in relationship to Steinkuehler and Duncan's (2008) previous informal scientific thinking work, and the "nuts and bolts" of justifying the content codes and then in selecting subsequent data for Discourse analysis. As this second case—what I call the "design project"—represents an attempt to extend the previous informal scientific thinking work (both theoretically and methodologically into a focus on game design through Discourse analysis), I provide a "blow by blow" account of how these methods evolved over time. In doing so, I hope to illustrate the choices made and challenges faced in extending this content coding approach toward the development of a process that could test not only researcher hypotheses, but elucidate the goals of the participants themselves.

INVESTIGATING DESIGN

The second case I outline here, the "design project," included multiple gaming spaces and different kinds of games and their fan communities, spanning a massively multiplayer online role-playing game (*World of Warcraft*), a narrative play game (*The Legend of Zelda*), as well as a community dedicated to the play and design of Flash-based games (the game hub *Kongregate*). Additionally, with the shift from scientific thinking to design, I brought a new, explicit emphasis on Discourse (Gee, 2014) to bear in these analyses, unpacking the ways that language—both the traditional textual and multimodal languages employed in the context of online discussions—was utilized to make meaning for participants within these spaces. I wanted to do more than simply identify the approach to design taken by participants within these spaces, but to also understand their framings of the design activities in which they were engaged along with the meanings they were making of their practices within these affinity spaces. By addressing the discussions in these forums using more than "counting approaches," the door was opened to engaging with the Discourse of these participants: Specifically, how did participants frame their activities within these forums, and what did they see themselves as contributing? In other words, what terminology did they use to describe what they were doing in the affinity spaces, and why?

Again, Chi's (1997) prescriptions for conducting analyses of verbal data were considered in order to develop a coding scheme that could potentially capture elements of the "messy data" of online discussions around design. While not following Chi's verbal analysis method specifically, her concerns with balancing quantitative and qualitative analyses were considered. It became clear that, in order to effectively meld quantitative and qualitative analyses, the type of designed artifact—narrative, ludic, or combined narrative/ludic game artifact—would need to be considered. Thus, a generalized coding scheme to capture "design talk" was developed. In our earlier analysis of informal scientific thinking, we faced a similar issue, opting to craft a coding scheme relatively distant from the original AAAS standards, instead focusing on a more abstracted level of practice. We stated:

> Our goal was to focus on scientific reasoning as "the building of houses" rather than the "collection of stones," per the vision of science practice articulated by Poincaré (1905/2001) and science education forwarded by Dewey (1910) and Schwab (1962). Therefore, important aspects to scientific understanding that are specific to content knowledge rather than practice per se (e.g. an understanding of natural forces) are notably absent. (Steinkuehler & Duncan, 2008, pp. 532–533)

Similarly, for this project, I followed the same emphases, shifting the focus of the analysis from informal science practices to informal design practices. While the "content" of gaming discussions may be quite different from the content privileged in academic and professional settings (science and design, respectively), I suspected that the fundamental practices of design might match those found in these contexts, building on the scientific thinking approach we took in Steinkuehler and Duncan (2008). If Gee's (2004) assessment of affinity spaces was correct, participants within these communities were drawn to these spaces perhaps *because* these spaces allowed for the enactment of complex practices such as scientific thinking and design, while not being wrapped up in the guise of academic language.

Content Coding

Toward this end, the investigations into professional design by Donald Schön (1983, 1988) served as a basis for a new coding scheme. Schön's emphasis on "design talk" in professional design mentorship was appealing in that several of the component factors—design "types" and "rules"—were abstracted categorizations of design practice not closely tied to the specific context of design from which they were gleaned. That is, while the category of "design reference" (one of Schön's types) evolved from his reading of architectural practice (for instance, using Frank Gehry's Experience Music Project museum as a case of "bad design" to justify deviations from that design), Schön's model allowed for a "design reference" to include "reference" in a very different design field (e.g., arguing that Valve's *Portal* provided a good reference for conceiving level structure in a new first-person "shooter" game). That is, the initial forms of "design" that served as the inspiration for this revised coding scheme were drawn from disciplines far afield from game design, but I suspected at the time that there could be useful commonalities between these conceptions and practices of design.

For the design project, Schön's design types and rules served as the initial basis for the revised coding scheme, developed and tested on a sample of forum posts for applicability. As per the content analysis and verbal analysis techniques first developed in Steinkuehler and Duncan (2008) and with consideration of Chi's (1997) guidelines for the analysis of verbal data, revisions to this coding scheme were necessary, in order to factor in more than the *a priori* framework from Schön's work. In particular, as the coding scheme was tested, it became clear that two other elements needed to be incorporated into the scheme—first, a means of capturing the co-construction of knowledge, argumentation, and development of ideas within the three forums under study and second, elements of "design talk" which were prevalent but not necessarily classified within the types/rules framework. This iterative revision of the coding scheme produced a more robust scheme that I suspected addressed the variety of design "talk" in these forums, as well as multiple levels of design processes within these communities. Though much of the structure of this revised coding scheme was similar to the previous informal scientific thinking project, the reframing of the codes (based on Schön's work) represented a significant shift toward capturing the explicit goals of gamer Discourse. As a consequence, the coding scheme was revised multiple times to attend more closely to elements of the "talk" present within each affinity space. The final set of codes was clustered into three major areas: *discursive practice*, *design practice*, and *narrative/ludic content* codes.

Following directly from Steinkuehler and Duncan's (2008) work, the coding scheme for informal design practices captured *discursive practices* employed by participants in the online discussion forums. These codes were directly lifted from the informal scientific reasoning project, as it was suspected that the forms of interaction between participants would be similar, including social knowledge construction, participants' building on each other's ideas, the use of counterarguments, uses of data/evidence, alternative explanations of data/evidence, and referencing outside resources in informal scientific reasoning discussions around *World of Warcraft*. Steinkuehler and Duncan's (2008) discursive practice codes effectively captured the co-construction of knowledge and argumentation practices prevalent in many online discussions, not just those found in informal scientific reasoning contexts. By utilizing this part of our earlier coding scheme, I sought to build explicitly on not just the approach but the specific coding scheme itself, with the goal being to test parts of the scheme's applicability to constructive, design-oriented discussions online while also consciously blurring the line between online science reasoning practices and online design practices. While the two studies featured very different goals, I hypothesized that both "science" and "design" employed many of the same common argumentation and discursive practices in these informal settings.

The set of codes developed to capture *design practices* were a distillation of Schön's design types and design rules (1988), with the addition of a subset of

Schön's (1983) design domains included as well. I started with the four design types specified in Schön (1988)—functional types, design references, *gestalts*, and experiential types—plus the identification of explicit design rules (or generalizable claims about design independent of specific design contexts). Next, I added three codes from Schön's (1983) description of design domains (i.e., "use," "structure/technology," and a combined code of "character/form" based on two design domains). In order to address inadequacies in the initial versions of the coding scheme, these design domains were brought in to capture forms of design talk found within these three forums' discussions. I also included Schön's emphasis upon intermediate representations that are brought into the design discussions, the statement of explicit design rules that arise out of these types, as well as three codes which are "closer to" the contexts of design. In this fashion, this part of the coding scheme was an attempt to address several levels of design talk in a manner not particular to a specific design context.

Finally, a set of simple *narrative/ludic content* codes was added to the coding scheme as a means of conducting a "manipulation check" for each case. By selecting each of these three cases (*World of Warcraft*, *The Legend of Zelda*, and *Kongregate*), I posited that talk in the forums I studied would be primarily ludic, primarily narrative, or combined narrative/ludic in nature, respectively. These codes were very simple and were used to identify if the design discussion in each forum post was about ludic elements of the game, game series, or platform under discussion; about issues of narrative around the game, game series, or platform under discussion; or if it was uncodable/ambiguous. I justified the choice of ludic, narrative, and combined context in Duncan (2010b), but for the purposes of this chapter, I wish to emphasize that these distinctions were used as a way to characterize the multiple types of "design" that might be found in gaming affinity spaces.

The final coding scheme, along with descriptions of each code, can be seen in Table 10.1. The scheme includes discursive practice, design practice, and narrative/ludic content codes. Individual codes reference American Association for the Advancement of Science standards (1993), Clark Chinn and Betina Malhotra (2002), and Schön's (1983, 1988) framework for understanding design.

In order to determine a rough measure of the reliability of this coding scheme, intercoder agreement was calculated between two coders on a subset of the data corpus for each of the three cases involved in my study. Two coders with significant experience in each setting, having each completed a *Zelda* game, and with several months' experience playing *World of Warcraft*, as well as familiarity with Flash/Actionscript development coded the data. Both coded the same data subset, which comprised approximately 9.5% of the data corpus (48 posts; 14 posts from the *Zelda* case, 20 posts from the *World of Warcraft* case, and 14 from the *Kongregate* case). The two coders reached a high degree of agreement—93.5% intercoder agreement using the coding scheme in Table 10.1.

Table 10.1. The Coding Scheme for the Design Project.

Code	Title	Description
		Discursive Practices
D1	Social Knowledge Construction	Designers construct knowledge in collaborative groups (AAAS.D.12.6 & 1.A.12.2; Chinn & Malhotra, 2002)
D2	Build on Others' Ideas	Participate in design discussions by restating or summarizing accurately what others have said, iterating designs (AAAS)
D3	Use of Counter-arguments	Suggest alternative claims or proposals, criticize arguments in which data, explanations, or conclusions are represented as the only ones worth consideration with no mention of other possibilities, suggest alternative trade-offs in decisions and designs, criticize designs in which major trade-offs are not acknowledged (AAAS.12.E)
D4	Uses Data/ Evidence	Use data or evidence in making arguments and claims (AAAS)
D5	Alternative Explanations of Data/Evidence	No matter how well one theory fits observations, a new theory might fit them just as well or better, or might fit a wider range of observations (AAAS.1.A.12.3, AAAS.12.A.8.3)
D6	References Outside Resources	References outside resources in making arguments and claims (e.g., other threads, online articles, databases)
		Design Practices
D7	Use	Designers address uses of designs; specifications for use (Schön, 1983)
D8	Structure/ Technology	Designers reference structures, technologies, and processes used in designing and implementation (Schön, 1983)
D9	Character/Form	Designers reference form of design or components, the character of a design, markings of organization of spatial relationships, and genre (Schön, 1983)
D10	Cost	Designers need to consider the cost of the design and construction of a design, both in terms of financial capital and human resources (Schön, 1983)
D11	Function	Designers refer to the function of designs, either functional elements of designs or the function of a design (Schön, 1988)
D12	Design References	Designers reference other designs, as exemplary "leading ideas" or as examples of designs to avoid (Schön, 1988)
D13	Gestalt	Designers refer to "coherent wholes," or the ways that subcomponents of a design fit together into larger systems and relationships (Schön, 1988)

Table 10.1. (*Continued*)

Code	Title	Description
		Discursive Practices
D14	**Experience**	Designers refer to the experiential significance, emotive power, or universality of designs (Schön, 1988)
D15	**Rules**	Designers state explicit design rules, maxims, or heuristics codifying good design practice (Schön, 1988)
D66	**Social Banter**	
D67	**Uncodable/ Ambiguous**	
		Narrative/Ludic Content
C1	**Narrative Play**	Is the content of the post about a narrative aspect of a game?
C2	**Ludic Play**	Is the content of the post about a ludic aspect of a game?
C66	**Not Relevant to Narrative/Ludic**	The content of the post does not discuss narrative or ludic elements of a game
C67	**Uncodable/ Ambiguous**	

In the development of this analysis, I found content analyses allowed for systematic assessment of design thinking across each case when using an analytic tool which, other than the ludic and narrative codes, was intended to be applicable to a wide range of design contexts, allowing claims to be made (if tentative) regarding the differences in design practices discerned across each case. However useful this methodology might be for assessing the prevalence of design practices in these spaces, the details of the back-and-forth interactions between participants were not fully interpretable with such a method, and the individual moments of meaning making between participants would presumably be largely occluded by such an approach. And so, an application of an idiographic method such as Discourse analysis—one in which I could pick apart the unique co-construction of knowledge and the negotiation of meaning within discussion threads—was needed to fully "flesh out" the analysis of design practices. In another sense, in order to value the agency and intentions of participants of these spaces, I turned to Discourse analysis (Gee, 2014) to provide a means for generating detailed and contextualized interpretation of their textual interactions.

Discourse Analysis

Gee's Discourse analysis methodology (2014) has shown itself to be a powerful tool for analyzing online social interaction (e.g., Steinkuehler, 2006a; Duncan,

2011). In the design project, I knew that I wanted to conduct Discourse analyses of selected threads and posts from online discussion forums drawn from each of the three affinity spaces under study. I was especially interested in focusing on the seven "building tasks" that Gee (2014) argued can guide the Discourse analyst's investigations of language-in-use. The foci of these tasks were: Significance, Activities, Identities, Relationships, Politics (the distribution of social goods), Connections, and Sign Systems and Knowledge. Each building task addressed a different aspect of language and social practice, and Gee developed sets of prompt questions to help guide targeted Discourse analyses (e.g., in analyzing Relationships, the researcher could ask: "What sort of relationship or relationships is this piece of language seeking to enact with others (present or not)?"). I wanted to employ these building tasks to unpack the ways that participants in these design-focused gamer discussion used traditional textual language and multimodal language involved in online discussions to make meaning with one another.

Specifically, I knew I would select productive exchanges from each of the three online forums under study with the goal of drawing data to further examine using Discourse analyses. Since all instances of meaning making with language are inherently socially and culturally situated, a first task of these Discourse analyses would be to characterize the ways that meaning was made by participants in the course of these discussions. Toward this end, I developed a set of guiding questions for each of Gee's seven building tasks (see Table 10.2), tied to each affinity space.

For each case of hypothesized design practice, then, the initial goal was to characterize Gee's building tasks using questions tailored to each specific affinity space. The methodological emphasis in these Discourse analyses was to explicate the discursive moves that helped "flesh out" the design contexts of each individual affinity space, rather than tracking common themes across the cases. Although explicit quantitative comparisons across cases were not made using the Discourse analyses, emergent themes nonetheless arose from these analyses. These Discourse analyses were intended to complement the content analyses, and were not intended to be comprehensive or to make hard-and-fast claims about differences between these communities. Rather, they were intended to provide detailed, principled accounts of individual cases of meaning making in each affinity space, and to provide qualitative support for the content analyses of discursive and design practices enacted within these spaces.

Connecting Methods

In this section, I describe how these two methods worked in tandem in the context of one example drawn from the design project, as well as some of the broader theoretic considerations at play here. I first attempted to wrestle with the connection between these two methods, and the goals for using both in Duncan (2010a). In

Table 10.2. Gee's (2014) "Seven Building Tasks," Applied to Each of the Three Affinity Spaces Under Study in the Design Project.

	Space 1: Zelda	Space 2: WoW	Space 3: Kongregate
	Narrative Play	Ludic Play	Game Design
What is the pertinent research question for this case?	"How does this community deal with new narrative elements and redesign timelines?"	"How does this community argue and iterate design proposals with the game's designers?"	"How do new game designers debate and design games using the *Kongregate Labs* tutorials?"
Significance	What "counts" as evidence in these activities?	What are valid elements of the game to redesign?	What aspects of game design should and can be focused upon?
Activities	How do participants flag narrative play vs. other activities?	How do players highlight their proposals vs. others?	What forms of mentorship have evolved in these forums?
Identities	What indication do we have that participants conceive of themselves as "designers?"		
Relationships	How are preexisting personal relationships between participants coded in their interactions?		
Politics	How is status (established poster vs. n00b) conveyed?	How is status (Blizzard employee vs. player) conveyed?	How is status (expert game designer/Flash programmer vs. novice) conveyed?
Connections	How do participants find connections between evidence and designs in their design arguments?		
Sign systems	How do participants utilize their community's own unique symbol systems for each design task?		

that piece, I argued that the content coding approach served to solve a key problem for Discourse analysis—the justification of data selection. For many Discourse analyses, the *choice* of which data to focus on has often remained essentially unjustified. Instead, it was often implicitly left to the judgment of the analyst to find the most "interesting" case to address. Consequently, it is often claimed that Discourse analysts rely too heavily upon their own judgment for the selection of data, and that "cherry picking" data of interest might lead to analyzing data that potentially do not represent the corpus.

Of course, unrepresentative data can still be quite useful and interesting, but without a clear depiction of the data selection's typicality, readers may be left not knowing how the data selected for analysis relate to the whole. In Duncan (2010a), I characterized the use of content analysis as a "filter" for selecting data for subsequent analysis. For instance, in the *World of Warcraft* data drawn from the design project, the content analysis provided a first look at the typicality of the hypothesized discursive practices and design talk within the selection of posts drawn from the official *World of Warcraft* forums. The coding saturation (codes applied to 242 randomly selected posts drawn from the "Damage Dealing" forums) can be seen in Figure 10.1. The coding served as the first step in the analysis, providing an indication of the typicality of several forms of design talk and discursive practice within this sample.

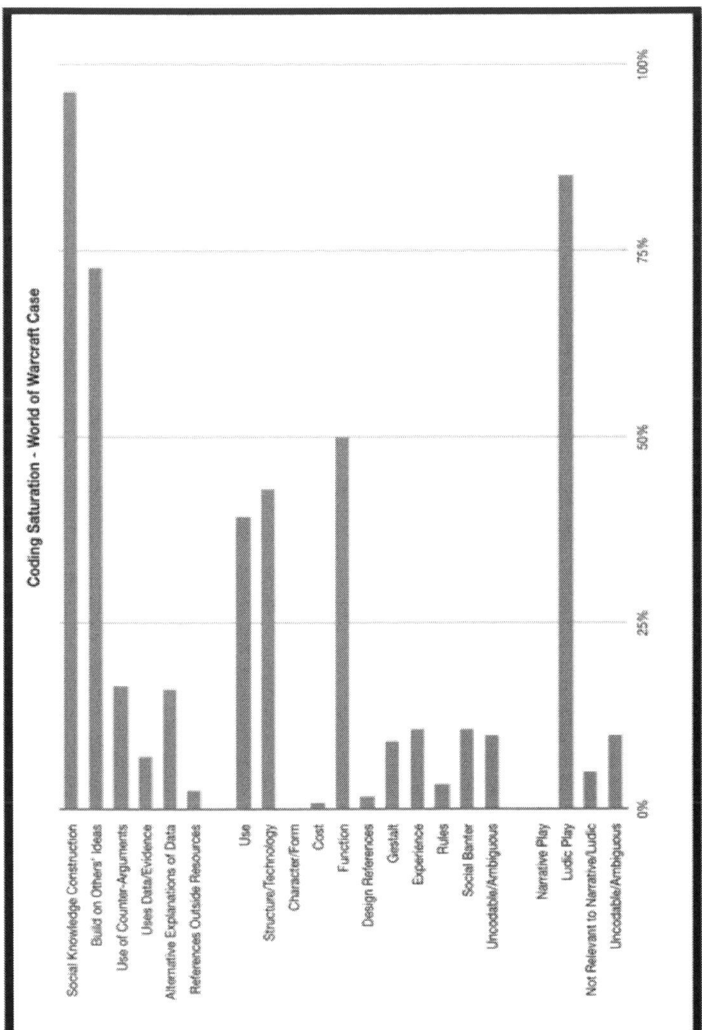

Fig. 10.1. A summary of the coding saturation for the *World of Warcraft* case.

As can be seen in the content coding, design codes such as discussions of "function," "use," and "structure/technology" were most highly coded. These differed from the other two cases in the study, and were seen as indicators that the discussions in this particular affinity space were geared toward the discussion of proposals to design the game's mechanical systems (the "function" and "structure/technology") with an eye toward how players would "use" these changes in the evolution of the game. Another interesting result that emerged was the degree to which these design proposals focused on arguments toward *one* individual—"Ghostcrawler" (Greg Street)—the then-lead designer of the game. Figure 10.2 shows that a total of 30% of the posts from the sample contained direct queries or responses to Ghostcrawler's posts.

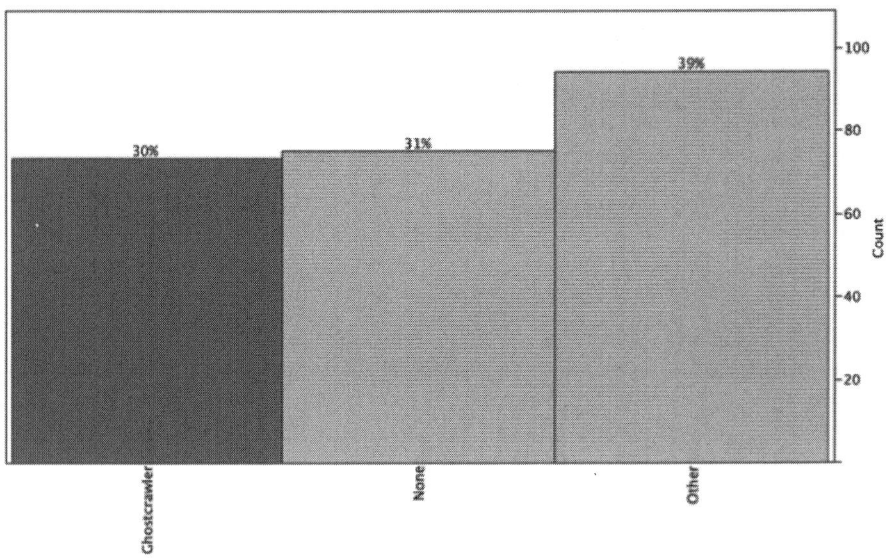

Fig. 10.2. An illustration of the high degree of engagement Ghostcrawler had within the affinity space.

Thus, we start to see how the method begins to winnow us down from a large-scale depiction of the types of design talk and discursive practices found within this particular case toward specific targets for us to investigate using more interpretive, qualitative methods. The initial content coding provided us with a description of the sample in aggregate, further pointing toward specific forms of design talk to look into. This led to the realization that a high number of responses was not simply fans talking about the game's design with other fans, but were fans in conversation with the game's lead designer. This in turn led to the selection of data that evinced the typical forms of design talk (characterized in the content analysis) that were centered on the game's lead designer. The content analysis method I used served as an important analytic precursor to help identify important exchanges for further investigation, using the interpretive approach of Discourse analysis.

In Duncan (2011), I conducted a detailed Discourse analysis drawn from this case. Space limitations preclude replicating it in any detail here, but suffice it to say, the Discourse analysis showed that there were interesting framings of the activity of participation within the affinity space that revealed tensions between Ghostcrawler and the fan participants in the space. In particular, using Gee's building tasks, the "activities," "identities," and "politics" questions quickly became quite salient in the selected data. Utilizing the original building tasks, adapted for these cases, I focused on a selection of data that was coded highly with "structure/technology," "use" and "function," and which *also* included posts that featured the direct involvement of Ghostcrawler.

The analysis was revealing. In particular, one discussion between a poster I call "Nawaf" and Ghostcrawler usefully captured an interesting tension between engaged fan practices and the goals of the company. Nawaf, a self-described physics graduate student, attempted to convince Ghostcrawler of the importance of player-collected data and player-driven data analysis using a fan-made "mod" to the game, *SimulationCraft*, framing their activity as a scientific investigation. In Table 10.3, I connect three of Gee's building tasks to insights drawn from the Discourse analyses. In a nutshell, Ghostcrawler presented a framing of fan activity in the affinity space as "engineering" that served to distance the fan-created meaning-making from the "real" designers, while Nawaf framed fan activities as "science" more so than design, as a means of legitimizing the work done in the affinity space.

Table 10.3. Discourse Analysis Building Tasks, with the Original, General Question to Summaries of Conclusions Drawn from These Analyses.

Building Task	Original Question	Conclusion
Activities	How do players highlight their proposals vs. others?	The use of scientific/scientized language is employed by fans to communicate game design proposals
Identities	What indication do we have that participants conceive of themselves as "designers?"	Fans view themselves as a "scientific community" more so than designers
Politics	How is status (Blizzard employee vs. player) conveyed?	Ghostcrawler frames players are "users" providing feedback, employing engineering framing over science framing

In Duncan (2013), I argued that understanding these tensions was key for understanding both the activities within affinity spaces and something about the design of the game itself. The tensions over the design of this game—and over the framing of what fans *do* with the game—revealed that the "ownership" of the game and its community was in contention. The staged approach to content analysis and Discourse analysis that I took provided a justified means for understanding the activities of participants in online affinity spaces, but at the same time, we should not ignore the fact that the very act of developing these methods can serve as an impetus to reconsider the boundaries of the "game" itself. My 2013 piece problematized what we considered to be the "game" (as typically limited to the boundaries of the interactions within the digital game space), and continues to highlight that analysis of these interactions "around" the game can provide a window into how the game is experienced by players and designers.

Moreover, I note that what I had suspected would be an interesting site for investigating design turned out to also reveal something interesting about informal scientific thinking after all. Whereas my original interest lay in investigating these spaces as a means to redress deficiencies in the earlier Steinkuehler and Duncan (2008) work, the question that arose from the analysis—"Is the fan activity best understood as science or design?"—was a surprise. The staged approach I describe allowed for the selection of data to be better justified, but also challenged preconceptions of the researcher. I initially wished to move beyond an *a priori* assumption that "science" was at play in these discussions, but through the process of analysis had perhaps replaced it with an *a priori* assumption that "design" was truly motivating the participants in these affinity spaces. By balancing both content coding and Discourse analysis, it became clear that the tension between these two framings of the fan activity itself was most important and interesting for understanding *World of Warcraft* as both a game and an impetus for affinity space discussions.

CONCLUSIONS AND FUTURE DIRECTIONS

Finally, I want to reflect briefly on what this evolving approach might tell us about two things: namely, how to "do" analyses within these spaces, and what they might represent in terms of allowing us to connect relatively disparate theoretical approaches in understanding affinity spaces. The evolving use of these linked methodologies is driven in part by the ground-level concerns of justifying data selection for one level of analysis. At the same time, the approach described in this chapter also represents an attempt to synthesize a number of theoretic concerns from multiple disciplines and interdisciplinary fields.

The design project described in greatest detail here was one where I wrestled with three key "families" of theoretic concerns. The first of these concerns focused on perspectives on design drawn from New Literacy Studies (e.g., Cope & Kalantzis, 2000; New London Group, 1996; Lankshear & Knobel, 2011; Street, 2003). The second concerned approaches that fit within the methodological home of the Learning Sciences (e.g., Chi, 1997). Third, given that the specific domain of study here was digital game affinity spaces, the interdisciplinary field of "Game Studies" (Aarseth, 2001; Steinkuehler, 2006b; Mäyrä, 2008) was also a concern. How might the approach advanced here help to meld these somewhat disparate families of research on learning in affinity spaces?

In Figure 10.3, I describe a "stage model" that synthesizes both Learning Sciences and New Literacy Studies approaches within a case justified by distinctions found in (admittedly, early) Game Studies literatures. In the design case in particular, this was characterized by a selection of cases distinguished by different forms of hypothesized play based loosely upon early Game Studies discussions of narratology vs. ludology (see Duncan, 2010b, for a more detailed justification).

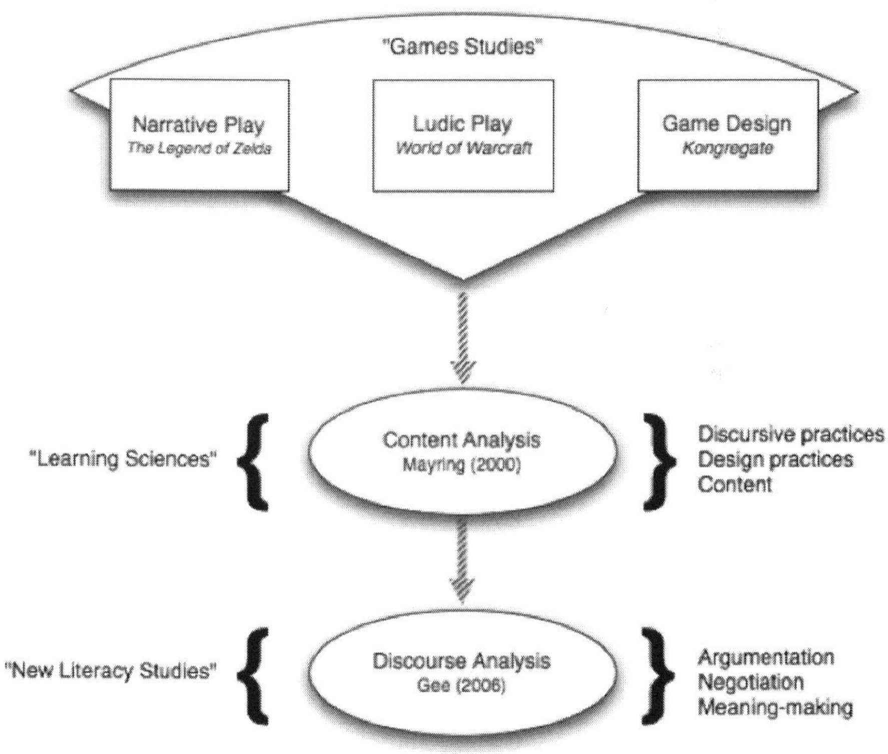

Fig. 10.3. A stage model of case selection, content analysis, and Discourse analysis, which informed Duncan (2010b). Relevant literatures that have informed each of these stages are present, as well as potential discursive and design phenomena under investigation.

Following site selection, the content analysis method allowed the characterization of phenomena typically considered within the realm of Learning Sciences: namely, discursive practices, design practices, and alignment to content. With content analysis enabling further refinement of the data selection for Discourse analysis, new phenomena were revealed. These included detailed accounts of argumentation, negotiation, and meaning making at a microstructural level.

The mappings of literatures to different stages of this process are admittedly loose (e.g., clearly the variety of methodologies used by Learning Sciences researchers should not be equated with content analysis alone). At the same time, such mapping helps illustrate ways in which theoretic concerns are present within a specific approach for understanding design in affinity spaces in the present chapter. I suggest that using multiple methodologies helps us within our research practice to synthesize multiple perspectives on design (in this specific case), and alignment between different scales of analysis (in general). Having tried to develop means for investigating participation in affinity spaces, I now conclude that we need to take seriously the different foci (literacy, learning, and games) in order to begin to construct approaches which can, at least potentially, drive the generation of new knowledge on their intersections. Within this framework, I have explicitly made room for generating emergent themes and findings from these analyses, to acknowledge that the methods presented here are but one way to understand learning and literacy within online gaming affinity spaces.

Consequently, my more recent work has taken a turn away from the Discourse analytic approaches described here, with a view to further exploring new methods that might enable even more interesting and productive understandings of these spaces to be developed. As part of a project funded by HASTAC that looked into the design and use of "digital badges" for learning (e.g., Halavais, 2012; Schenke, Tran, & Hickey, 2013), my lab conducted multiple content coding analyses through this approach with three new affinity space datasets, two of which were not related to gaming. We investigated political discussions on Reddit's /r/politics subreddit, computational thinking in StackOverflow, and systems thinking in the affinity spaces around the competitive game *Dota 2*. Our aim was to track the connections between the designed recognition systems within these spaces—in particular, digital badges, along with other systems for recognizing participation and engagement within the spaces, such as upvoting/downvoting. Through this process, we developed new coding schemes to capture political negotiation, computational thinking, and systems thinking within these spaces, while shying away from Discourse analytic approaches.

A key reason for this shift has been to try and understand the role that the design of these spaces themselves played in understanding the interactions within them. Gee's early work (and much of my work reported here) was largely agnostic toward the role(s) that the designed elements of the affinity spaces played in the practices within them. Further understanding of the roles of the design of the spaces themselves may dictate additional methodological concerns to be iterated. Hence, while the design study was an attempt to innovate in the direction of connecting content coding to the lived experiences of participants in these affinity spaces, there is still much work to be done in the opposite direction. To date, the technological substrates of these spaces have been only barely documented and explored. While it is naïve to assume that these spaces simplistically determine the kinds of activities that happen within them, many opportunities lie ahead for more rigorous investigation of the ways that designed elements of affinity spaces may influence and shape participation within them.

This may lead to adding further methods to our toolkits for investigating participation in online affinity spaces. Employing learning analytics and educational data mining methods (Siemens & Baker, 2012; Berland, Baker, & Blikstein, 2014) is the obvious next step that may provide more revealing approaches to large affinity space datasets, uncovering regularities that would otherwise be too difficult for qualitative analysis to uncover. With the future of the study of affinity spaces appearing rich with possibilities for understanding participation and learning within them, I conclude with the hope that we may consider multiple methodologies in the study of affinity spaces, and continue to forge meaningful linkages between them.

REFERENCES

American Association for the Advancement of Science (AAAS) (1993). *Benchmarks for science literacy.* Oxford University Press, New York.

Aarseth, E. (2001). Computer game studies, year one. *Game Studies,* 1(1), 1–15.

Berland, M., Baker, R., & Blikstein, P. (2014). Educational data mining and learning analytics: Applications to constructionist research. *Technology, Knowledge and Learning,* 19(1–2), 205–220.

Chi, M. (1997). Quantifying qualitative analyses of verbal data: A practical guide. *Journal of the Learning Sciences,* 6, 271–315.

Chinn, C., & Malhotra, B. (2002). Epistemologically authentic inquiry in schools: A theoretical framework for evaluating inquiry tasks. *Science Education,* 86(2), 175–218.

Cope, B., & Kalantzis, M. (2000). *Multiliteracies: Literacy learning and the design of social futures.* London: Routledge.

Dewey, J. (1910). Science as subject matter and as method. *Science,* 31(787), 121–127.

Duncan, S. (2010a). A dual-level approach for investigating design in online affinity spaces. In K. Gomez, L. Lyons, & J. Radinsky (Eds.), *Learning in the disciplines: Proceedings of the 9th international conference of the learning sciences (ICLS 2010) - Volume 2, short papers, symposia, and selected abstracts* (pp. 346–347). Chicago, IL: International Society of the Learning Sciences.

Duncan, S. (2010b). Gamers as designers: A framework for investigating design in gaming affinity spaces. *E- Learning and Digital Media,* 7(1), 21–34.

Duncan, S. (2011). World of Warcraft and "the World of Science": Ludic play in an online affinity space. In T. Wright, D. Embrick, & A. Lukacs (Eds.), *Social exclusion, power and video game play: New research in digital media and technology* (pp. 177–198). New York: Lexington Press.

Duncan, S. (2013). Well-played and well-debated: Understanding perspective in contested affinity spaces. *Well-Played*, 2(2), 37–58.

Duncan, S. (2016). "Games with learning": Adpositions and the lusory attitude. *On the Horizon*, 24(3), 246–256.

Gee, J. (2004). *Situated language and learning: A critique of traditional schooling*. London: Routledge.

Gee, J. (2005). Semiotic social spaces and affinity spaces. In D. Barton, & K. Tusting (Eds.), *Beyond communities of practice: Language power and social context* (pp. 214–232). Cambridge, UK: Cambridge University Press.

Gee, J. (2014). *An introduction to discourse analysis: Theory and method* (4th ed.). New York: Routledge.

Halavais, A. (2012). A genealogy of badges: Inherited meaning and monstrous moral hybrids. *Information, Communication & Society*, 15(3), 354–373.

Hayes, E. & Duncan, S. (Eds.) (2012). *Learning in video game affinity spaces*. New York: Peter Lang.

Kuhn, D. (1991). *The skills of argument*. Cambridge, UK: Cambridge University Press.

Lammers, J., Curwood, J., & Magnifico, A. (2012). Toward an affinity space methodology: Considerations for literacy research. *English Teaching*, 11(2), 44–58.

Lankshear, C. & Knobel, M. (2011). *New literacies: Everyday practices and social learning* (3rd ed.). New York: McGraw-Hill.

Mäyrä, F. (2008). *An introduction to game studies*. New York: Sage.

Mayring, P. (2000). Qualitative content analysis. *Forum: Qualitative Social Research*, 1(2). Available from: http://www.qualitative-research.net/index.php/fqs/article/view/1089/2385

New London Group. (1996). A pedagogy of multiliteracies: Designing social futures. *Harvard Educational Review*, 66(1), 60–93.

Poincaré, H. (1905/2001). Science and hypothesis. In S. Gould (Ed.), *The value of science: Essential writings of Henri Poincaré* (pp. 7–180). New York: The Modern Library.

Schenke, K., Tran, C., & Hickey, D. (2013). Design principles for motivating learning with digital badges. *HASTAC Blog*. Available from: https://www.hastac.org/blogs/kschenke/2013/06/05/design-principles-motivating-learning-digital-badges

Schön, D. (1983). *The reflective practitioner*. New York: Basic Books.

Schön, D. (1988). Designing: Rules, types, and worlds. *Design Studies*, 9(3), 181–190.

Schwab J. (1962). *The teaching of science as enquiry*. Cambridge, MA: Harvard University Press.

Siemens, G., & Baker, R. (2012). Learning analytics and educational data mining: Towards communication and collaboration. In *Proceedings of the 2nd international conference on learning analytics and knowledge* (pp. 252–254). New York: ACM Publications.

Steinkuehler, C. & Chmiel, M. (2006). Fostering scientific habits of mind in the context of online play. In S. Barab, K. Hay, N. Songer, & D. Hickey (Eds.), *Proceedings of the International Conference of the Learning Sciences* (pp. 723–729). Mahwah NJ: Erlbaum.

Steinkuehler, C. (2006a). Massively multiplayer online videogaming as participation in a Discourse. *Mind, Culture, & Activity*, 13(1), 38–52.

Steinkuehler, C. (2006b). Why game (culture) studies now? *Games and Culture*, 1(1), 97–102.

Steinkuehler, C., & Duncan, S. (2008). Scientific habits of mind in virtual worlds. *Journal of Science Education and Technology*, 17(6), 530–543.

Steinkuehler, C., & Squire, K. (2014). Videogames and learning. In K. Sawyer (Ed). *The Cambridge handbook of the learning sciences* (pp. 377–396), Cambridge, UK: Cambridge University Press.

Street, B. (2003). What's "new" in New Literacy Studies? Critical approaches to literacy in theory and practice. *Current Issues in Comparative Education*, 5(2), 77–91.

CHAPTER ELEVEN

"There's A Relationship"

Negotiating Cell Phone Use in the High School Classroom

ANITA S. CHARLES

I glance around the classroom of undergraduate students. I notice the girl with her iPhone conspicuously in the open, thumbs moving rapidly across the screen; the young man at the back who has pulled his own phone from a pocket to check the time; the two students who are smiling over something on a laptop screen. Together, we are embedded in societal realities and cultural artifacts that define (and are defined by) our interactions with each other. Smartphones and other digital spaces are ubiquitous—my own iPhone rests on the desk in front of me. It serves as my timekeeper, note-taker, and calendar, a source of quickly accessible information, and—yes—sometimes a repository of messages to and from others. But how do I establish and enforce rules around such devices in a classroom setting? I struggle with the balance between an authoritarian zero-tolerance policy and a laissez-faire permissive response to what I know I cannot control.

In countless daily moments similar to this scenario described here, teachers at every level—elementary, secondary, and beyond—and in every type of school across the U.S. struggle to define rules around the use of digital devices. Teachers must reflect on their own attitudes and beliefs around the purpose of these tools; on technology's impact, for better or worse, on student learning; on their (the teachers') own will and capacity to enforce basic protocols. What to do about cell phones and other digital tools in the classroom? There is no easy answer to this question that unsettles us.

The intent of the research project described in this chapter was to explore how adolescents engage in—and make meaning from—literacy activities across multiple contexts that are ever-evolving in a technology-rich world. How do teens negotiate interactions with various types of texts across social spaces? How do they learn to be literate across a range of social, academic, print, and digital discourses?

Teens—and earlier ages every year—maneuver with varying degrees of success across multiple literacy and discourse tools, including school-sponsored devices; smartphones with "texting" capacity; academic textbooks and worksheets, both on-screen and in hard-copy print formats; novels for English class and for pleasure, again located both on-screen and in hard-copy; flipped classroom lectures accessed virtually; and online social media sites, such as Facebook, Instagram, Twitter, and blogs; among other texts and spaces. This interactive movement is situated within spaces where new literacies are invented and transformed, beyond the limits of static, print-centric models of literacy.

Other researchers seek answers to questions similar to my own: How are youths making sense of the world around them, and with what texts and tools (Bell, 1993; Kress, 2000a, 2000b)? How are these new semiotic, multimodal resources impacting pedagogy in K-12 schools (Lewis & Fabos, 2005; Luke, 2000)? How do teens define and bridge these complex social and academic worlds (Ito et al., 2008; Lenhart, Smith, Macgill, & Arafeh, 2008)? How does discourse interweave with these new literacies (Gee, 2005; Lankshear & Knobel, 2003)?

CRITICAL SOCIOCULTURAL THEORY

Lev Vygotsky's (1978) "zone of proximal development" construct was defined by him as "the distance between the actual developmental level [of the learner] as determined by independent problem solving and the level of potential development as determined through problem solving under adult guidance, or in collaboration with more capable peers" (p. 86). This construct engages what some researchers call "intersubjectivity" between teacher and student (Wertsch, 1984, p. 10) and what Paulo Freire called the teacher–learner dialogical relationship (Hare & Portelli, 2001), rather than a unidirectional transfer of knowledge from teacher to learner. Rogoff (1990) perceived "guided participation" as a collaborative process between children and adults with an intersubjectivity defined as a *sharing of focus and purpose* between children and more skilled partners in a given activity, thereby encouraging growth in the direction "offered by cultural and social values" (p. 142).

However, sociocultural perspectives can be problematic, leaving little room for agency in relation to culture, and not doing enough to address the larger ideological assumptions and power structures within situated communities (Lewis, Enciso, & Moje, 2007, p. xv). A critical inquiry stance in the classroom perceives it as a transactional space (Fecho & Meacham, 2007). Agency is "the strategic making and remaking of selves, identities, activities, relationships, cultural tools and resources, and histories, as embedded within relations of power" (Moje & Lewis, 2007, p. 18). In this present study, my intent was to listen to teen voices as they reflected on their own choices and how they situated themselves, in juxtaposition with sociocultural influences at work in their lives, both in and out of school.

METHODOLOGY

Participants

Throughout the 2008–2009 school year, I studied seven youths, all but one of who were in the 10th grade at local public high schools. I also interviewed and observed the classrooms of three Grade 10 English teachers, each from a different public or private high school.

Riverpark High School is located in a middle class community in New England (U.S.A.). Mr. Scott had been teaching English at Riverpark High School for four years. In nearby Centreville, a town that is more culturally diverse and with a lower socioeconomic reality than Riverpark, I observed Mrs. Andrews, a warm and personable 10th-grade English teacher who had been teaching for more than 15 years. The third teacher I observed and interviewed was Ms. Fisk, a gentle, friendly young woman in her first year of teaching at a private coed day school. Table 1 summarizes these participants.

Table 11.1. Summary of Participant Information.

Student Name	School	Grade	English Teacher
Carrie	Riverpark	10	Mr. Scott
David	Riverpark	10	Mr. Scott
Maria	Riverpark	10	Mr. Scott
Haley	Riverpark	10	*Mr. Frangeli
Nicholas	Riverpark	11	*Mr. Frangeli
Jamal	Centreville	10	Mrs. Andrews
Jeffrey	Centreville	10	*Ms. Deere
[No-one]	Welltown Academy	10	Ms. Fisk

*These teachers were *not* interviewed or observed, as they were not participants in my study.

Rationale for Sample Population

Typically within the U.S., 10th-grade students are not in transition from or to a different school environment or "classification" (e.g., elementary to middle school);

conversely, they also are not yet enmeshed in the world of college planning and life beyond high school. Tenth-grade students tend to be eager to learn, maturing but not yet distanced from authority figures, and, while certainly entrenched in patterns of social and academic behavior, they tend to still be open to change and self-reflection.

English is a required course during all four years of high school; consequently, English classes tend to represent the norms of the school as a whole and provide numerous opportunities for students to engage in texts, both through writing and reading.

Rationale for an Ethnographic Approach

Qualitative research is context situated, emerging from an understanding that participants and activities exist in relation to "the circumstances in which and through which" they occur (Schram, 2006, p. 9), and can acknowledge subjective or partial truths. Specifically, this type of work seeks to explore the following questions, as taken directly from Thomas Schram (2006, p. 86):

- What specific social actions and events are happening within this particular setting?
- What do actions, events, and ideas mean to the people engaged in and with them, and how do these understandings influence their behavior?
- How are events, actions, and meanings influenced by the particular context or unique circumstances in which they occur?

These questions provided vitally important guidance to me through three levels of analysis—descriptive, interpretive, and theoretical—allowing movement from local description toward broader theory, exploring the interconnections between meaning and context (Agar, 2006a, 2006b). They do not replace my initial research questions; rather, they complement them by making the larger theoretical questions accessible.

Observations

I completed eight nonparticipant classroom observations within three different classrooms, with a minimum of two observations in each.

Interviews

Interviews co-construct meaning as guided by the researcher (Poland, 2002; Silverman, 2007) and provide rich sources of data. Observations and interviews can work together to enhance our understanding of how participants make meaning of their experiences (Atkinson, Coffey, & Delamont, 2003); in this case, how teens negotiate meaning across and within literacy and discourse contexts. Interviews provide access to knowledge that extends into the realms of the affective and moral, and involve the researcher in a careful listening for "gaps, inconsistencies, and associations" (Luttrell, 2000, p. 517). Conversations with the youths helped to provide coherence throughout my work and to frame a narrative storyline (Riessman, 2008). Lastly, interviews permit discourse analysis of transcripts (Gee, 2005), with the researcher noting elements of, and patterns within, youths' discourses during interviews, and seeking out the "remarkable in the mundane" (Silverman, 2007, p. 13).

I completed a total of 17 semi-structured interviews, between one and three interviews for each of my ten participants: three teachers and seven students.

Gee's "Building Tasks"

James Paul Gee's (2005) approach to discourse analysis is both a theory of language-in-use and a method of research. Gee focuses on how language is used within Discourses, with a capital D, which he defines as not just language-in-use (discourse with a small d), but also the values, beliefs, interactions, tools, objects, symbols, and all components that "enact a particular sort of socially recognizable identity" (p. 21). Gee (2005) has claimed that literacy and discourse activity involves elements or "building tasks" of language. In my work, I focused on aspects of *significance*; *activities*; *identities*; *relationships*; and *sign systems*. Gee provided a detailed subset of questions for each of these domains, which enabled me to move seamlessly from theory to practice and back again to theory. Figure 11.1 illustrates the interplay among the levels and types of questions I used to gather and explore data.

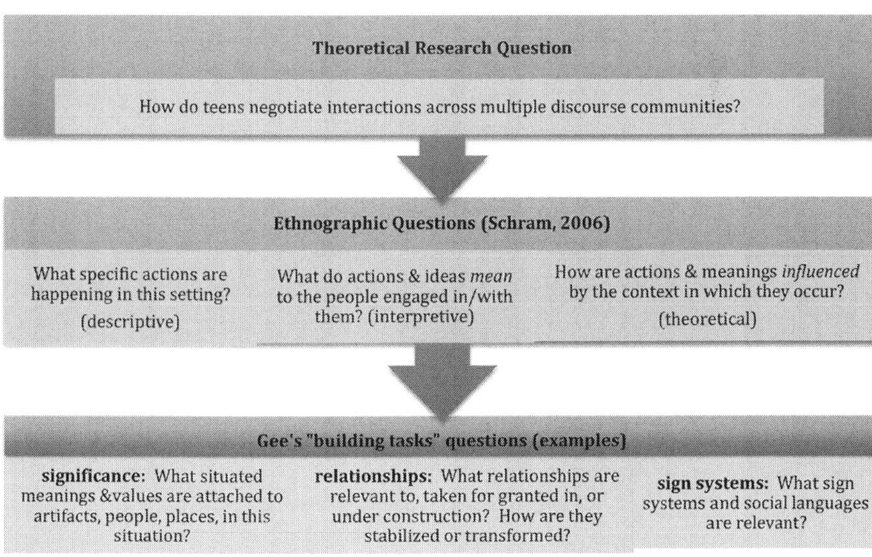

Fig. 11.1. Interrelationship of research questions.

Gee's (2005) "building task" questions align perfectly with Michael Agar's (2006b) framing of ethnographic research. Agar (2006a) explained that we must identify the differences and conflicts between points of views (differences in meaning), and then construct a logic-in-use (context) that makes sense, in order to build coherence. In other words, "You select a surprising F and construct an H to explain it. *F is the meaning; H is the context*" (Agar, 2006b, p. 20, italics his). Gee (1996) explained the intersection of context and meaning in this way: "The behaviors of any individual person, at a specific time and place, are meaningful only against the Discourse or, more often, set of complementary or competing Discourses, that can 'recognize' and give 'meaning' and 'value' to that behavior" (p. 166).

Data Management

Interviews were recorded and transferred as audio files to my laptop where I transcribed them into written documents. Each interview was given a code—first and last initial of participant, plus interview number—and pages were numbered. Field notes were labeled with date, time and place, and pseudonyms, and artifacts had identifying information altered.

Data Analysis

Observations

Observational field notes involved jottings from real-time participation as well as a written record of the events as soon as possible after the events (Emerson, Fretz, & Shaw, 1995). My reflections on and memos about my field notes and interviews (Kleinman & Copp, 1993) allowed me to explore my relationship to the data, feelings and perspectives, assumptions and attitudes.

Coding

For interview transcripts, I followed the open coding process as detailed by Robert Emerson, Rachel Fretz, and Linda Shaw (1995). Open coding allowed me to find patterns and surprises that emerged in the data, remaining open to possibilities and not limiting myself too early in the process of analysis (see 11.2).

Interpretation of Data

Once I had coded the interviews, I shifted to an analytic stance, guided by Gee's building task questions. I organized data around thematic codes (important either through their commonality or through their indication of a possible surprising "rich point") to develop theoretical interpretation. *Rich points* are defined by Agar

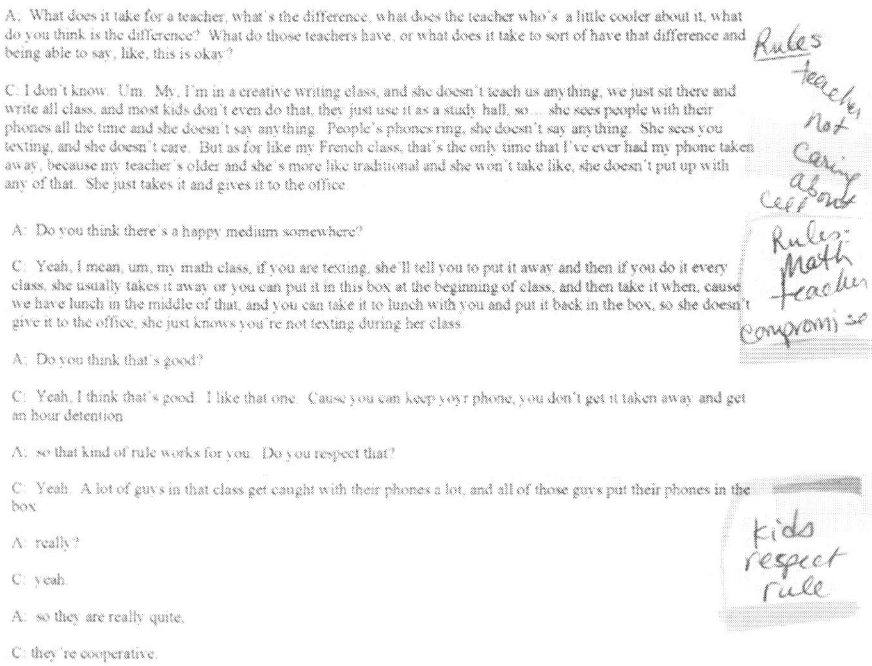

A; What does it take for a teacher, what's the difference, what does the teacher who's a little cooler about it, what do you think is the difference? What do those teachers have, or what does it take to sort of have that difference and being able to say, like, this is okay?

C: I don't know. Um. My, I'm in a creative writing class, and she doesn't teach us anything, we just sit there and write all class, and most kids don't even do that, they just use it as a study hall, so… she sees people with their phones all the time and she doesn't say anything. People's phones ring, she doesn't say anything. She sees you texting, and she doesn't care. But as for like my French class, that's the only time that I've ever had my phone taken away, because my teacher's older and she's more like traditional and she won't take like, she doesn't put up with any of that. She just takes it and gives it to the office.

A: Do you think there's a happy medium somewhere?

C: Yeah, I mean, um, my math class, if you are texting, she'll tell you to put it away and then if you do it every class, she usually takes it away or you can put it in this box at the beginning of class, and then take it when, cause we have lunch in the middle of that, and you can take it to lunch with you and put it back in the box, so she doesn't give it to the office, she just knows you're not texting during her class.

A; Do you think that's good?

C: Yeah, I think that's good. I like that one. Cause you can keep yoyr phone, you don't get it taken away and get an hour detention.

A: so that kind of rule works for you. Do you respect that?

C: Yeah. A lot of guys in that class get caught with their phones a lot, and all of those guys put their phones in the box.

A: really?

C: yeah.

A: so they are really quite,

C: they're cooperative.

Fig. 11.2. Coding samples.

(2006a) as "those surprises, those departures from an outsider's expectations" (p. 2) that indicate differences between cultures and that provide new direction in analysis and theorizing. I grouped my open coding into six broad thematic categories (see Table 11.2), which I then color-coded. As an aside, I am not particularly inclined toward color-coding and was skeptical about sustaining such a system. As it turned out, the color-coding enabled me to comb through transcripts numerous times through different lenses, to color-tab each occurrence within transcripts for ease of access, and to visually organize my work within thematically organized documents throughout the data analysis process.

I also added a section for notes I labeled "also to think about," with miscellaneous ideas such as economic and gender differences, swearing, and use of handwriting.

Table 11.2. Six Major Themes Developed from Open Coding of Interview Transcripts.

Meaning and Value of Literacy	Institutional Discourses and Rules
Meaning and Value of Texting/Social Media	Sign Systems and Social Discourses
Relationships—Trust and Respect	Systems of Knowledge—Moving across Discourses

I combed through the transcripts yet again, highlighting notes and excerpts according to these six themes, and transferred the information to a word document. Figure 11.3 illustrates an example of this organizational strategy. Furthermore, I constructed data tables around themes and subthemes. (For an example of a data table, see Table 11.3.)

INSTITUTIONS/DISCOURSES (school and cyber): (PINK)
<u>Understanding school rules, breaking rules, expressing different teacher reactions</u>
School rules, and rules being broken
Rules:
    M1.2
    NE1.5/18/20
    CG1.2/3/15, CG2.15
    DJ1.5
    HM1.2, HM1.3, 1.22, HM1.26
Everyone doing it:
    M1.3
    NE1.19
    CG1.19
    HM1.3
Got caught in art CG1.2, and in French CG1.3
TXTING MOM HM1.3

Some teachers oblivious: CG2.18, HM1.5

Some teachers bend the rules, compromise: CG3.2, 3.3, HM1.11, HM1.22
*This may link to "trust" (green)

Certain boundaries for when/why: CG3.2 (rude when teacher talks), HM1.3
*This may link to "knowledge system" (blue)
Boundaries are GOOD: CG3.3

No texting in math! HM1.2 (MESSAGES FROM TEACHERS ABOUT CYBER STUFF)

Fig. 11.3. Example of data organization strategy.

At this point, I had done the initial open coding followed by a consolidated arrangement of the codes into themes. The next step was to develop assertions that stretched the data into the realm of interpretation of what was happening in "real life." My intent was to draw links among the six categories, to begin to examine the "so what" around them, to find places where they intersected or collided. I did so by exploring various permutations of placing two different themes together.

Ultimately, I developed four assertions, including two that developed into key findings exploring teens' use of social media in the classroom. These two were:

1. Teens are able to manage multiple discourses, sometimes simultaneously. They not only multitask throughout their day, interacting with various types of texts within short spans of time, but they also are able to articulate and understand the boundedness of these discourse systems.
2. While institutions and authority figures set rules and protocols that define appropriate behaviors with social digital networks, students, teachers, and parents frequently negotiate the boundaries through relationships founded on trust and respect.

INTERSECTION OF NEW AND OLD LITERACIES

If traditional literacy means being able to both read and write within print-bound formats, then "new literacy," or literacy 2.0, means being able to read and write new media forms, including sound, graphics, and moving images in addition to text, shifting away from static and print-centric texts (O'Brien, 2006; Ohler, 2009). Multimodal communication may be interactive, alive, fluid, and multidimensional. New digital literacies "challenge how schools traditionally have valued a single author laboriously working alone to create a unique text" (Knobel & Wilber, 2009, p. 22). This interaction is about production and participation, not just "consumption and spectatorship" (Gee & Levine, 2009, p. 49). Such engagement represents a paradigm shift in actions and possibly a shift in epistemological mindset (Knobel & Wilber, 2009). Generally, Web 2.0 media have at their center a strong sense of interaction, collaboration, adaptability, and innovation (Burke, 2007; Palfrey & Gasser, 2008).

What Belongs in a Classroom?

Certain communicative and networking tools, particularly Instant Messaging (IM) and cell phones, are on the very social end of the interactive technology spectrum, and may not be valuable within academic realms of learning. While some researchers (Gee, 2004; Kress, 2003) believe these social digital tools might well be integrated into a classroom experience, it's not the purpose of such technologies. Some digital media, such as blogging or iMovie, might add a new dimension to learning in ways that creatively promote "participation, collaboration, and distribution" (Knobel & Wilber, 2009, p. 21). As Margaret Weigel and Howard Gardner (2009) have explained, such networking interests should only be contextualized within classrooms when they are "both developmentally and pedagogically suitable" (p. 40). The digital technologies of the day may be more or less suitable for deliberate classroom adaptation depending on a variety of factors—accessibility, teacher knowledge and comfort level, and curricular goals and objectives. However, this pedagogical use is in stark contrast to the nonteacher-directed actions of students on such devices within classrooms.

Discourse and discourse: Understanding the Difference

Social networking interactions run the gamut in terms of surface-level, standard English "correctness" for syntax, grammar, and usage. However, these digital social spaces also vary, not only in terms of discourse with a small "d," but also in terms of their capital-D Discourse—that is, their contextualized appropriateness and sense of larger framework for where, when, and how to use these discourses (Gee, 2005). Schools confront not only the tension between standardized and nonstandardized language-in-use (small-d discourse) but also the intersections of Discourse (capital-D) communities.

Figure 11.4 illustrates these tensions, the Y-axis representing the "discourse" continuum from casual/social to formal/academic, and the X-axis being the larger context or Discourse community. In simplified terms, we might think of the Y-axis

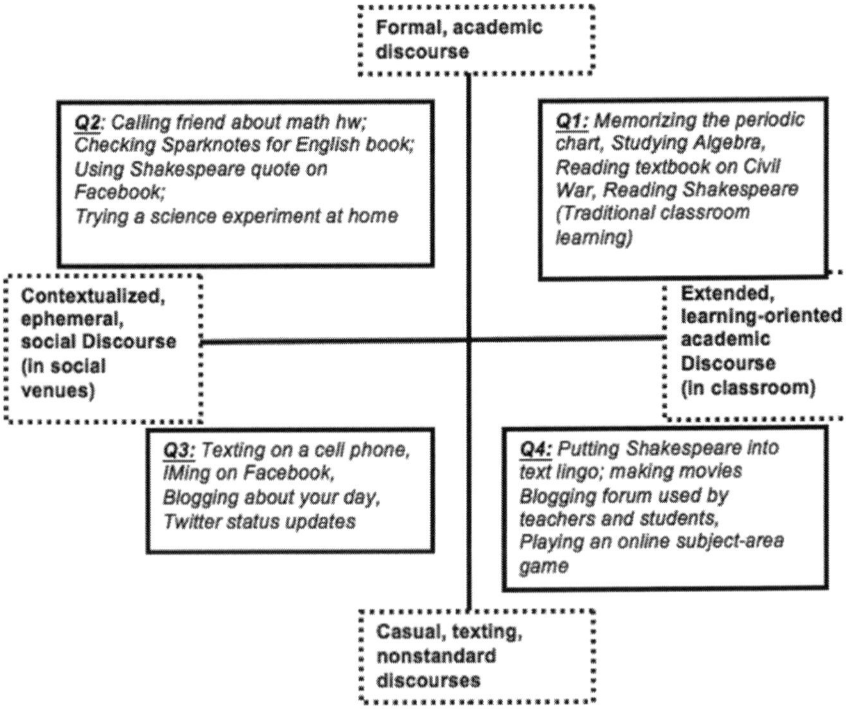

Fig. 11.4. Intersections of Discourses and discourses.

as being the "what" of language, how we talk about something, whereas the X-axis is the "where" that such language happens, that is, the "right" time and place.

Each quadrant gives sample activities that might occur. Quadrant 1 is structured formally both in terms of language use and location, and the activities tend to be traditional classroom learning, such as textbook activities. Quadrant 2 retains much of the formal nature of language itself, but is placed into more social contexts, such as getting help from a friend with homework or reproducing a science experiment at home. Quadrant 3 is social and informal both in terms of language and place, representing social networking activities. Quadrant 4 represents the formal setting of the classroom with the inclusion of social digital tools.

While the texting activities in Quadrant 3 are, in theory, intended to take place outside the classroom walls, it is clear that such activity is happening within the schools as well. Thus, students do not perceive a physical barrier of space and time for partitioning this social media as separate from academic engagement.

This paradoxical overlapping of discourses and Discourses lies at the heart of my work: How is it that some teens seem to be able to maneuver across and among these literacies and discourses successfully? How do they understand both the fluid and bounded nature of these disparate arenas?

FINDINGS

A New Mindset: "It's Just Part of What We Do"

One of my participants, Maria, spent hours on social media platforms, and explained, "It's just part of what we do." David, with virtually no regular access to Literacy 2.0 tools, said, "We were born in the age of technology."

The three teachers I visited also recognized this embeddedness. Mrs. Andrews, a longtime teacher at Centreville, stated, in an uncanny replication of the students' words, "They see [digital media] as an everyday tool, it's an extension of themselves, and just part of what they're doing … It's something they've had their entire life, [in contrast to something] they're being taught." The youngest teacher interviewed, Ms. Fisk, in her first year of teaching at a private school, saw herself as part of a bridging generation between the two worlds, able to embed herself in the new tools, even without access to them throughout her childhood.

Teacher Use of Social Digital Media

In an interesting twist, student participants reported that teachers, usually younger ones, engaged in social media, such as Facebook or texting, even those who were not incorporating new technologies directly into the classroom. Haley laughed,

"It's funny when teachers get a phone call or they get a text, and they're just like, 'uh, keep talking,' or 'what's that? Chchch.' [makes sound of the teacher secretly texting]. It depends on what kind of teacher. Is it a cool teacher or is it an old-school teacher?" Nicholas laughed about a music teacher who was "notorious for taking out her phone and texting. … She's in her twenties."

The two younger teachers I interviewed told me that they used these tools at school, although both denied doing so during academic class time. Mr. Scott checked his Facebook page while monitoring study hall, and Ms. Fisk texted during the day when she was not teaching. As teachers gain familiarity with new tools, they too are figuring out the overlaps and boundaries of such activities in the classroom.

Additionally, some teachers were willing to learn more about new technologies from the students themselves. Haley described a moment when she and her friends introduced a teacher to a new online source they were looking at. Mrs. Andrews had an experience when a student took out a cell phone to show her an application:

> He said, I'm gonna show you, and he had it out and was on the internet. And I said, wow, you can do that? And he said yes. And I said, but you know you're not supposed to have your cell phone out. So we're in this conflict … He's already disturbed class … But I had no idea he could do all this on his phone. It's incredible.

Still, confusion remains over how to best address the continuum of literacies and discourses in classrooms. Haley summed up the tension when she stated, "I think everyone has their own opinions on how much technology should be involved in your life and your studies. If it's more academic or it's more personal and I think there's a fine line." Mrs. Andrews also reflected on the lack of integration among these discourses:

> Part of that is the training we [teachers] have as well. If you were to take the degree as a literacy specialist, you are going to be inundated with reading classes, and writing, and all of the methods and means by which we read. But nobody's going to sit you down to a computer and have you do chats and IMs and you know, they're not. With the society that we have today … why isn't everybody receiving, you know, [a] technology literacy class? Because we look at them as mutually exclusive. We see different things in different forms, and we've got nice neat little boxes that we place them in.

Here, she alludes to helping teachers better understand multiple discourse and literacy communities, noting that we put different "forms" into different "boxes."

Social and Academic Discourses

Students were unified in their belief that texting on cell phones was more about casual chatting than embedding any literacy value. Texting was seen as an ephemeral, nonformal, verbal activity, more so than an enduring written one.

In contrast to the students, the teachers did view digital networking as a form of literacy, albeit one with a distinct discourse and context for use. In fact, the interviews revealed an interesting mismatch: students overwhelmingly felt that their teachers and parents neither valued texting discourse nor would consider it literacy, whereas teachers tended to acknowledge it both as literacy-related as well as valuable within its own context. Mrs. Andrews and Mr. Scott both realized that students were unlikely to see texting as literacy, in part because of their schooling and messages, both implicit and explicit, received from teachers and schools. Mrs. Andrews poignantly summed up this tension when she mused,

> I think we're governed by our traditions. We're moving toward, and we talk about, becoming literate with technologies, but we haven't been able yet to truly see that, because who's defining what we need to learn? It's people who are like our age, people who aren't abreast of all the technologies, the ability, and instead of embracing what we could be doing with the technology, we forbid it. You [the student] may not have your iPod, you may not have your cell phone. You may not have this that and the other thing. We can write you up because you have it out.

Students seem to have received this message, but may also be defining and appropriating their own understandings of multiple discourses. This point of separation between simple and complex, informal and formal, ephemeral nature and enduring coherence, became an important aspect of defining components and categories of literacy for all of the participants, and was a factor in or heuristic for building competence in negotiating across discourses.

Rule-Setting, Rule-Breaking, and Relationships

The issue of cell phone use in school became an insistently recurring topic of conversation throughout the interviews in surprising ways, leading to unexpected findings and assertions, including important understandings of teacher–student negotiations within institutional structures. My research took a dramatic turn when I started to attend carefully to what the students were telling me about the cell phone rules that schools and teachers make, the rampant breaking of these rules, the self-imposed boundaries that students internalize, and the negotiating of rules based on building relationships of trust and respect.

Setting the rules: "The school's pretty strict about it"

Smartphones, iPads, and similar web-enabled devices seem to be a pervasive disruption to the purposes and functioning of classrooms, despite the fact that schools are scrambling to implement protocols that address this ever-evolving realm of student activity. However, while schools and teachers set rules that define appropriate behaviors with digital social networks, it also appears that students and teachers frequently negotiate the boundaries in relationship with each other. The three schools in my study set rules that come as no surprise: no cell phones during class time; and generally, no cell phones during the school day, from first to last bell. iPods and other mp3 music players were more difficult to regulate.

I asked participants what the rules were for their schools. Confusion abounded across participants and schools about the official rules governing lunchtime, hallways, and before and after school time, spaces that aligned more with social interaction than academic work. Some participants indicated that the cell phone rule was about visibility (needing to be out of sight), whereas others claimed that the rule was to have them turned off entirely. Welltown Academy had the strictest policy by far, banning all handheld technological devices throughout the entire day. As we will see, however, actual enforcement at Welltown becomes a different matter altogether in practice.

Breaking the rules: "Everyone basically texts all the time"

As established previously, students readily admitted to breaking the school rules for cell phones. Mimi Ito et al.'s (2008) study found:

> In response to … regulations, most teenagers developed "work-arounds" or ways to subvert institutional, social and technical barriers to hanging out … [T]eens become adept at maintaining a continuous presence, or co-presence, in multiple contexts. (p. 13)

The teachers in my study recognized that students were texting throughout the day, blatantly disregarding school policy. Mr. Scott's solution to this problem was to have students place phones on their desks during class time so that they were visible. However, within days an administrator told him that such a rule violated the school policy!

Ms. Fisk, the youngest of my teacher participants, said she was well aware of the texting going on in her classroom, even given the strong nonusage policy at Welltown Academy. She laughed about her keen ability to spot the texters, in part, she claimed, because of her own closeness in age to them. She knew the tricks of students to avoid detection: "I know that when they're looking in their pencil case for 30 seconds that they're not looking for a pencil … Or when they're looking in their coat pocket … I'm like, oh what do you have in your pocket?"

Mr. Scott, one of the teachers who held to a strict no-use policy, recognized the challenges and said, "I think our rules are more reactive than proactive. I don't know how we could do it any different." Mrs. Andrews at Centreville reflected,

> It's the modern question. [Texting] is very difficult to monitor. You know, it's the same thing that happens when we take kids to a computer lab. We expect them to be on task and only visiting the sites that we tell them to see, and unless you have that monitor to

> watch everyone else, you won't know that they just minimized the screen. So you always have to be monitoring. Are there going to be abuses? I think there will always be abuses. What you have to make clear is where your standards are, that you recognize that this is a tool that can help them with the task you have at hand, and there are parameters where you can use that.

Mrs. Andrews understood that there needed to be some room for negotiation with students, as well as for guiding students in understanding reasonable parameters.

Ms. Fisk at Welltown valued a negotiation approach: "If it's something like in study hall, I'd sort of think [that's okay]. I think at two p.m. it should be okay. Two p.m., cell phones out. I don't see a problem." She added, "I guess I don't totally understand the policy."

Students and teachers alike were aware of the rule-breaking going on, and consistent enforcement seldom occurred.

Self-imposed rules: "I find it rude to text during classes"

Reassuringly, the students themselves were able to articulate boundaries for themselves around cell phone rule breaking. Although they seldom did so for, as Jeffrey said, "moral" reasons, they did have guidelines for themselves around use, some of which were grounded in protocols of politeness.

Most students defined cell phone use during certain class activities as "rude," a finding supported by Ito et al. (2008) who found that "a consensus is emerging about socially appropriate behavior that largely mirrors what is socially appropriate in offline contexts" (p. 18). The youths in my study shared a desire to participate in academic learning, and some classes required uninterrupted concentration, especially math. Some of the students set boundaries based on proximity to the teacher and the fear of the consequences of being caught.

In a world where young people are making complex decisions throughout their day concerning usage of new technologies, we might take comfort in the recognition that these particular students, at the very least, are setting reasonable boundaries for themselves, even as they resist institutional rules that they feel are ineffective and unenforceable.

Variance in teacher enforcement: "She took my phone"

A rule in theory is only as strong as its enforcement in practice. All of my participants, teachers and students alike, recognized that teachers enforced the cell phone rules differentially. Teachers varied on how strict they were in upholding the policy, in how they approached different classes, and in what the consequences were for getting caught. The level of tolerance often correlated with age range, with younger teachers more forgiving and flexible about the cell phone policy

Table 11.3. Teacher Enforcement of Cell Phone Policy.

Strict Enforcement	
Carrie	"At the end of [art] class, I was texting somebody just before the bell rang and she took my phone and gave it to the office. It sucked not to have my phone the rest of my day."
	"I've had my phone taken away during French too … My [French] teacher's older and she's more traditional and … she doesn't put up with any of that. She just takes it and gives it to the office."
	"If [the social studies teacher] sees it he'll take it and give you a detention. So I try not to text during that class."
Haley	"You can't be texting during class … But there's some parts where I've seen kids get their cell phone taken away and it isn't a time to, like [the teacher] had no reason to. Like if they're checking what time it was, or it's the end of class."
Maria	"Mrs. Henry, my science teacher, she doesn't like it at all … If she catches people in the bathroom on their phone, she'll take it, or in the hallway. She's taken mine before."
Nicholas	"[My science teacher] is a huge no-texter. If she sees your phone, she'll absolutely take it away, no questions asked."
Jeffrey	"My chemistry teacher always confiscates phones, but he's the only one I know."
Jamal	"Some teachers are really strict about rules. Some of the teachers say that if the principal were to happen to walk in and see this, they'd be fired or get in trouble. I've never seen that. I've never seen the principal in a class."
Less-Strict Enforcement	
Carrie	"[The social studies teacher] sees people with their cell phones all the time and she doesn't say anything. People's phones ring, she doesn't say anything. She sees you texting, and she doesn't care." [DO YOU THINK THAT'S GOOD OR BAD?] "Not good. No."
Haley	"[Mr. Frangeli] will be like, get off the computer. Or truthfully, those kids will be spark-noting right before we have a discussion and he'll go right up behind them too. He'll see it and be like, guys, stop spark-noting … He's not very assertive." "[When he sees kids texting] [he'll say] 'put it away' and they put it away and then when he turns it's back out."
Maria	"Mr. Scott, he's obviously one extreme [strict], and my yearbook teacher, we can have our phone out, like on the table texting and she sees us doing it and she just doesn't care."
	"Mrs. Stone, everyone texts in that class, she just doesn't notice. She's not aware. I don't think she's looking for it as often."
	"I like Mrs. Ross as a teacher … I like having that [rule that texting is allowed]. Instead of trying to be sneaky about it, we're just open."

Less-Strict Enforcement	
Nicholas	"I would probably say at any given time I could take out my phone and text and [Mr. Frangeli] wouldn't, it's not that he doesn't care, it's just that he wouldn't notice. I don't think he pays attention to that." "I've seen teachers who have seen students texting and they haven't said anything." [During band] "I do [text]. On my music stand I put my phone down so I can see if somebody does text me. A lot of kids, the entire band, everybody has their phone on their stand. They'll check their time. [The teacher] will see them out, but she won't say anything unless you're actually texting. Even [the teacher] has her phone right there on the stand." [DOES SHE TEXT?] "I know she texts, but not during the band class. No." [BUT SHE HAS IT OUT]. "Uhhuh." [Same teacher, during an after school chorus rehearsal], "If we're just around the piano singing and it's not your turn to be singing, then you can usually take out your phone and just text. If it's like a casual day, she won't mind too much. 'Cause even she will take out her phone and text."
Jeffrey	"[If teachers catch someone], they'll say, I need you to put your phone away. And [students are] like, oh sorry, and put the phone away. They almost never [confiscate it.]"

than older teachers. Table 11.3 provides a rich variety of responses about teacher enforcement.

These responses illustrate a continuum from strictly authoritative, through reasonably restrictive, through laissez-faire, to oblivious with respect to their teachers. The top half of Table 11.3 describes teachers who have a no-nonsense, non-negotiable response to upholding the school's cell phone policy. Mr. Scott fell into this category. In fact, his policy, according to his students, was that if one student was caught with a cell phone, not only did the phone get confiscated, but the class needed to write a paper about cell phone use in class. Haley was frustrated by teachers who took cell phones away, even when the circumstances might be reasonable.

The bottom half of the table is more difficult to tease apart. This less restrictive enforcement seems to comprise several different approaches. Some teachers did not tolerate the phones, but were gentler in their response, asking simply that they be put away. This approach was the one that Ms. Fisk and Mrs. Andrews tended to take.

Other teachers permitted cell phones in their classes, but this also divided into two approaches: those who permitted cell phones to the point of disruption, and those who permitted cell phones because the particular class or activity could accommodate them without disruption to management. When Carrie described her social studies teacher by saying "she doesn't care," she presented a very different attitude to Maria, who described her yearbook teacher by saying "she just doesn't care." Carrie judged her teacher harshly, disapproving of her lack of management. Maria, on the other hand, described an atmosphere for building the yearbook that was informal, and she respected the decision of the teacher not to be punitive about cell phone use. Haley passed judgment on a teacher who she felt made only feeble attempts to quell cell phone use. Maria, however, conveyed a different attitude entirely about a teacher when she said, "I like having that [rule that texting is allowed]. Instead of trying to be sneaky about it, we're just open." Understanding the students' feelings and attitudes that underlie their words is an important aspect of interpretation in these instances (Gee, 1996, 2005).

Lastly, there were some teachers who, according to the students, simply were not aware of cell phone usage and therefore didn't enforce a rule they didn't see being broken.

Contrasting styles: "It's a big teacher thing"

Students and teachers were able to reflect philosophically about the differences among teacher regulation. Haley, for example, shared this insightful reflection:

> I feel if there's two people, there's always going to be one really cool one and there's always going to be one that doesn't trust people, 'cause we're all teens, we do crazy stuff. [Some teachers are] very old fashioned … and there's certain morals that people should keep.

Jamal, too, mused about the issue, stating, "I think the really mean [teachers] are just mad, and the nice ones just let us go because you can't stop everything in the world." The responses from students indicate an understanding of adolescent behavior—"we do crazy stuff"—as well as of why teacher response to rule infractions might vary. The contrast of styles tends to be aligned with teachers who are "cool" or "nice" versus those who are "old fashioned" or "mad."

Even Mr. Scott felt the confusion around enforcement. He said, "Study hall expectations at this school are so varied from individual teacher to teacher … It's really a monitoring issue. In my own [study hall], I've had kids on Facebook when I was on Facebook."

I realized that at the heart of rule enforcement and flexibility was an intuitive understanding of teacher–student negotiation. The degree of enforcement varied based primarily on the one-on-one (or one-on-classroom) relationships involved.

Negotiation and trust, student views: "There's a relationship"

Boundaries around digital social media in the school environment get negotiated through relationships of trust and respect. This finding emerged with crystal clarity as the students and teachers talked more about the apparent lack of consistency in enforcing rules about devices such as laptops, cell phones, and iPods, as well as computer use of Facebook, Myspace, game sites, and other interactive programs. Rules are only as good as their enforcement, but enforcement hinges primarily on relational trust.

Teachers and students worked together to establish protocols for the particular class or situation. Maria stated, "I think it depends on the student, and I think it depends on the class. Work ethics of the class." She continued, "It's kind of a trust thing. … The teacher is trusting that, even though you are texting, you're still gonna do what you need to do to get [your work] done. But where there's a class that doesn't do their work, you're not trusting that they're going to get it done, and that they're gonna goof off." Nicholas reflected, "I know a lot of kids who don't really get themselves in trouble, so if they need to [text], the teacher won't give them a hard time." Haley said she had been given leeway from teachers before because "they know that I have good intentions … I'm not trying to fool anyone. I'm not trying to take advantage." Haley also spoke of the rule-setting as being about "a relationship" built in part on respect *for* the teacher and flexibility, based on trust, *from* the teacher.

Negotiation and trust, teacher views: "A judgment call"

The teachers reiterated the value of relationships in establishing workable protocols within classrooms. As Mr. Scott affirmed, "I think 90 percent of education is probably trust. It's trust from the educators, but it's respect from the students." Mrs. Andrews echoed, "I think so much of that [handing over responsibility] comes from respect. If you respect them, and in turn they respect you, I think you go a long way." She explained further:

> There cannot be hard and fast rules … I think each teacher needs to be open to the possibilities, creative enough to see the implications, and a sergeant in the sense of maintaining control in the classroom while still, like a parent. You give your kids parameters, but then you expect them to make decisions within that.

Ms. Fisk agreed:

> I feel like there are rules, but it's also a judgment call. Like, I don't get mad … if it's a good student who's doing it. If it's a student that's goofing around all the time who says, oh I'm just putting my homework in my phone, I'd be like no you're not. But with a good student, I might say, you're not supposed to have this and they'd say I know. And I might just say okay.

She further explained, "I'm pretty cool with them, lenient, and since I have that kind of relationship, I go about it more 'I'm disappointed.'"

Each of the teachers described examples of their own flexibility in establishing policies around social digital tools. Mr. Scott was willing, during study hall, to permit students to be on social networking sites, but only "for some students who have done their work" and who do not "distract other students." Mrs. Andrews described a moment:

> I have a young lady who has misplaced her agenda book, and she automatically grabs her cell phone one day when I'm handing out the homework, and she's just, 'I'm not texting, this is my calendar. I'll show you, I'll stand right beside you.' And I know this girl very well, and she was using it to record. It's instant, it's an extension. They *are* organized, they just are not organized in the way we tell them to be.

Based on this response, I later asked Ms. Fisk, "Would it be against school rules to record homework on the cell phone?" "Probably," she replied. "Because they're not supposed to have a cell phone in the classroom at all. But if it's already in the room ..." Her voice dwindled, understanding the need for flexibility in these circumstances.

Ms. Fisk did, however, describe a moment where the student took advantage of her trust:

> I had someone make a phone call in the middle of study hall, ordering a pizza or something ridiculous, and of course I took the phone for that, 'cause I was so mad that someone would do that ... I felt a little betrayed because I'm a pretty cool teacher and someone would do that in my room, because I'm not completely, you know, hawking them, watching them ... And it was a good student that did it.

In this instance, her feeling of betrayal by the student comes through strongly, amplified by the fact that "it was a good student" who made the call, indicating a break in the relationship that she felt had been established. Ms. Fisk admitted that she might be perceived as being "too trusting," but she was willing to err on the side of students.

Both Ms. Fisk and Mrs. Andrews discussed moments of compromise with students. Ms. Fisk stated, "I've had kids come in and say, can I call my mom in here? And I'm like, okay, because I'm not going to make them go all the way downstairs to call their mom." Mrs. Andrews said, "You know, a kid has forgotten that he had to stay after school for make up. Send him to the office to make a call? And that's going to take 15 minutes. Or say go outside the door and use your cell phone, it's more expedient. It's more efficient."

The teachers I spoke to did not want to be complicit in activities that are illegal, unethical, or unfair to others, such as cheating using digital devices and smartphones, or the problem of cyberbullying, defined as cruelty to others through "sending or posting harmful material online or through a cell phone or engaging in other cruel or hurtful actions [resulting in] significant emotional harm to others" (Willard, 2006, p. 3). Two students also described being aware of inappropriate sexual activity, or "sexting," through cell phones, such as photographs or text that conveys sexually suggestive material (Willard, 2006).

Regardless of potential dangers, teachers and students in my study felt the need for a reasonable and balanced perspective on the issue of rules for new technologies. Mrs. Andrews reflected philosophically, "I think we all just carve out what we can live with and abide by, and carve out the intent of the rule." Thus, while schools and teachers set rules and protocols that define appropriate behaviors with social digital tools, students and teachers frequently negotiate the boundaries through relationships founded on trust and respect.

KEEP DISCOURSES STRAIGHT: "YOU JUST DON'T CROSS THEM"

To return to the earlier exploration of the intersections of discourses and Discourses, I found myself probing students about their ability to maneuver across and among discourses competently. How do adolescents engage in this skill with greater or lesser degrees of success, and how do they come to understand both the fluid and bounded nature of contextualized literacies?

A common societal concern exists that the texting discourse will taint irreparably—and on numerous levels—the academic writing happening in schools. Yet, there is little evidence that this actuality has come to pass. With the exception of David and Jamal, my student participants were successful students *and* successful texters. I asked students to explain to me how they were able to be successful in both contexts without detrimentally impacting their schoolwork or social activity. Students explained that texting is, in some ways, a different "language." The students seemed intuitively to sense this notion of discourse, even without naming it explicitly.

The ways in which they described this different "language" crossed both the sense of structure and purpose. Structurally, participants were able to see a clear distinction in the two discourses. Carrie said, "[School writing] has to do with I think vocabulary and the way that you set up your sentence. When I'm writing a paper, I use longer sentences. I pay attention to what I'm doing, but if I'm just texting someone or IMing them, it's just like I'm talking to them in person." Jamal explained, "English is English. The way it makes sense is using proper grammar, [what students] should do for school." And Jeffrey's words delineated differences in vocabulary, grammar, and usage:

> The language [of texting] isn't the standard grammar rules that you're taught in English class, and a lot of the words are different. When we go to school, we'll learn standard usage, grammar and whatever, that kind of stuff, vocabulary lists with correct spellings on them, and then outside in social environments we can learn these other things, like [texting] or whatever.

Maria summed up the distinction in discourse this way:

> I think of English as like a formal thing, I just see this [social media] is like a casual hanging, friends ... When people use different slang terms and stuff, you would never use those things writing. Like you wouldn't see it in a book most likely. You wouldn't see it in the newspaper or something like that. People just don't use that form of language.

Along with an intuitive understanding of discourse comes a distinction of purpose as well. Here again is the sense of orality with social media that aligns it more closely with spoken language than with written. Carrie said, "It's like, if I'm talking to one of my friends in person, I'm not going to try to make myself sound good." Nicholas said, "If you were talking to your friends, you wouldn't usually [be formal]."

I discovered that these youths have developed an uncanny and nuanced understanding of discourses that permeates their day, a "mindset" that was ever present.

Carrie said, "I never [confused the two]. Even when I first started IMing and using Myspace I didn't start writing papers like IMing ... I don't know how someone can mix them up! They're so different to me. It's just like, I don't know, an automatic thing for me that when I'm in school, when I'm doing a paper, I use better vocabulary, I actually try, and then when I'm with my friends, it doesn't really matter." Maria told me, "They are separated. Conversation and a formal paper that I'm handing in for a grade. I just know, like you just don't cross them." "You don't cross what?" I probed. "The language," she replied. Jeffrey explained, "When you learn something in a certain context, you only use it in that context I guess."

Haley, both social and studious, confidently affirmed the same message: " [The two are] different worlds ... No, no confusion." She continued, "Maybe it's my mindset and the way my brain functions and that I'm very good at doing two different things at once, and I can keep them pretty separate. I don't confuse them."

Rather than finding that those doing more texting were less successful in their English classes, I found the opposite correlation, indicating a strong ability to move across multiple discourse communities. Thus, I was curious as to how Jamal, who not only didn't text but also did not perform well on English papers, might see this issue of different discourses getting mixed up. He told me that, even though he struggled to write well for school, he would not put texting language into a paper. I asked him why not. He replied, "Because it wouldn't make sense. [The teacher] wouldn't get it."

CONCLUSION

The idea of sensemaking for a particular audience and context is in part what literacy is about, and these youths seem to understand that from their years of schooling. Their ability to articulate and enact the distinctive nature of different interactions with text for varying purposes and audiences points to future success with multiple literacies. This understanding stems from both their own agentic experiences and from explicit messages from teachers and other adults within sociocultural realities.

Given the ubiquitous nature of cell phones and other new social media tools within school settings, teachers and students are learning to engage in democratic negotiation and conversation to develop rules and protocols collaboratively. This interactive process is based on relationships of trust and respect, and therefore flexibly adapted based on context and circumstances.

REFERENCES

Agar, M. (2006a). Culture: Can you take it anywhere? *International Journal of Qualitative Methods*, 5(2), 1–16.

Agar, M. (2006b). An ethnography by any other name … *Forum: Qualitative Social Research*, 7(4), 1–23.

Atkinson, P., Coffey, A., & Delamont, S. (2003). *Key themes in qualitative research: Continuities and changes*. Walnut Creek, CA: AltaMira Press.

Bell, J. (1993). Finding the commonplaces of literacy. *Curriculum Inquiry*, 23(2), 131–153.

Burke, J. (2007). Teaching English language arts in a "flat" world. In K. Beers, R. Probst, & L. Rief (Eds.), *Adolescent literacy: Turning promise into practice* (pp. 149–165). Portsmouth, NH: Heinemann.

Emerson, R., Fretz, R., & Shaw, L. (1995). *Writing ethnographic fieldnotes*. Chicago, IL: University of Chicago Press.

Fecho, B., & Meacham, S. (2007). Learning to play and playing to learn: Research sites as transactional spaces. In C. Lewis, P. Enciso, & E. Moje (Eds.), *Reframing sociocultural research on literacy: Identity, agency, and power* (pp. 164–187). Mahwah, NJ: Lawrence Erlbaum.

Freire, P. (2001). Reading the world and reading the word: An interview with Paulo Freire. In W. Hare & J. Portelli (Eds.), *Philosophy of education: Introductory readings* (revised 3rd ed.). Calgary, Alb.: Detselig Enterprises.

Gee, J. (1996). *Social linguistics and literacies: Ideology in discourses* (2nd ed.). New York, NY: RoutledgeFalmer.

Gee, J. (2004). *Situated language and learning: A critique of traditional schooling*. New York, NY: Routledge.

Gee, J. (2005). *An introduction to discourse analysis: Theory and method* (2nd ed.). New York, NY: Routledge.

Gee, J., & Levine, M. (2009). Welcome to our virtual worlds. *Educational Leadership*, 66(6), 48–53.

Ito, M., Horst, H., Bittanti, M., boyd, d., Herr-Stephenson, B., Lange, P. G., Pascoe, C. J., & Robinson, L. (2008). Living and learning with new media: Summary of findings from the Digital Youth Project, white paper. The John D. and Catherine T. MacArthur Foundation Reports on Digital Media and Learning. Chicago, IL. Nov.

Kleinman, S., & Copp, M. A. (1993). *Emotions and fieldwork*. Newbury Park, CA: Sage.

Knobel, M., & Wilber, D. (2009). Let's talk 2.0. *Educational Leadership*, 66(6), 20–25.

Kress, G. (2000a). Design and transformation: New theories of meaning. In B. Cope, & M. Kalantzis (Eds.), *Multiliteracies: Literacy learning and the design of social futures* (pp. 153–161). New York, NY: Routledge.

Kress, G. (2000b). Multimodality. In B. Cope, & M. Kalantzis (Eds.), *Multiliteracies: Literacy learning and the design of social futures* (pp. 182–202). New York, NY: Routledge.

Kress, G. (2003). *Literacy in the new media age.* New York, NY: Routledge.

Lankshear, C., & Knobel, M. (2003). *New literacies: Changing knowledge and classroom learning.* New York, NY: Open University Press.

Lenhart, A., Smith, A., Macgill, A., & Arafeh, S. (2008). *Writing, technology and teens.* Washington, DC: Pew Research Center.

Lewis, C. & Fabos, B. (2005). Instant messaging, literacies, and social identities. *Reading Research Quarterly,* 40(4), 470–501.

Lewis, C., Enciso, P., & Moje, E. (2007). Introduction: Reframing sociocultural research on literacy. In C. Lewis, P. Enciso & E. Moje (Eds.), *Reframing sociocultural research on literacy: Identity, agency, and power* (pp. 1–11). Mahwah, NJ: Lawrence Erlbaum.

Luke, C. (2000). Cyber-shooting and technological change: Multiliteracies for new times. In B. Cope, & M. Kalantzis (Eds.), *Multiliteracies: Literacy learning and the design of social futures* (pp. 69–91). New York, NY: Routledge.

Luttrell, W. (2000). "Good enough" methods for ethnographic research. *Harvard Educational Review,* 70(4), 499–523.

Moje, E., & Lewis, C. (2007). Examining opportunities to learn literacy: The role of critical sociocultural literacy research. In C. Lewis, P. Enciso, & E. B. Moje (Eds.), *Reframing sociocultural research on literacy: Identity, agency, and power* (pp. 15–48). Mahwah, NJ: Lawrence Erlbaum.

O'Brien, D. (2006). "Struggling" adolescents' engagement in multimediating: Countering the institutional construction of incompetence. In D. Alvermann, K. Hinchman, D. Moore, S. Phelps, & D. Waff (Eds.), *Reconceptualizing the literacies in adolescents' lives* (2nd ed.) (pp. 29–46). Mahwah, NJ: Lawrence Erlbaum.

Ohler, J. (2009). Orchestrating the media collage. *Educational Leadership,* 66(6), 8–13.

Palfrey, J., & Gasser, U. (2008). *Born digital: Understanding the first generation of digital natives.* New York, NY: Basic Books.

Poland, B. (2002). Transcription quality. In J. Gubrium, & J. Holstein (Eds.), *Handbook of interview research* (pp. 622–650). Thousand Oaks, CA: Sage.

Riessman, C. (2008). *Narrative methods for the human sciences.* Los Angeles, CA: Sage.

Rogoff, B. (1990). *Apprenticeship in thinking.* New York: Oxford University Press.

Schram, T. (2006). *Conceptualizing and proposing qualitative research* (2nd ed.). Upper Saddle River, NJ: Pearson.

Silverman, D. (2007). *A very short, fairly interesting and reasonably cheap book about qualitative research.* Thousand Oaks, CA: Sage Publications.

Vygotsky, L. (1978). *Mind in society: The development of higher psychological processes.* Cambridge, MA: Harvard University Press.

Weigel, M., & Gardner, H. (2009). The best of both literacies. *Educational Leadership,* 66(6), 38–41.

Wertsch, J. (1984). The zone of proximal development: Some conceptual issues. In B. Rogoff & J. Wertsch (Eds.), *Children's learning in the zone of proximal development* (pp. 7–18). Hoboken, NJ: Jossey-Bass Inc.

Willard, N. (2006). A briefing for educators: Online social networking communities and youth risk. *Center for Safe and Responsible Internet Use.* Available from: http://csriu.org/cyberbully/docs/youthriskonlinealert.pdf

Contributors

Ibrar Bhatt is a Lecturer in Education at Queen's University Belfast, Northern Ireland. His PhD was completed at the University of Leeds (UK), and his current research interests include digital literacy and writing, and how these relate to education and knowledge production. He is author of the book *Assignments as controversies: Digital literacy and writing in classroom practice* (2017).

Carly Biddolph recently graduated with a Bachelor of Education (Honors) and a Bachelor of Arts from the University of Sydney, Australia. She currently teaches English and History to secondary students, and she is interested in educational research related to new literacies and social media. She has coauthored a chapter in *New Literacies and Teacher Learning* (Peter Lang, 2016).

Rebecca Black is an Associate Professor in the Department of Informatics at the University of California, Irvine (USA). Her research interests center on how young people use media and technology to learn, create, and communicate. Her most recent collaborative project, funded by the U.S. Department of Education, involves designing technology tools to help students improve their academic literacy skills. Her work has appeared in *Reading Research Quarterly*, *Research in the Teaching of English*, *Journal of Adolescent and Adult Literacy*, *International Journal of Learning and Media*, and *E-learning*, and she has authored the book *Adolescents and Online Fan Fiction (Peter Lang, 2008).*

Andrew Burn is Professor of English, Media and Drama at the Institute of Education, University College London. His research is in young people's engagement with the media, mainly through forms of digital production in film, animation, and videogames. He also researches the related topics of media literacy, multimodality, and play. His publications include *Media Literacy in Schools: Practice, Production, Progression* (2007, with James Durran); *Making New Media* (2009), and *Children's Play in the Age of New Media* (2014, edited with Chris Richards).

Anita S. Charles is Director of Teacher Education and Lecturer at Bates College in Lewiston, Maine. She has a B.A. from Dartmouth College, an M.Ed. from Harvard, and a Ph.D. from the University of New Hampshire. Her dissertation explored the ways in which adolescents negotiate multiple discourse practices, including social, digital, and academic ones. She was recently a Fulbright scholar in India where she taught college courses and studied aspects of education. Research interests include early and adolescent literacy, special education, and early childhood education. She has had numerous articles published as well as a chapter in an anthology entitled *The First Year of Teaching: Real World Stories from America's Teachers* (ed P. Kane, 1991).

Mark Chen is an independent games researcher and designer and part-time professor of games and learning, qualitative research, and games studies. He is also the director of Pepperdine University's Gameful Design Lab where he promotes social change, activism, and personal agency through the development of expertise in gaming practice and game design. He earned a PhD in Learning Sciences/Educational Technology from the University of Washington and a BA in Studio Art from Reed College. In a previous life, Mark was a webmaster and game designer for the Oregon Museum of Science and Industry. Mark wants a die-cast 1st generation Soundwave for Christmas. You can read more about Mark on his blog at http://markdangerchen.net and reach him @mcdanger.

Jen Scott Curwood is a senior lecturer in English education and media studies at the University of Sydney, Australia. Her research focuses on literacy, technology, and teacher professional development, and her work has appeared in the *Journal of Literacy Research*, *Journal of Adolescent and Adult Literacy*, *Asia-Pacific Journal of Teacher Education*, and *Teaching Education.* She also coauthored the book *Conducting Qualitative Research of Learning in Online Spaces* (Sage, 2017).

Sean Duncan is Assistant Professor of the Learning Sciences in the Department of Counseling and Educational Psychology at Indiana University. His research focuses on learning as embedded within cultures of play and learning, focusing on learning within game play, through game design, and within participation in gaming affinity spaces. He is coeditor (with Elisabeth Hayes) of *Learning in Gaming Affinity Spaces* (Peter Lang, 2012).

Aaron Hung is Assistant Professor of Educational Technology within the Department of Curriculum and Instruction at Adelphi University. His research interests include understanding and describing how people make sense of their technological environments, and studying how people learn through play. His publication includes *The Work of Play*, published by Peter Lang.

Michele Knobel is Professor of Literacy within the Department of Early Childhood, Elementary and Literacy Education at Montclair State University (USA). Her research interests include studying everyday practices involving literacies and digital technologies. Her publications include *New Literacies* (2011, 3rd edn; with Colin Lankshear), *A New Literacies Reader* (Peter Lang, 2013; edited with Colin Lankshear), and *A Handbook for Teacher Research* (2004, with Colin Lankshear), among others.

Jayne C. Lammers is an Assistant Professor and director of the secondary English teacher preparation program in the Warner Graduate School of Education and Human Development at University of Rochester (USA). Her research explores adolescents' writing and literacy practices, particularly in online spaces. Her recent scholarship has appeared in *Research in the Teaching of English*, *Journal of Adolescent & Adult Literacy*, and *Literacy*.

Colin Lankshear is an independent education researcher and writer based in Mexico. He is coauthor of *Literacies: Social, Cultural and Historical Perspectives* (Peter Lang, 2011). His most recent publications include entries (cowritten with Michele Knobel) to *The Routledge Companion to English Studies* (2014), *The Routledge Handbook of Language and Digital Communication* (2016), and *The Routledge Handbook of Language and Creativity* (2016).

Alecia Marie Magnifico is an assistant professor of English teaching at the University of New Hampshire (USA). Her research interests focus on understanding, supporting, and encouraging writing across digital and face-to-face contexts and audiences. She is a coauthor of *Conducting Qualitative Research in Learning in Online Spaces* (2017; with Hannah Gerber, Sandra Abrams, and Jen Scott Curwood), and recent articles have appeared in *Literacy* and the *Journal of Adolescent and Adult Literacy.*

Names index

Subject Index

new literacies ¶ AND DIGITAL EPISTEMOLOGIES

Colin Lankshear & Michele Knobel
General Editors

New literacies emerge and evolve apace as people from all walks of life engage with new technologies, shifting values and institutional change, and increasingly assume 'postmodern' orientations toward their everyday worlds. Despite many efforts to take account of such changes, educational institutions largely remain out of touch with the range of new ways of making and sharing meanings that increasingly mediate and shape the lives of the young people they teach and the futures they face. This series aims to explore some key dimensions of the changes occurring within social practices of literacy and the educational challenges they present, with a view to informing educational practice in helpful ways. It asks what are new literacies, how do they impact on life in schools, homes, communities, workplaces, sites of leisure, and other key settings of human cultural engagement, and what significance do new literacies have for how people learn and how they understand and construct knowledge. It aims to challenge established and 'official' ways of framing literacy, and to ask what it means for literacies to be powerful, effective, and enabling under current and foreseeable conditions. Collectively, the works in this series will help to reorient literacy debates and literacy education agendas.

For further information about the series and submitting manuscripts, please contact:

Michele Knobel & Colin Lankshear
Montclair State University
Dept. of Education and Human Services
3173 University Hall
Montclair, NJ 07043
michele@coatepec.net

To order other books in this series, please contact our Customer Service Department at:

(800) 770-LANG (within the U.S.)
(212) 647-7706 (outside the U.S.)
(212) 647-7707 FAX

Or browse online by series at:

www.peterlang.com